A COMPANY OF HEROES

A Company of Heroes

THE AMERICAN FRONTIER

1775–1783

DALE VAN EVERY

Author of Forth to the Wilderness

Quill

William Morrow

New York

Library of Congress Cataloging-in-Publication Data

Van Every, Dale, 1896–
A company of heroes: the American frontier, 1775–1783/Dale Van
Every.
p. cm.
ISBN 0-688-07523-1
1. Northeast, Old—History—Revolution, 1775–1783. 2. United
States—Territorial expansion. I. Title.
E263.N84V3 1988   87-27769
CIP

Printed in the United States of America

First Quill Edition

1 2 3 4 5 6 7 8 9 10

Contents

MAPS

A COMPANY OF HEROES

THE WEST IN 1775

I

៩

The Choice

ON MAY 4, 1775, the *Virginia Gazette* was displaying an adver-
tisement announcing that George Washington was offering a
"Forty Dollars Reward" for the return of "two servant men" who
had escaped on April 19th. They were recent immigrants, Thomas
Spears, a 20-year-old cabinetmaker from England, and William
Webster, a 30-year-old bricklayer from Scotland. The colonies' extraordinary increase in population of the past half century had been
much accelerated by a surge of immigrants seeking the wider opportunities of the new world. Most had arrived lacking other means of
paying their Atlantic passage than by indenturing themselves to
seven years' service to whatever employer elected to buy their con-
tracts from the ship's captain.

In the same issue of the *Gazette* were more momentous references
to a more memorable escape which had been embarked upon that
same April 19th. At Lexington and Concord Patriot militia by firing
upon English regulars had committed all Americans to a course
from which there was likewise to be no willing return. Of this more

portentous hazard Washington that May was writing George Fairfax, "though the once happy and peaceful plains of America are
either to be drenched with Blood or Inhabited by Slaves . . . can a
virtuous Man hesitate in his choice?"

In both the lesser and the greater cases there was the same knife-
edged compulsion to choose. On the one hand was constraint and
security, on the other freedom and perils too numerous and diverse
to contemplate. At Mount Vernon the two young bondsmen had
been well fed, well clothed, well housed, and well treated. Nevertheless, they embraced the hardships and dangers of flight through
a countryside in which every magistrate, sheriff, constable, employer,
traveler, innkeeper, even every reward-seeking fellow bondsman,
was an enemy bent on their apprehension. Their hope to retain their
freedom depended upon their gaining the frontier where, however,
they would find the hardships and dangers multiplied a hundred-
fold. The great majority of Americans when confronted by the
same need to assess the value of freedom made the same choice.
They, too, exchanged the certainty of comfort and security for the
hazards of an unknowable future. Until that last moment their
grievances had not seemed so deep as to require more than persisten.
remonstrance and protest and petition. But the blaze of Concord
and Lexington had emitted a pitiless glare of reality. Before every
man loomed the sudden desperate dilemma. He must at once, with
every eye in the community upon him, take his stand as a man
bound to reaffirm his allegiance to his king or as one ready to take
up arms against that king.

It was a hard choice for most. Washington that May was referring
to the New England minutemen as "the Provincials" and to their
red-coated antagonists as "the Ministerial Troops." In his letter to
Fairfax expressing his repugnance to slavery he was also writing,
"for we do not, nor cannot yet, prevail upon ourselves to call them
the King's Troops." But the hard choice could not be long evaded.
Soon Washington and most of his fellow countrymen had made it.
In so doing they were choosing a seven-year war in which, as Washington had forecast, the plains of America were to be drenched with

blood. Boston, New York, Philadelphia, Charleston, and Savannah were occupied by royal troops. The Hudson Valley became the war's chief theater. Armies marched and countermarched across New Jersey. The coasts of Rhode Island, Connecticut, and Virginia were laid waste. The southern states were tormented by a succession of peculiarly brutal campaigns. This procession of disasters weighed upon all Americans, rebel and loyalist alike. But nowhere did these general vicissitudes of war afflicting the whole country bear down so cruelly as upon the struggling new nation's long and incredibly exposed western frontier.

Upon the more populous eastern communities the war struck as a succession of violent but passing storms. But for the inhabitants of the western border the sky remained always dark, the bolts forever descending. While Washington and Congress strove to keep an army in the field, their difficulties were made less extreme by recurrent intervals in the demands made upon them. Washington's main army was obliged to fight no major battles between Monmouth in June of 1778 and his institution of the siege of Yorktown in September of 1781. Boston was evacuated by enemy troops nine months after Bunker Hill, and Philadelphia was returned to American custody after an occupation that lasted no longer. The campaigns in the south did not begin until 1780 and Piedmont Virginia was not invaded until 1781. Meanwhile, in the whole seven long years of the war there were for the frontier people to be no such intervals, no relief from danger, no surcease from dread. For them the day that passed without an attack was nevertheless always a day when an attack might be but an hour away. Theirs was to remain a conflict in which victory was beyond the reach of valor. Their enemy was not a ponderous army of disciplined and uniformed soldiers commanded by civilized officers, but packs of painted savages, capable of springing at any moment from the wilderness to burn a homestead and butcher a family and then of disappearing again as suddenly into the wilderness. This enemy's method of waging war was as fearful as his terrifying antics and macabre appearance. His favorite weapons were surprise, ambush, mutilation, the war whoop, the knife, the hatchet, and the burning stake. As the years of such a war rolled on, they were to impose upon these Americans of the frontier a strain more nearly unendurable than any to which any other people have ever been subjected.

The protraction of their suffering was not occasioned by chance or circumstance or the uncertain caprice of vindictive Indians. It was a planned and purposeful feature of the war. In the east the major strategy of the English high command varied from time to time. It was first planned to cut the revolting colonies in two by marching an army from Canada down the Hudson, then to dismay the rebels by capturing the rebel capital, Philadelphia, then to stifle rebel shipping by harassing the rebel coasts, and finally to seize and hold as hostages the southern provinces. But on the western frontier the English plan remained always the same. It was to ravage the screen of scattered western settlements until their necessary abandonment had opened the way for the descent of hordes of savages upon the less hardy inhabitants east of the mountains and thereby to provoke such widespread terror as must once and for all discourage the rebellion. The resolution with which the frontier people clung to their clearings and stockades, year after year against odds which appeared ever more hopeless, frustrated this design. Their desperate resistance was a service to the national cause that played no inconsiderable part in the nation's final victory.

Yet, immense as was this service, it was not their principal contribution. Their resolution served their country in an even more decisive and vital fashion. American independence was eventually won on the seaboard by the indomitable Washington's long-suffering Continental Army and the skill with which, when the moment came, he took advantage of the allied French army and fleet. But on the morrow of victory at Yorktown, there was no faintest assurance that the independence now for the first time clearly in sight was to extend beyond those inhabited portions of the original thirteen provinces lying east of the mountains. That the dominion of the new United States was about to be recognized as extending all the way to the Great Lakes and the Mississippi was entirely due to the achievement of the frontier people in having seized, just in time, their lodgments west of the mountain barrier and in having held those scattered American outposts through all the desperate years of the Revolution. An attempt to examine this achievement, this transcendent contribution to their country's destiny, is the object of this book.

II

⟨ornament⟩

The Frontier of 1775

THE INHABITED TERRITORY of the thirteen colonies, extending in a long, threadlike strip from the southeast coast of Maine to the southeast coast of Georgia, was the home of a maritime people for whom it was natural to face toward the sea. The shore of the Atlantic was a dominating factor in the conduct of their daily as well as their most important affairs. Most of them lived near it or near rivers leading to it. Their principal commercial enterprises were connected with trade with Europe, the West Indies, and the slave coast of Africa. Most of their trade with each other was likewise seaborne. Their only cities were seaports. Every merchant, banker, and planter thought as much in terms of bottoms and cargoes as did shippers and shipbuilders. Every inland farmer who was situated too far from a river to float his produce to market found himself thereby handicapped. The most impoverished, most recently arrived immigrant had been able to take his modest place in the community only because the sea had made his passage relatively inexpensive. The sail-dotted sea lanes of the Atlantic had kept the transplanted European in America aware of his European background and had delayed a recognition of his new status as the citizen of a new country.

Compared to the impact upon the public consciousness of this eastern sea frontier, the opposite land frontier to the west appeared, except to the few people who lived along it, to have but trifling significance. It was commonly referred to, always disparagingly, as the "back country." According to prevailing opinion only people unequipped with ordinary good sense ever committed themselves to an existence burdened by difficulties so crushing as were there inescapable. That these few foolhardy "back woods men," persisting stubbornly in their occupation of the edges of the wilderness, had already begun to shape the future of the United States and were to continue to do so for the next hundred years was a development not yet evident to anybody.

The sea frontier was broken by innumerable indentations, bays, estuaries, and offshore islands, a circumstance which greatly increased its usefulness to its inhabitants. Due largely to the inconsistencies which had marked Indian resistance since the white man's first coming, the land frontier followed a course very nearly as irregular, a companion circumstance which by as much decreased the likelihood of its inhabitants' survival. Considering the westward limit of settlement as an approximate line along which the more advanced holdings were within a half-day's travel of the one next nearest, the western frontier of 1775 stretched from German Flats, 70 miles west of Albany, southeastward in a valley-hopping circuit around the eastern flank of the Catskills to the New Jersey line 30 miles west of the lower Hudson, thence veered erratically westward to the forks of the Susquehanna, thence angled southwestward to follow Forbes' Road from near Bedford across the unsettled ranges of the Appalachians, thereafter angled northwestward to the northern bend of the Ohio above Pittsburgh, thence kept along the eastern bank of the river to the vicinity of the present Moundsville, West Virginia, thence, swinging away from the Ohio, zigzagged southeastward through narrow mountain valleys to the western wall of the Valley of Virginia, west of the present Harrisonburg, thence bore off southwestward through parts of the Greenbrier and

New river valleys to roughly the point at which Clinch River crosses the present Tennessee line, thence turned sharply southeast to the present North Carolina line near Grandfather Mountain, thence kept southwestward along the eastern slopes of the mountains across the western tip of South Carolina to the Savannah River, thence ran southeast in a fairly straight course to the Georgia seacoast at the Florida line.

Fantastically eccentric as were the geographical meanderings of this outer line of settlement, which were to obstruct so much every effort to attach any semblance of organization to its defense, another inherent weakness was even more disturbing. Its inhabitants were still preoccupied with the precarious initial stage of getting themselves established in their new homes. Among the more advanced locations between New Jersey and North Carolina, along the whole westward bulge of the frontier, not one was held by a settler who had occupied it for more than five years, and many had been held for less than one. Beset by the task of keeping his family fed and sheltered until he had completed a cabin and cleared enough ground for a corn crop, usually separated by miles from his nearest neighbor, in many cases still unacquainted with the region into which he had ventured, such a settler found himself, his wife, and his children suddenly exposed to every shock and dread of a general Indian war. Among these anomalies of location and unreadiness, seemingly certain to invite irresistible assault, no aberration was as outwardly absurd as in the case of Kentucky. Thrust far westward into the continent's central wilderness, separated by 200 miles of all but impassable forested mountains from their nearest neighbors to the eastward on the main frontier line, hemmed in on all sides by Indian enemies, four little settlements were being founded there the very month that Concord and Lexington were bringing on the war.

This singularly awkward posture into which the frontier had stumbled was due to the conjunction of a land speculators' conspiracy with Indian disunion, governmental indecision, and settler audacity. Disturbed by the immensity of the frontier defense problem revealed by the French War and Pontiac's War, the government of England had by the King's Proclamation of 1763 decreed the crest of the Appalachians to be the western limit of settlement. There had been no colonial objection to this limitation for there was as yet no population pressure east of the mountains to require an outlet west of them. Establishment of the Line was at first of interest only to the land companies who needed time to perfect their designs to profit by eventual sales of western lands in the still distant future, to Indian traders who hoped that the advance of western settlement might be indefinitely retarded, to Indian nations who were determined to hold the white frontier at the mountain barrier, and to the English regular army which had been assigned the task of keeping the peace in the wilderness. For a time the army sought by forceful dispossessions and cabin burnings to turn back the few peculiarly hardy squatters who ventured beyond the mountains in defiance of the king's edict, provincial statutes, and Indian threats. Soon, however, incensed by colonial refusal to share the cost of frontier defense, the English government resolved to relinquish responsibility for wilderness peace and instead to concentrate the army in eastern seaports where it might be more usefully employed as a check upon incipient colonial sedition. As the army was relaxing its hold, the mountain barrier was likewise being temporarily neglected by its natural defenders, the Indians. The land companies had instantly recognized their opportunity.

Under the shrewd supervision of Sir William Johnson, the great English proconsul to the Indians, the 1768 Treaty of Fort Stanwix was negotiated with the Iroquois who had become suddenly willing to sell for the equivalent of $50,000 their every claim to all land east and south of the Ohio River.* The Iroquois, in sacrificing the general Indian interest and what was presently to prove their own interests, had not been the totally unwitting dupes of Johnson and his fellow conspirators. The Iroquois claim to the land involved was based on century-old conquests. They had no practical use for it. Other nations had meanwhile become accustomed to hunt in it. The underlying purpose of the arrogant Iroquois was to channel what they regarded as the eventually inevitable future advance of

* This episode is more fully treated in Chapter 17 of Dale Van Every's previous book, Forth to the Wilderness, New York, 1961.

white settlement off toward the Ohio and away from their own homeland in northern Pennsylvania and western New York. In the south the Cherokee, the next most important center of Indian military power, had taken their cue from the Iroquois. They, too, began to sell their claims to western lands for which they, too, had no immediate use in order to turn the future white advance away from their homeland. Their dealings, chiefly with land companies, culminated in a sale to the Transylvania Company which opened the way to the establishment of Boonesborough.

It was not long, however, before the news of the Treaty of Fort Stanwix had stirred among many individual settlers east of the mountains a feverish apprehension that, if they delayed making their move, the most favorable locations west of the mountains might be taken by others. The sudden disorganized land rush that ensued frustrated every design of the land companies which had instigated the treaty. While the mountain barrier remained unguarded by Indian nations who were quarreling among themselves and by the English army which was pulling out, hordes of excited settlers were pouring over the mountains to seize for themselves every choice site in what is now southwestern Pennsylvania. The Shawnee, whose hunting grounds were being invaded by this entirely unexpected influx, had been abandoned by their former Indian allies and were forced to acquiesce in this breach of the mountain barrier by a self-organized frontier army from the Valley of Virginia that marched 200 miles down the Kanawha to win at Point Pleasant one of the most stubborn battles ever fought between red men and white. These had been among the unexpected and unforeseen circumstances which had led to a greater advance of the frontier in the five years preceding 1775 than had been accomplished in the previous century. They had also led to placing it in such a state of sprawled imbalance as to arouse every doubt that it could possibly be defended.

Upon these basic physical disadvantages suffered by the frontier of 1775 at the outbreak of the war were superimposed almost every other conceivable disadvantage. The demands of war would require the accumulation of supplies to keep even the most primitive home-guard in the field or in garrison, but this was made all but impossible by mountain ranges dividing all of the more advanced and more exposed settlements from supply sources in the east. These settlements were in turn separated from each other by distances made longer by the lack of roads. Each location threatened was held by at most a few families while its isolation kept even the support of its nearest equally weak neighbor too often too late. The inhabitants forced to undertake their own defense were not soldiers but men burdened with families who, however grave the threat, were obliged to continue to plant and reap in order to subsist. Most had been destitute when they came and war was certain to make a barest livelihood more than ever uncertain. From the outset gunpowder, the most imperative of all necessities, was everywhere lacking.

If all of them had withdrawn from their isolated clearings to take refuge in the more populated areas to the east as the threat of war became an imminent certainty, it could only have been accepted as a normally prudent recourse with which every sensible observer must have agreed. That so many of them chose instead to hold their ground and to continue to hold it through seven agonizing years of war was regarded as incredible then, and must still seem so.

They were not encouraged, even at first, by ignorance of the magnitude of the threat that impended. Memories of the terrible Indian inroads of Pontiac's War only ten years before were still too fresh. Immediately before that had been the prolonged border horrors of the French War. In those two so recent wars thousands of frontier men, women, and children had perished and thousands of square miles of border farmland been laid waste. Few families occupying this new frontier of 1775 had not lost members in those former devastations. It was soon evident, moreover, that this new onslaught might prove even more frightful. No longer was there a mountain barrier between the white border and the Indian country. This time the barrier was behind them. This time there would be no English regular armies marching to the rescue. On the contrary, this time the English army was to be not the guardian but the enemy of the frontier. The Indians whose former attacks had been characteristically intermittent and spasmodic were this time to be organized and supplied as a permanent auxiliary of the English war effort and to be led and accompanied by Tory rangers, animated by an aversion to their former Patriot neighbors very nearly as bitter as was the Indian aversion to white settlers. All this the frontier people of 1775 could see coming at them; still most of them held their ground.

Forbidding as was the menace hanging over the border as a whole, each segment of the frontier was harassed by special local problems. In New York's Mohawk Valley, the effective organization of defense was handicapped by the white population's division among three racial strains, English, Dutch, and German. Here also the animosities between Tory and Patriot inhabitants had already reached a pitch of intensity never equaled elsewhere until the closing years of the war in the south. And, most threatening of all, here the Indian enemy was on their very doorstep. Elsewhere, Indian attackers must come from a distance, but in New York there were towns of the Iroquois within an hour's march. Moreover, the Iroquois were the most powerful of all Indian nations, the most closely allied to English interests, and could be the most effectively kept in the field by their proximity to English military supply bases in Canada.

In Pennsylvania, any attempt to provide for frontier defense was distracted by boundary disputes with other provinces. Connecticut had laid claim to Wyoming, the area now occupied by the cities of Wilkes-Barre and Scranton, and to implement the claim had introduced Connecticut settlers. Pennsylvania indignantly denied the claim, and the first field operation of Pennsylvania militia in 1775 was the dispatch of an expedition to dispossess the Connecticut intruders. West of the mountains the Pennsylvania claim to the entire area about Pittsburgh was violently disputed by Virginia. This was the area into which during the past five years there had been the sudden, unforeseen, chaotic rush of settlers from both provinces. The rival jurisdictional claims became increasingly embittered and again and again approached the brink of armed conflict. Each state established competing counties and courts. The magistrates of each were arrested and imprisoned by the other. Virginia seized Pittsburgh and rebuilt Fort Pitt which had in 1772 been abandoned and dismantled by the English army. Throughout the Revolution this interstate conflict was to continue to disorganize every frontier defense effort on the upper Ohio.

Virginia in 1775 had among all the states by far the longest and most exposed frontier to defend. The dispute with Pennsylvania in the northwest was only one of the jurisdictional difficulties by which it was distracted. Virginians from the Valley of Virginia had pushed southward down the Holston, braving Cherokee resentment, denunciation by royal authorities, and disapproval of Carolinians who regarded the intrusion as certain to bring on another Indian war. They were scarcely settled on the Watauga and the Nolichucky before they were disconcerted by the disclosure in the western prolongation of the survey of the Virginia-North Carolina line that their new situations were south of it. They were no longer Virginians and yet were divided from North Carolina by a range of mountains which denied them effective support from that province even were it disposed to assist them. The most isolated and presumably the least defensible segment of Virginia's frontier, Kentucky, was the area most of all plagued by jurisdictional confusion. Virginia claimed the region by her interpretation of her original charter which could be construed to include all territory to the west and northwest as far as the western ocean. This original assertion of rights to Kentucky had been reinforced through the years by the early interest among Virginians in western land speculation. Representatives of Virginia land companies, Thomas Walker and Christopher Gist, had in 1750 and 1751 been the first Englishmen of record to enter Kentucky. Long hunters from Virginia had explored Kentucky. Surveyors commissioned by Virginia's Fincastle County had surveyed much of central Kentucky in 1773, and in 1774 Virginians had fought the Shawnee for access to Kentucky. Nevertheless, of the first two actual settlements in Kentucky in the spring of 1775 neither had been established under Virginia auspices. Harrodsburg had been founded the year before and was now being reoccupied by a party of independent settlers led by James Harrod, a Pennsylvanian, and Boonesborough was being built under the sponsorship of the Transylvania Company, most of whose corporate members were North Carolinians.

As a result of this literally universal jurisdictional disorder extending from New Jersey to South Carolina, the transmountain frontiersman of 1775 could not know in what province, if in any, he resided or the laws of what government, if any, he should recognize as applying to him. This legal vacuum which had so recently precipitated his rush westward had been given an infinitely less inviting aspect by the sudden imminence of war. Were he a constitutional lawyer, he could assume that he might be outside the jurisdiction of any province and unlawfully in territory under the direct rule of the imperial English government. Yet this theory was not supported by the presence in the territory of a single magistrate, sheriff, or functioning representative of that government to take the place of the English army officers who had been its only former manifestation of authority in the wilderness until the army's recent withdrawal to the seaboard. The King's one remaining representative west of the mountains was Alexander McKee, deputy Indian Agent at Pittsburgh, whose duty it was to deal not with settlers but with traders and Indians. This frontiersman of 1775 could, therefore, know that unless he reaffirmed his loyalty England loomed as his certain enemy, but he could not know what province, if any, might feel responsibility for contributing to his defense in the event he adhered to the Patriot cause.

Among all these confusions one seemed to him of paramount concern. In venturing to cross the mountains into the wilderness he had realized that he was taking a course in which he must look to his own safety. But he had come to take up land, whether a pretentious tract or enough for a corn patch, and the confusion meant that after all his effort he could not yet know how and when, if ever, his title to it might be accepted as valid. So far his right to the land he was clearing was being denied by the royal government, by one or more provinces, by land companies, often by rival settlers, and inveterately by the Indians.

His own way through this jurisdictional maze in which there seemed to be no umbrella of legality over any of his actions was simple, direct, and immediate. He was as ready to govern himself as to shift for himself in every other way. He had not come to the

wilderness to become a wild man. Instinctively he chose not to live
outside the law but to make his own laws. The first impulse of every
new settlement, before land was cleared, cabins built, or stockade
raised, was to hold a town meeting in which every man old enough
to bear arms voted by majority rule for regulations governing social
conduct, assignment of community tasks, and mutual defense. In
1772 the Holston settlers, realizing they were no longer in Virginia
and might not be accepted by North Carolina, had formed the
Watauga Association to deal with Cherokee hostility and the English
ministry's objections to their occupation, and at the same time with
their every self-government need from the raising of militia to the
sanctification of marriages. Before they had yet heard of Concord
and Lexington, 18 representatives of the four settlements then being
established in Kentucky in the spring of 1775 had met in convention
at Boonesborough to declare their assumption of the right to govern
themselves and to vote ordinances extending even to the preserva-
tion of game. Having been informed of the outbreak of hostilities
in Massachusetts, the settlers of Hannastown and Pittsburgh ignored
for the moment their differences as Virginians and Pennsylvanians,
and met on May 16th to declare their sympathies with their eastern
fellow countrymen and to form, respectively, the Westmoreland
Association and the West Augusta Committee to take charge of the
raising of such military forces as might prove needed.

Nothing so sharply distinguishes these first settlements west of
the mountains as this immediate readiness to assume political responsibilities. From time immemorial new, weak, and struggling colonies
have tended to look back toward the land from which they have
sprung for support, guidance, and, above all, for governmental decision. But these few small communities, scattered through the fear-
haunted forest of the continent's vast interior, invariably and
unhesitatingly, from the first moment of their existence, considered
themselves endowed with the right to decide all for themselves. Their
political self-sufficiency was to prove an enormously strengthening
element in the total political fabric of the new nation of which they
were in time to become a part.

This insistence in the west upon the inherent right of self-government was to intensify during the Revolution and persist thereafter. The extraordinary self-reliance of the frontiersman, which extended from making his own shoes to doctoring his own ills, was in no way evidenced so forcefully as by his readiness to make his own laws. His persistence in the demand that his right to do this be recognized by the slowly coalescing central government of the new United States led to what was the greatest of all his contributions to the shaping of the new nation—the doctrine of the progressive and successive admission of new and equal states to the union of the original thirteen. No constitutional device in all the history of nations has ever opened a way so successful to a growth so rapid.

This monumental self-reliance was the dominating and the only common trait of the frontier people of 1775. Without it they could not have existed even from day to day. In other respects they were as diverse as the population east of the mountains from which they had separated themselves. There were among them, however, certain discernible groupings in which there were more similarities than dissimilarities.

Providing the frontal edge and the outer defense line of the new frontier were the original frontier people, themselves a new and altogether distinct kind of people whose extraordinary hardiness had been forged in the fires of the past twenty years of border wars. They were members of families who had occupied the former frontier east of the mountains for two and in some instances three generations. They were a people already long familiar with the demands of existence in the edges of the wilderness. They had already experienced all the border horrors of the French War and Pontiac's War. They knew as could no one else the reality of the danger awaiting beyond the 200-mile leap over the mountain barrier into the great central wilderness. Yet they were the first to make it. They were attracted by an appeal that they could not resist and saw no sufficient reason to try to resist. It was not so much new land that they sought as it was room in which to live the life that they had learned to prefer. The man who had grown up on the frontier had learned to value the personal freedom of action of the frontier way of life more than he might ever value the accumulation of possessions, the enjoyment of ease, or the relaxation of safety. He wanted to continue to feel completely his own master, to feel able to hunt when he chose, to feel able to work only when he chose, and, above all, to feel able to move on when he chose. He wanted to continue to enjoy these privileges of life in the wilds without being required to sacrifice the privilege of keeping his family with him. This unique conjunction of privileges had already begun to be displaced east of the mountains by advancing civilization's clutter of such constraints as rents, wages, taxes, and law suits. To regain them it was necessary to press on into the wilderness. That danger was the companion of the freedom awaiting there, only added zest to the quests.

Aside from these born and bred frontier people, three other general types on the frontier were noteworthy: the long hunter, the land seeker, and the refugee. The long hunter was the frontier's forerunner who had learned to take to the wilderness as naturally as an Indian or a wolf. Most of the time he was scarcely a part of the frontier which he visited only at intervals in his distant roaming, but he was essential to it as occasional guide and advisor and, during Indian wars, he was its surest shield. Roving, often alone, sometimes with one or two companions, for months and years at a stretch, a practice which had gained him his name, always far in advance of the advancing frontier, he was never to yield to domestication, and in the next generation was to keep on westward to become the Missouri trapper and then the mountain man.

The land seeker was at the other end of the scale. He was a man impelled not to enjoy the wilderness but to dispel it, not to continue to wander but to find a place to sink ever stronger and deeper roots. In rare instances he was a man who owned a considerable acreage east of the mountains who sought at a bound to increase his eastern five hundred acres to a western five thousand or fifty thousand. Such more substantial pioneers were often men of some intellect and great vigor, and as a class they were to furnish most of the frontier's natural standard bearers, the founders of settlements, colonels of militia, delegates to the Continental Congress, and the first governors of western states. The more usual case among land seekers was that of a man who had had little or no land and who was determined to seize, before it had passed, this opportunity to acquire as much and as good land as he considered he needed. In either case the land seeker had come to possess the country. He was to become the architect of its progress.

Of the more general types of people discernible on the frontier, the refugee was by far the most widely represented. He had been led there less by what he hoped to gain than driven by what he hoped to escape. He might be a bankrupt, a runaway bondsman, a disappointed lover, a fugitive from the law, a nondescript failure at all he had essayed before, a man with a family too large to support by any means formerly at his command, or a footloose youth merely eager to postpone settling down anywhere. This refugee class came in swarms. It was also the first to flee eastward in times of stress.

Whatever had been his origin or were his expectations, the average frontiersman of 1775 lived in a stump-dotted clearing of two or three acres in a one-room, earthen-floored cabin which had just taken the place of last year's half-faced camp, the brush-thatched sapling leanto with a cooking fire built in the open side, which had been his family's first shelter. His furniture was contrived of hand-hewn slabs of wood, his bed a tick filled with corn shucks, and his hearth a structure of mud-plastered sticks which were forever catching fire. His tools, utensils, and personal possessions were limited to the weight that could have been carried over the mountains on the backs of himself, his wife, and his horse, if he had a horse. If he had a cow he had had to butcher her the previous winter to save his family from starving. The handful of gunpowder remaining to him could not these past many months be used for hunting but had had to be conserved for graver emergencies. With spring now stretching into summer, however, there would be enough to eat for months to come, what with squash and beans from the garden and greens and berries from the forest, and this year there was promise of enough of a corn crop to last through the coming winter. His children were in rags but his wife would probably regain enough strength after her spring childbearing to weave the nettles he had gathered into a hemplike cloth, and he would have to find time to make them leather shirts before the cold set in. The dark forest encircling the little clearing laid grim emphasis on the solitude that dominated his existence. He might be a while even hearing of the war that was starting, for days and often weeks passed without his seeing any human being not a member of his family. His nearest neighbor was in a similar clearing three miles away on the other side of a ridge; the nearest town, the abode of six families, eleven miles away over a trail passable only in dry weather. Supposing his corn crop this season were to include a surplus or his traps this next winter to yield a good fur catch, there would nevertheless remain for him the task of getting to a market in which to exchange his produce for the powder and salt, the new hoe and the new ax, he had for the last year so sadly needed.

Any speculation by others, including us today, on whatever could have moved this frontiersman of 1775 to choose an existence so harsh and desolate, and thereafter so fiercely to cling to it in the face of unspeakable dangers, must first take into account the driving force of his preconceptions. Since childhood he had heard through occasional contacts with long hunters, traders, returned soldiers, or friendly Indians, stories of the grandeur of that far country beyond the mountains. It had become a country that had taken on in his youthful imagination dimensions and attributes more vivid than those attached to the reality of anything he had ever himself experienced. It was a country where not only was any amount of land to be had but such land as man had never before enjoyed. It was a country in which everything was bigger, the rivers, the lakes, the trees, the springs, the meadows, the fish, the game, even the grass. The cane grew to thirty feet and the grapevines so luxuriantly that their great clusters of fruit hung from the tops of the tallest trees. His hunter's soul had been delighted by accounts of the herds of buffalo, elk, and deer, the multitudes of bear, the packs of wolves, the number of panthers, the unending files of turkeys, the infinite variety of fish, the limitless flocks of waterfowl, the sky-darkening flights of pigeons. The air was purer, the soil richer, the water sweeter, the sky bluer. It was a country further set apart from lesser climes by mysteries and wonders, boiling springs, immense caverns, mounds reared by giants, the bones of monsters. It was a country

the mere contemplation of which suggested a future in which anything was possible. Above all, it was a big country with room in it
for a man who, above all, wanted room.

Having undertaken the great venture of crossing the mountains
to see for himself, he was discovering that all the stories had been
true. But other and grimmer discoveries were also awaiting him. In
the vast loneliness of the seemingly boundless wilderness there were
already established other powers and other occupants, all of whom
regarded him as an alien intruder. The prospective outbreak of war
gave to these objections to his presence a sudden arresting significance.

Of overwhelmingly first concern, and to continue to occasion him
an equal concern for the next twenty years, were the Indians who
considered the wilderness their homeland and him the most flagrant
of trespassers. About the perimeter of the new transmountain frontier were ranged twenty-six Indian nations who were in the process
of composing their former disputes with one another, were from
now on to be supplied from English military depots, and could
therefore soon be expected to make a united assault.

It was not the multitude of their warriors that made their hostility
so ominous. The population of all twenty-six nations totaled not
much more than a hundred thousand compared to the thirteen
colonies' more than two and a half million. But at the outset of the
war they greatly outnumbered the settlers west of the mountain
and their method of waging war made their enmity a maximum
menace. They were able to sortie at will from their distant towns,
to traverse the intervening forest undetected, to select objectives at
will, to strike with sudden fury and surprise, to kill and ravage,
and then to withdraw as suddenly back into the forest before a
countering force could be assembled. The pressures of such a war
upon the settlements were continuous and relentless. Any homestead
or station that continued to escape destruction must remain in perpetual dread that the dawn of each new day might bring with it the
end of that chance immunity.

The strategic location of the centers of Indian power added tremendously to the task of coping with the threat. On the New York

frontier the dreaded Iroquois,* historically the most warlike of all Indian nations, who after posing for more than a century as the friend of that frontier had now become its most bitter enemy, were in a position to ravage it by attacks against which there could be literally no adequate defense. When, tormented beyond endurance, the frontier, with help from the Continental Army, painfully assembled a force of sufficient strength to mount a counteroffensive, the Iroquois had need only to withdraw to the sanctuary of the English bases in Canada after which they were able to return, almost on the heels of the retiring American army, to resume their depredations.

The deep salient of the middle frontier, extending from its base along the Virginia-Pennsylvania mountains to its tip in Kentucky, was nakedly vulnerable at the points where any salient is most sensitive to attack, its shoulders and its principal lines of communication. North and west of the Pittsburgh area were arrayed the Seneca, the Mingo, the Delaware, the Wyandot, and the Shawnee in a threatening semicircle from the headwaters of the Allegheny in western New York to the mouth of the Scioto in what is now the state of Ohio. Their warriors had been among Pontiac's fiercest followers, and had in his war been schooled in all the preferred techniques of ravaging the white man's border. From their forest strongholds they were able to descend at any moment of their choice not only on the settlements between the mountains and the Ohio but on the western stretches of Forbes' and Braddock's roads and on the long Ohio River route to Kentucky which together constituted the salient's northern life line. Behind these "near" Indians, as the frontier termed them, were the "far" Indians, the nations of the Lakes, guaranteed by distance against any faintest fear of frontier retaliation, who were as avidly ready as in Pontiac's time to make the long journey through the wilderness toward the waiting satisfactions of harassing the white man. On the southern flank of the salient were the Cherokee, crouched in their mountain fastnesses

---

* The composite nations of the Iroquois confederation, the Six Nations as it was often called, were, from the headwaters of the Delaware in the east to Niagara in the west: the Mohawk, the Oneida, the Tuscarora, the Onondaga, the Cayuga, and the Seneca. Iroquois colonists who had taken semipermanent residence in what is now eastern Ohio had become known as the Mingo.

overlooking the Holston, the Clinch, and the Wilderness Road, the frontier's other life line. The Cherokee, too, were veterans of recent wars against the whites. The fringe of outlying settlements and the 200-mile-long mountain trail leading to the pitifully few cabins in Kentucky offered them an irresistible opportunity to settle innumerable ancient grudges. The strategic situation of the Creek, next to the south, enabled them to maintain endurable relations with the adjacent Georgia and South Carolina border while continuing covertly to dispatch war parties through the Cherokee country to join in the attacks on the Holston and the Kentucky.

This arc of Indian pressures was but the inner shell of the menace. During the Revolution, and for the next ten years after it, the frontier was required to regard the Indians as merely the nearer enemy. More threatening and unassailable even than the Indian centers of power were the distant English military bases which kept the Indians supplied with the food, guns, and gunpowder which they required if they were to persevere in their attacks. At English army posts at Oswego, Niagara, Detroit, and Mackinac in the north, and at Mobile and Pensacola in the south, English regular officers and Tory partisan leaders entertained, counseled, and exhorted congregating packs of Indian warriors, speeded and often accompanied their expeditions against the American settlements, welcomed and rewarded their return.

Equally distant across the far reaches of the wilderness were scattered other prior and alien occupants, these of a different and softer breed who wavered between friendliness, neutrality, and hostility but whose existence under any circumstances multiplied frontier uncertainties and confusions. The little French communities at Detroit, Vincennes, Kaskaskia, and Cahokia exerted an influence on their Indian neighbors which tended to favor the American frontier when it appeared strong and as readily turned the other way when it appeared to weaken. They were vestiges of the onetime French dominion which had extended in a great crescent across the continent's interior from the mouth of the St. Lawrence to the mouth of the Mississippi. All of it east of the Mississippi France had relinquished to England as recently as 1763 at which time the rest of France's continental possessions had been ceded to Spain, a gesture that had promptly made Spain a third power reaching for the Mississippi Valley. This was a passing but, while it lasted, a far from idle threat. The immense Spanish-American empire extended in one vast, unbroken sweep from the southernmost reaches of South America to the headwaters of the Mississippi, and there were Spanish garrisons at New Orleans, Fort Arkansas, Ste. Genevieve, and St. Louis. During the Revolution Spain was at first benevolently neutral and thereafter ostensibly an ally. But from the moment in 1779 that Spain entered the war against England, her every military and diplomatic move was directed toward gaining possession of the entire region west of the mountains. In this design Spain was actively supported by France, the other and the indispensable ally of the United States.

Among the widely scattered Indian towns, English forts, French villages, and Spanish garrisons that shared occupancy of the 1775 western wilderness with the American settlers' stockades, there was one eccentricity even more startling than the stark isolation of the Kentucky settlements. Along the bluffs above the Mississippi at Natchez stretched the rude new plantations of a few score American settlers from Connecticut, New Jersey, the Carolinas, and Georgia. They had been attracted to a situation so remote by that sole opportunity to obtain a valid title west of the mountains offered by the exception in the Proclamation of 1763 which permitted settlements west of the Line if in West Florida. Having considered the fantastic opportunity, they had undertaken the stupendous journey to their new homes, some by Forbes' Road, the Ohio, and the Mississippi, some by way of the Holston, the Tennessee, and the Mississippi, and a few by striking out across the intervening 600 miles of wilderness between the southern seaboard and the Mississippi.

Among all these varied confusions contributing to the frontier's uncertainties, none was more demoralizing at the outbreak of the war than the lack on either side of outstanding leaders capable of commanding sufficient recognition to shape the course of events. Of the towering figures who had dominated the frontier world during the past two decades, all had passed or were passing from the scene. Sir William Johnson, Henry Bouquet, and Pontiac were dead. George Croghan, once more bankrupted, this time by the collapse of his grandiose land schemes, was slipping into a seclusion plagued by poverty and ill health. His offers of service to the Patriot cause were rejected. Widely held suspicions of the sincerity of his sympathies were prompted by his past associations with the Johnsons and the Indians, the current Tory activities of his nephew, John Connolly, and his deputy, Alexander McKee, and the service of his son-in-law, Captain Augustine Prevost, in the English army. John Stuart, forced by Patriots to flee from Charleston and oppressed by an illness to which he was soon to succumb, had not yet been able to re-establish his headquarters at Pensacola. The brilliant and aggressive frontier county colonels in the Valley of Virginia and the Holston who had so masterfully waged the Shawnee War, Andrew Lewis, William Fleming, Evan Shelby, William Christian, and their like, were as active and vigorous as ever, but each was too absorbed by the defense demands of his immediate locality to be ready for a more general role. Among the Indian chiefs there was none whose personality or reputation suggested a possible fitness for Pontiac's mantle. Cornstalk's star had been dimmed by his defeat at Point Pleasant, Dragging Canoe was frustrated by his superannuated seniors in the Cherokee hierarchy, and Alexander McGillivray was still more trader than chief.

The extreme stresses of frontier war, however, were about to raise two young men, hitherto unknown, to awesome heights of responsibility and to demand of each an inexorable reckoning of his innate capacity to command. They were antagonists, each the indicated champion of his people, in an irreconcilable conflict between total ways of life as well as races and nations, in which defeat meant for the vanquished the end of his world. Each was a hero in the ancient and epic sense in that he had won recognition as his people's champion by extraordinary personal feats of courage, stamina, and violence. As with all epic heroes, their careers were distinguished by prodigious perils and triumphs and in the end darkened by trials heavier than men can sustain.

George Rogers Clark, the Virginian, and Joseph Brant, the Mohawk, so clearly represented, as well as decisively commanded, the principal opposing forces that the frontier war took on many of the aspects of a personal duel. Any attempt to examine the wilderness campaigns of the Revolution must devote continuous attention to their vital successes and failures.

III

꧁

Brant

THERE HAVE BEEN many remarkable Indians but, in the long and storied roll from Powhatan and King Philip to Pontiac and Tecumseh and on to Crazy Horse and Geronimo, none was as remarkable as Joseph Brant. No other Indian so narrowly approached leading his people to a successful resistance to the fate made inevitable by the coming of a stronger race. None evidenced a personality so complex or was compelled to meet challenges so varied. The careers of few men of any race or time have been marked by changes and contrasts so striking. His experiences enclosed within the compass of a single lifetime a kind of recapitulation of the history of mankind, from the simplicities of barbarism to the perplexities of the Industrial Age.

The first impressions of his childhood were of the primitive rigors of an Indian hunting camp in the depths of the wilderness. As a youth he was subjected to a white man's education and became a convert to the white man's religion. As a young man he was the consort of missionaries and a translator of the scriptures. As a mature man he was expelled from this cloistered atmosphere into an outer world of tumult and crisis in which he was laden with

[26]

public responsibilities he was to bear to the end of his life. His emotional nature developed a capacity for the deepest friendships and an idyllic marriage. In London, he became the intimate of scholars, artists, peers, and cabinet ministers. Such was the respect in which he was held even by his enemies that he could be received by Washington with all the ceremony due a visiting head of state. Yet this man who had acquired so many civilized and cultured instincts was for years the aggressive and dedicated commander of bands of Indian marauders whose depredations were more atrocious than any others in the long and fearful record of frontier warfare.

We know more about the personal detail of his career than we do of any other great Indian. Though not an hereditary sachem, he came to be regarded by the English and American governments, by other Indian nations, and by the Iroquois themselves as the responsible spokesman for and the acknowledged leader of the Iroquois nation. In the greater Indian crisis precipitated by the outcome of the Revolution, he became the recognized spokesman for all Indians. Throughout his adult life, therefore, his actions and decisions, even his apparent motives and intentions, were a recorded and essential part of the history of his times.

His origin and pedigree, nevertheless, remain shrouded in fascinating mystery. His name indicated him to be the son of Nichaus Brant. But Nichaus, an elderly and much respected Mohawk, was Joseph's mother's second husband and she married him some time after Joseph's birth. It was generally assumed at the time on both sides of the frontier that Sir William Johnson was his actual father. This was an easy assumption inasmuch as during his long and ardent wooing of the Iroquois nation Sir William was reputed to have fathered upwards of a hundred Indian children. It is evident that Johnson would have been delighted could this assumption have been confirmed. He took the boy into his household, kept him at his side even when he was in the field at the head of armies, made himself responsible for his education, and in his will mentioned him repeatedly, affectionately, and generously. Neither man, however, ever publicly acknowledged a blood relationship. The conclusion is inescapable that the only unimpeachable testimony, that of Joseph's mother, remained inconclusive.

Little light is thrown on the mystery by the known circumstances of Brant's * birth. He was born in 1742 in the forests of the upper Ohio, 500 miles to the west of his clan's long-established residence at Canajoharie. It was not unusual for Iroquois to make long hunting trips to the Ohio, attracted by the more plentiful game in that wilder region. Many Iroquois families were so strongly attracted that they remained there for years at a time, and some remained there permanently, becoming known as the Mingo. But what led Brant's mother to make so arduous a journey while expecting a child is not indicated. This, the fourth year after Johnson's tempestuous arrival on the Mohawk frontier, was the year his white son, John, later Sir John, was born to him by his indentured German servant girl, Catherine Weissenburg, whom he married three years later on her death bed.

Whatever Brant's mother's motives in choosing at this time this remote western residence, her sojourn there bestowed upon Brant all the satisfactions of a wilderness childhood. In Canajoharie, a semi-civilized town with wooden houses and barns, cattle, poultry, tilled fields and orchards, existence had for generations been influenced by contacts with the adjacent white frontier, but life on the Ohio was as wild as beyond the shores of the farthest Lakes. Here he was able to enjoy to the fullest the traditional delights of an Indian boyhood.

The Indian boy was one of the most favored of all beings. He was not only permitted but expected and encouraged to do all of the things any boy might most want to do, while being required to

---

* Indians ordinarily had several names, the one given them in childhood being superseded by others as they attained maturity or distinction. The names by which Indians are known to history are almost without exception the names, or nicknames, by which they were commonly known to their white contemporaries. Brant was known to his fellow Mohawk as Thayendanegea. In Johnson's will he was referred to as "young Brant, alias Kaghneghta of Canajoharie." Nichaus' English family name, Brant, had been in use for several generations, supposedly as a consequence of a much earlier and uncertainly recorded association with a white family named Barnet. Nichaus' father, known to the pamphleteers of the era as "King Brant," had made a much publicized London visit in 1710.

do nothing to which any boy might take the slightest exception. He was urged to spend his time fishing, hunting, swimming, trapping, canoeing, roaming, playing games, gorging himself, and in every way aping the employment and deportment of an adult hunter-warrior. If he chose to waste days in idleness he was not scolded. Sulkiness, disobedience, misbehavior, fits of temper were tolerantly accepted as signs of budding manhood. His elders took a constant interest in his progress. His first kill, though no more than a chipmunk, was celebrated by a feast to commemorate the achievement, and his first bear and first buffalo by communal rejoicing. As he grew in strength and stature his opportunities widened. He was invited to participate in more elaborate and demanding exploits. Whether he awakened to a day to be devoted in collaboration with older companions to netting wildfowl, spearing sturgeon, snaring eagles, invading a bear's den, firing the forest for a deer drive, chasing elk on snowshoes, or experimenting with various fashions of painting his face, it was a life filled with satisfactions. In Brant's case it was also a life that by developing forest skills and physical stamina was equipping him for a later career in which he was able to command the devotion of his warrior followers by those qualities of self-confidence, endurance, cunning, and contempt for danger which they most respected.

Among the lessons of this boyhood apprenticeship which prepared the Indian boy to become the Indian man, most satisfying of all was his dawning realization that the process of becoming a man was a process of learning to take the fullest advantage of a completely uninhibited personal freedom. Everything he could sense in the world about him contributed to this realization. He could contemplate gleaming streams, leaping waterfalls, forest glades, sunlit lakes, cloud-wreathed mountains, star-filled skies—a limitless and beautiful world bountifully supplied with fish, game, and fruits to provide for his needs as well as delight his senses. He learned to appreciate these natural beauties and bounties with a religious fervor. His conception of the deity was of a supreme power which had created this world solely for his benefit and then had set him free in it to enjoy it entirely according to his bent.

This preoccupation with personal freedom with which the Indian boy was indoctrinated from his earliest years was not an unalloyed blessing. It was as well the source of that principal Indian weakness which so much accelerated the rate of the Indian downfall. It was natural for the Indian boy to do only what he pleased and to be most pleased by whatever caused him the least mental or moral effort, but this became an equally natural attitude of the Indian man. From his youth on he became increasingly inclined to shirk irksome tasks, to indulge himself in the present, to postpone hard decisions, and to remain oblivious to the inexorable passage of time. He regarded complete personal freedom as the essential attribute of manhood but along with the nobility of this aspiration he felt free, either whenever he chose or as a lifelong practice, to waste in idle feasting a winter's store of food, to exhaust his health and goods in drunkenness and gambling, or to leave to others the duties of community defense. That Brant was able to surmount these handicaps of his early training was possibly due in part to inborn traits of character exceptional in an Indian, but probably in a larger part to the stimulation of his energies by later and more varied demands.

The region about the Forks of the Ohio which was so soon to become the most strategically important on the continent was, during Brant's childhood there, one of the least inhabited. It had been depopulated during the Iroquois wars of conquest in the previous century and since then had been kept unpopulated by Iroquois policy. Only within the last generation had Delaware and Shawnee from eastern Pennsylvania and a few Iroquois hunting groups from New York begun to filter into it by Iroquois sufferance. Isolated in their little forest communities, separated from the white frontier by the mountain barrier and from other Indian nations by distance, the recently arrived inhabitants were able to live pleasantly free of outside interference, to hunt and fish and plant in peace and seclusion. Outside influences were soon to beat upon their sylvan tranquillity in a series of waves that eventually became tidal, but at first they needed only to consider the unlikely chance of a foray incident to the permanent state of desultory war between northern and southern Indians. For generations Catawba and Cherokee war parties from the far Carolina mountains had intermittently journeyed north to raid the edges of the Iroquois country, and retaliating Iroquois war parties had as meticulously returned the insult.

Among Brant's earliest and most vivid memories were those connected with a second and, at the time, more welcome intrusion. White traders who had served the Delaware and Shawnee in their former homes on the Susquehanna were beginning to follow them across the mountains to show their wares on the Ohio. No occurrence was more intriguing to a remote Indian community than the arrival of a trader. In his packs was a store of glittering treasures so coveted that their value seemed unlimited. Needles, mirrors, brass kettles, steel knives and hatchets, glass beads, silver brooches, everything the trader had on display was an article of almost supernatural excellence which the Indian intensely desired, could not produce for himself, and could acquire only by a trader's beneficence. Valued above any possible price was a gun, the possession of which raised instantly, as by the tap of a magician's wand, the status and the prowess of the hunter and warrior to a height of which without one he could never have dreamed.

The feasting to celebrate the trader's arrival, enlivened by the trader's distribution of rum, added to the gala atmosphere of the occasion. Such periodic traders' visits represented for Brant the first of those contacts with the white man's world which were to increase and develop until the white man's way of life had become almost completely his own. There is no record of his later recall of any meeting with George Croghan, the great Pennsylvania trader and royal administrator, at this time. But during Brant's boyhood Croghan had established his Pine Creek trading post and was circulating continuously among the Indians of the upper Ohio. They must have met, and the boy Brant could only have been much impressed by each reappearance of this fabulous figure seemingly possessed of inexhaustible wealth. Later their association was to be long and intimate and Croghan was to become more important to him than any other man except Johnson.

The third intrusion put a catastrophic and permanent end to forest peace. The French had determined to assert their dominion over the upper Ohio at the same moment the Virginians had determined to reach for land west of the mountains. The clash of these colliding forces brought on a world war in which the Indians of the Ohio were required, willing or no, to take sides. Many Ohio Iroquois, faithful to their friend and advisor, Croghan, offered their services to the English and, after the initial English defeats, were obliged to withdraw to their native New York. Other Ohio Iroquois, the genuine Mingo, cut their ties with their parent nation, joined the Delaware and Shawnee in enlisting with the French, and took part in the ensuing prolonged devastation of the white frontier east of the mountains.

Meanwhile, Brant had already left the Ohio as a result of a sudden alteration in his prospects of equally earth-shaking proportions, so far as his personal fortunes were concerned. During a visit to the Mohawk homeland, Molly, his spirited sixteen-year-old half-sister, had chanced to catch Johnson's perpetually roving eye. Johnson was never a man slow to make up his mind. He promptly established her in his home, Mount Johnson. Molly became nominally his housekeeper but was indulged by him with every deference due a wife. She surpervised his household, presided at his table, received his guests, permitted no rivals, and bore him eight children. Contemporary gossip agrees that their life together was happy to the day of his death twenty-one years later.

Johnson's attachment to Molly drew his attention to Brant, and the boy was accepted in the household, then consisting of Johnson and his three white children, Nancy, John, and Polly, with as much consideration as though he, too, had become a member of the family. This was a sensational transition from the crudities of his former wilderness background. There was more to the transformation than the physical novelty of stone dwelling, mahogany furniture, table silver, polished boots, and six-horse carriage. Johnson, the master of all this, the father image, the all but king, with his personal charm, his robust manner, his overwhelming personality, was the dominating new impression in this floodtide of new impressions. He had long been regarded by the Iroquois as the greatest living white man. The outbreak of the new war with France was making him seem almost as important in the eyes of England. He was charged by the king with supervision of all Indian relations, given the command of armies, made a baronet, and generally recognized as certainly the most significant figure in the colonies. In his fortified house, now called Fort Johnson, guarded by armed Highlander retainers, served by scores of Negro slaves, courted by swarms of Indian delegates, he received a continuous procession of distinguished guests, English generals, colonial governors, and traveling European scholars, peers, and scientists.

For a twelve-year-old Indian boy fresh out of the Ohio wilderness all this provided a bewildering and dazzling introduction to the complexities of life in the white man's world. But, possibly given assurance by Johnson's kindness, he appeared to have no great difficulty adjusting himself to it. With an Indian's peculiar imitative facility in detecting and repeating sounds, including even those of a strange language, his English soon became sufficiently fluent to make him useful as an interpreter. Whatever his inner doubts of his paternity, Johnson made the boy as much a companion as though he knew him certainly to be his son. At thirteen Brant was with Johnson at the Battle of Lake George when the as yet untried commander was achieving the first and only land victory that England was to win in the first five years of the French War. Brant continued to exhibit a boy's natural affinity for military color and excitement. At sixteen he ran away from home in order surreptitiously to join the Indian contingent accompanying the great English naval raid on Fort Frontenac. At seventeen he was with Johnson on his Niagara campaign and participated with mentioned credit in the fierce Iroquois onslaught along the forested brink of the famous gorge which determined dominion over half a continent.

Victory and peace raised Johnson to new heights of power and success. His influence over the Iroquois had now been extended over an imperial expanse to include the Indians of the St. Lawrence, the Ohio, and the Great Lakes. The projected new home, Johnson Hall, into which he proposed to move with Molly and their growing brood, was by frontier standards to be a palace. The number of his Highlander retainers, his slaves, his flocks and herds, his acres of land, had increased threefold. By now he was lord of a virtual principality. The future opening to his protégé, Brant, was one that demanded a more orthodox preparation than he had so far gained among Indians, traders, and soldiers. He packed the young man, now nineteen, off to the Indian school at Lebanon, Connecticut, along with William of Canajoharie, Johnson's acknowledged natural son, the product of a brief attachment to Caroline, niece of Hendrick, the old Mohawk hero killed at the Battle of Lake George.

Eleazer Wheelock, the school's enterprising founder, attempted to recruit other Iroquois youths but of the twenty or more who appeared from time to time most were never at ease and only Brant took sufficient advantage of his opportunities to attain the rank of famous alumnus. He appeared to find no more difficulty in turning from the martial din of camp and field to the monastic quiet of study and chapel than he had in stepping from the outer wilderness into Johnson's feudal household. His capacity readily to adapt himself to the unfamiliar demands of a totally new environment had no parallel among Indians of his generation and has been rare enough among representatives of any race. In writing Johnson reports on Brant's progress, Wheelock was particularly struck by this evidently unexpected trait in the disposition of the young savage: "Joseph is indeed an excellent youth, he has much endeared himself to me, as well as to his Master, and everybody else, by his good behavior."

While at school Brant profited by other than classroom lessons. He was soon being welcomed as friend in the homes of many of his teachers. Among these extracurricular contacts was Samuel Kirkland, later the heroic missionary to the Oneida. With him Brant passed from the role of disciple to that of assistant in Kirkland's studies of the Iroquois tongue in which Kirkland was presently so eloquently to preach. Another of Brant's increasingly intimate associates was his personal tutor, Charles Jeffrey Smith, a young man of some means with an earnest desire to become a missionary to the Indians. Smith hoped to devote the next school vacation to a preliminary tour of the Iroquois country with Brant, his favorite student, serving as guide and interpreter. In his letter of January 19,

1763, asking Johnson's approval he shed more light on the twenty-one-year-old Brant's character as it appeared to the most attentive observers, as well as on how lively were the hopes of his teachers for his future as a scholar:

"I have contracted an intimate Acquaintance with Joseph who I understand is high in your affection and esteem, and has Wisdom and Prudence to resign himself to your Direction and Conduct—as He is a promising Youth, of a sprightly Genius, singular Modesty, and a Serious Turn, I know of none so well calculated to answer my End as He is—in which Design He woud very Willingly and cheerfully engage shoud Your Honour consent to and approve of it. He has so much endeared Himself to me by his Amiable Deportment; his Laudable Thirst after and Progress in Learning: that did I not apprehend this woud be as beneficial to Him, as advantageous to me, I shoud neither desire his Assistance nor solicit Your Approbation ... The present Excursion is designed only for a few months after which He can return again to this School, so that I imagine if its of no Advantage, it can be but of little disadvantage to him."

There is certainly little in this appreciation of the eager, gentle, amenable scholar by one who knew him well to foreshadow his becoming the blood-stained scourge of the border. Instead, there is the conviction that here was almost perfect material, ready to be shaped into an instrument for the advancement of learning and the dissemination of the gospel. Those who knew him as a young man describe him as tall, erect, muscular, paler than the average Indian, with mobile and expressive features and an alert and confident bearing. His several portraits, indicating a softly rounded countenance, suggest more of a philosopher's thoughtfulness than of a warrior's ferocity. Wheelock was planning further to widen Brant's acquaintance with the conventions and civilities of white society by taking him with him on a June trip to Boston and Portsmouth in connection with the projected relocation of the school at Hanover, New Hampshire, where it was shortly to become Dartmouth College.

But all of these amiable and scholastic concerns were disrupted by the sudden roll of thunder out of the west. Pontiac had raised his standard, and the whole Indian world was aflame with revolt. On

May 15, 1763, there arrived at Lebanon a cryptic letter from Molly to Brant, under Johnson's seal but written in what Wheelock supposed to be Mohawk, peremptorily ordering his return. Word of Pontiac's investment of Detroit six days earlier could not possibly have reached Fort Johnson, his first attacks on the white frontier were not to begin for another three weeks, and he had concealed his preparations with such success that even men who knew Indians as well as did Johnson and Croghan were to be stunned by their first news of the upheaval. But Molly was still an Indian and, for all her preoccupation with her involved domestic and social duties, had been able correctly to sense the suddenly rising tension. This seemed to her no time for as important a young Mohawk as her brother to be idling away his days among white men at a white school. Wheelock's earnest attempt to detain him was unsuccessful. Brant went home. His school days were over.

He found the complicated Johnson established in the process of a sweeping realignment of its residential order. The previous year Johnson had arranged the marriage of his older daughter, Nancy, to Daniel Claus, his assistant, and this spring of his younger daughter, Polly, to Guy Johnson, his nephew. Daniel and Nancy had been assigned the original Mount Johnson house as their domicile; a new house, Guy Park, was being built for Guy and Polly; and Fort Johnson was being turned over to John, his housekeeper, Clara Putnam, and their two daughters. Johnson and Molly were moving into the nearly completed Johnson Hall, the normal confusion of the transfer being greatly augmented by the sudden necessity that the new edifice be at the same time fortified and garrisoned.

For Brant had returned to a greater change than any in the Johnson domestic arrangements. Johnson's influence over the Indians which, as recently as April, had appeared to extend to the farthest reaches of the wilderness had, within a matter of days, so completely collapsed that he could no longer be sure even of his long-faithful Iroquois. The Seneca, most numerous and most warlike of the Six Nations, had already gone over to Pontiac. The Cayuga and Onondaga were threatening to follow. Even the Mohawk were restless.

Brant lent his fervent support to Johnson's frantic efforts to restrain at least the eastern Iroquois. He was twenty-one and ready for
a man's responsibilities. His services were particularly useful among
his fellow Mohawk. There had been much disparaging comment on
his going away to school, but now that he stood again among them
they were soon listening to him with a respect they had not granted
to any other Indian since the passing of the immortal Hendrick. His
co-operation with Johnson's desperate efforts culminated in his accompanying an expedition of Mohawk and Oneida volunteers, led
by Andrew Montour but planned and organized by Johnson, which
made midwinter surprise attacks on the nearer Indian towns loyal
to Pontiac. Four upper Susquehanna villages were destroyed, together with their stores of corn, and 41 prisoners taken, including
Captain Bull, a noted Delaware chief. This armed aggression by the
historically dreaded Iroquois upon fellow Indians whose only offense
had been their opposition to white men proved a stunning blow to
the morale of Pontiac's Indian confederation and restored some of
Johnson's prestige. His pacification negotiations of the following
summer dragged on for months, but finally resulted in a renewed
recognition of his authority by the Seneca and the Indians of the
Lakes.

But it was also an episode the memory of which was to haunt
Brant in later years when he, in his turn, was struggling to set up
a general Indian confederation to oppose the same white enemy
Pontiac had opposed. Too many older Indians could never quite
forget that in the days of Pontiac's great gamble Brant had taken
arms in defense of that enemy. Yet at the time of Pontiac's War
Brant could have felt little compunction. He may have been influenced by his dominating benefactor, Johnson, but the position he
had taken was the identical one to which the Iroquois nation had
clung for more than a century. According to this ancient and time-
honored doctrine, Iroquois security depended upon peace with the
white men on the Hudson, whether they be the Dutch or the English, in order to keep open this trade source of guns and gunpowder
and thus to free them to turn their perpetually hostile attention in
the other direction upon all fur-gathering trade rivals, whether they

be the French or western Indians. This was a policy in which the Iroquois had such confidence that in the past they had embarked upon war after war to sustain it. By it they had been guided to extraordinary successes. Even in the infinitely perplexing crisis of the recent French War it had led them to ally themselves with the eventual victor. Now, when English power was entrenched more firmly than ever, seemed certainly no time to abandon it. Again their course seemed to have been proved wise. The furies of Pontiac's War, which for a time had inflamed the heavens, soon diminished. And once more Iroquois pre-eminence remained unchallenged.

Brant's confidence in the principle that Iroquois interests were best guarded by holding to the time-tested Anglo-Iroquois alliance was not even shaken by the Treaty of Fort Stanwix. That the stupendous Iroquois land cession injured other Indians immediately and disastrously did not at the time impress the Iroquois. Historically other Indians had often been trade rivals and hence the necessary objects of Iroquois hostility. For the friendship or support of other Indians the lordly Iroquois had never had need. No Iroquois was as yet able to foresee that there might ever be a need.

Though the threats of Pontiac's War were subsiding, Brant did not return to school. Nearer and more insidious threats had persuaded him that, however engrossing his white interests, the interests of his own people required his attention. In past years the Mohawk had yielded again and again to the temptation to sell strips of land to the continuously land-hungry white frontier. They had heedlessly continued the prodigal practice until their lower castle, Fort Hunter, had been completely surrounded by white settlement and their middle castle, Canajoharie, was now being encircled. Their belated disinclination to continue to sell merely increased the pressures. The proximity of the frontier had long since emptied the area of game. Mohawk families had been driven to dependence upon farming. While their remaining land had thus become more necessary to them, they were more than ever harassed by new white encroachments, boundary disputes, title questionings, law suits, irregular surveys, forged deeds. Brant's first direct service to his people was his intervention as advisor and advocate in their land difficulties. His position as an official Indian Service interpreter, his access to Johnson's attention, and his firsthand acquaintance with the way white men spoke and thought added to the effectiveness of his efforts.

At twenty-two he was also ready to assume other and more private responsibilities. He settled in a small frame house at Canajoharie, tilled a hundred-acre farm, raised horses and cattle, and married Christine, the daughter of an Oneida chief who had become a Christian convert and a noted native preacher. By Christine he had two children, Isaac * and Christiana. Their life together was far removed from the austerities of the wigwam. Their scale of living included beds, dishes, chairs, and other comforts with which ordinary Indians were unfamiliar and which were as well far above the standard of the average white settler. One account of a visitor who was much impressed by the hospitality with which he was received in the Brant menage remarks on Brant's fine suit of blue broadcloth and his wife's chintz gown decorated by tiers of silver brooches. Christine's health was not robust and her disposition was reputed to be difficult. Brant, though, must have been suited for when she died after eight years he promptly married her sister. Within another year she, too, fell victim to tuberculosis, an affliction to which Indians were notably subject.

During this period of domesticity and comparative calm Brant became increasingly interested in religious affairs. As early as 1753 Johnson had begun advocating the introduction of missionaries among the Iroquois. His interest was largely utilitarian. In addition to making Indians more manageable, he considered English pastors a useful counterweight to the influence of the French priests who were constantly slipping into the Iroquois country from the Canadian side. In the 1760's this English missionary effort was intensified and expanded with rising enthusiasm. A wave of zealous young New England evangelists rushed into the field. Brant gave his ardent

---

* As Isaac grew older he became increasingly irresponsible and twice was accused of killing companions during drinking bouts. At the age of twenty he attacked his own father in a drunken rage and during the scuffle suffered a blow on the head from which three days later he died. Brant was stricken by remorse though he was held guiltless both by public authority and public opinion.

support to this effort to Christianize his fellow Indians. His own conversion was presently being triumphantly announced by Wheelock, his former headmaster who had continued to be his friend and spiritual advisor. Brant made his Canajoharie home a headquarters for the mission movement, tutored aspiring missionaries in the Iroquois language, collaborated in the translation of the prayer book and the scriptures, superintended the building of Mohawk chapels, and occasionally himself conducted the kind of hymn-singing services which most readily engaged and held the attention of Indian congregations.

One Arcadian interlude brightened this period in Brant's career just before it was entirely absorbed by the necessities of war. Croghan had patented a hundred thousand acres in what is now Otsego County, New York, as one of the rewards stemming from his participation in the Fort Stanwix negotiations.* Brant was a frequent and delighted visitor in those years immediately after 1769 when Croghan was enthusiastically establishing his new home on the shore of beautiful Otsego Lake beside the outfall of the sparkling Susquehanna. Croghan had often before raised edifices in the wilderness, including particularly his major posts at Augwick, Pine Creek, and Pickawillany, but this was to be a more pretentious effort in keeping with his new status as almost certainly the owner of more land than any other man in the world. Direct Indian grants made personally to him totaled more than 300,000 acres, while his land-company interests could be expected to assure him fully three times as much more. He had introduced swarms of workmen and was energetically rushing the construction of a new house, already given the manorial name of Croghan Forest, a dozen lesser houses for his retainers, a mill, a bridge, a ship to sail the lake, and wagon roads to connect his still isolated but so suddenly burgeoning wilderness domain with

* Croghan was forced soon to realize that he had assumed obligations more extensive than he could meet. He was required first to mortgage, then to sell his Otsego lands and presently lost as well all of the other tremendous grants that had seemed to be within his grasp. Shortly after the Revolution a large portion of this tract passed into the possession of Judge William Cooper, whose son, James Fenimore Cooper, was brought here to live when still an infant. Much of the wilderness lore and color enlivening the Leather Stocking Tales were inspired by Cooper's boyhood experiences on the forested shores of the lake.

the white frontier. As an Indian Brant should have been horrified by all this furious activity. Every such clamor of new clearing and building, every such new disruption of the forest's former quiet, represented a renewed and ever more dangerous threat to the Indian way of life. But he had by now so far lost touch with the ordinary Indian point of view that he could comprehend and sympathize with his old friend's vaulting ambitions. He could even conceive that the day might come when he himself might become such a planner and builder.

Across the gleaming blue lake stood the somewhat more modest establishment of Lieutenant Augustine Prevost, son of the noted English general, who had married Croghan's white daughter, Susannah. Brant was powerfully drawn to the personable and cultivated young Swiss, who though two years his junior had had so much wider experience with the world beyond this wilderness. There developed between them a fervent friendship which on Brant's part amounted almost to idolatry. For seventeen years he had been surrounded by white influences. In Johnson's household, at the Lebanon school, and among his mission companions at Canajoharie he had become accustomed to behaving more like a white man than like an Indian. His attachment to Prevost marked the high tide of this inclination to consider himself as possibly belonging more to the white than to the Indian world. To have been accepted as an equal by this gifted and ingratiating European seemed to him not only a crowning gratification but a crowning reassurance. The sense that, as an Indian, he must never lose sight of the fact that there could never be any conceivable accommodation between the races had for the moment escaped him. The ebb and flow of this recurring impulse to envisage himself as a civilized man of the world whose more natural place was in white society was more important than any search for personal equilibrium. Upon the outcome of his inner struggle were soon to hang thousands of lives.

Whatever his aspirations and illusions during those pleasant years at Otsego Lake, they were jarred by Prevost's sudden recall to active duty and his abrupt departure overseas. Brant was literally prostrated by grief. For months he was inconsolable. Slowly he began to realize that the friendship which had seemed to him so consequential had seemed much less so to Prevost. The shock was a sobering reminder that he was after all an Indian and that he could not ignore his personal share in Indian concerns. A concurrent circumstance of those years at Otsego could have provided him with another presage of the real nature of the future awaiting him. Croghan's Indian daughter, Catherine, was then a slender, big-eyed, olive-skinned child of twelve. Absorbed in his relationships with Croghan and Prevost, Brant appears to have taken little notice of her. But she was to develop into a stately and beautiful woman of exceptional force and intelligence, to become the wife of his mature manhood, and to prove his constant and beloved helpmate through every grief and crisis to the day of his death in 1807.

The years of preparation which had granted him opportunity and leisure to measure the comforts and values of education, domesticity, religion, and widely varying social contacts were drawing to a close. Widowed for a second time and deprived of his Otsego associations, he was the more ready to yield to the aging Johnson's insistence that he take a larger part in Iroquois affairs. Johnson, leaving in the fall of 1773 for what was to prove his final visit to England, delegated to Brant responsibility for the diplomatic isolation of the Shawnee. Obedient to Johnson's instructions he spent months among the western Indians, making certain that the Mingo, Delaware, and Wyandot continued to abandon the Shawnee to bear alone the assaults of the Virginians. But, in common with many other perceptive Iroquois, he was by now appalled by the unforeseen dimensions of the settlers' rush into the Pittsburgh area after the Fort Stanwix land cession. It was beginning to become glaringly apparent that Iroquois misjudgment at Stanwix had released a tide which could threaten Iroquois security along with that of other Indians. At the Iroquois grand council that fall he delivered a powerful address warning his nation that it must soon take the chief responsibility for holding the advance of the white frontier at the Ohio.

Upon Johnson's return from England in the spring of 1774 Brant pressed this view upon him. Johnson continued to insist upon the sacrifice of the Shawnee, but in one of his last letters to the Earl of Dartmouth, secretary for the colonies, he was reminding him, as he had himself so often been reminded by Dartmouth's predecessors, that the Proclamation Line represented the legal limit of settlement and that any attempt to cross the Ohio might precipitate united Indian resistance. The Indians, he said, were well aware that the Line decreed by the king, establishing a boundary between white and Indian territory, had by the Treaty of Fort Stanwix merely been diverted to the Ohio, and they might well prove to be as determined to hold the new limit as they had been to hold the old one in Pontiac's time. Johnson's premonitions were more than justified. For the ensuing twenty years the Indians waged desperate war, successfully until near the end of the period, to maintain the Ohio boundary.

Johnson's death July 11, 1774, magnified rather than reduced Brant's official importance. Guy Johnson, succeeding his uncle as Indian Superintendent, realized by how much he failed to match Sir William's influence either with his own government or with the Iroquois and hastily appointed Brant his secretary. Actually it was Brant, now thirty-two years old, who succeeded Sir William Johnson as uncrowned king of the Iroquois. How enormous was the responsibility descending upon his broad young shoulders was revealed by the news from Lexington and Concord. Upon his decisions depended the fate of his people together with the lives and fortunes of every settler on the New York-Pennsylvania frontier.

IV

℘

Clark

IN THE FAR LONGER and more storied roll of remarkable frontiersmen, there has been not one whose exploits and achievements
have ever approached those of George Rogers Clark. For the frontier's ten most dangerous years he was the defender toward whom
all turned in every recurrent crisis. It was largely due to his tireless
exertions and the extraordinary force of his personality that, during
the Revolution, the westernmost frontier was everywhere held in
the face of odds which so apparently dictated a retreat.

He came later to the scene than other great leaders of the early
frontier. He was born 32 years after Andrew Lewis, 23 years after
William Preston and William Fleming, 20 years after Washington,
and 10 years after James Robertson and William Christian. But once
he had appeared he lost little time making his presence felt. At
twenty he was descending the Ohio by canoe, exploring shores
notoriously perilous to all white men other than a few Indian-toler-
ated traders. He was surveying in Kentucky while the stockade
poles of Harrodsburg and Boonesborough were just beginning to
rise. At the outbreak of the Revolution, leadership was thrust upon
him by the handful of Kentucky settlers the defense of whose four

weak and scattered stations seemed beyond the range of human capacities. He conducted that defense so aggressively that he was soon embarking upon the only successful invasion of enemy territory achieved by American forces during the Revolution. In six wilderness campaigns—a form of warfare demonstrated during the preceding century and a half of border conflict to be the most difficult and precarious of all military undertakings—he was never surprised, never discomfited. Again and again he snatched victory when by every circumstance defeat appeared foreordained. Lafayette, with ample opportunity to judge, rated him as second only to Washington among American commanders. Certainly no one after Washington served the Revolutionary cause with more enduring effect. His unflagging defense of Kentucky, his inspired trans-Ohio conquests, and his persistent demoralization of the western Indians gave unanticipated substance to American postwar claims to the west. The Mississippi boundary, conceded at the peace table, seems to us now an English surrender somewhat less fantastic than it was then universally considered, because of his efforts. All this he achieved before he was thirty.

Unlike the Indian, Brant, whose pre-eminence among Indians stemmed from attributes of character and intelligence which set him apart from other Indians, in the frontiersman, Clark, there appeared fully developed every quality which most clearly identified him as a completely representative frontiersman. In the depths of the wilderness he was as much in his element as any Indian or long hunter. He was a master of those accomplishments, skills, and crafts most valued on the frontier. In physique, strength, and endurance he had few equals and in the common frontier predisposition to violence, belligerence, and reckless daring he had none. He was able to command the devotion of his normally recalcitrant and insubordinate followers by a continuing demonstration that whether in the woods, on the river, on the march, or in forest battle he was more ready than any other man for every wilderness test. High among the fashions in which he appealed to them was the degree to which he shared their contempt for consequences, moral as well as physical, and their volcanic impatience with every restraint, notably that of governmental authority. Perhaps strongest of all his appeals to them was that he shared the nearly universal frontier inclination, in whatever situation, to look first for personal advantage, an inclination that reached its apogee in an insatiable hunger for land, including land already claimed by another settler, previously granted to a land company, or repeatedly pronounced Indian by treaties.

Yet absolute self-reliance, the key virtue in the frontier character, could reach an extreme from which flowed more weakness than strength. Clark did not escape this extravagance. His impatience of restraint led him during his most brilliant campaigns to keep official accounts so heedlessly that his personal affairs never recovered from the disorder; his scorn of authority, particularly the plodding decisions of the central government, led him to independent enterprises which bordered on treason; and, eventually, frustrations of his freedom of action led him to alcoholic excesses which undermined his health. But these were weaknesses that became manifest later. During the Revolution, when the fate of his country and of his countrymen on the frontier rested so heavily upon him, he rose unfailingly to every demand.

His preparation as a child and boy to meet these demands upon his young manhood could not have been more effective had it been consciously planned with that end in view. He was born November 19, 1752, in a cabin on the banks of the Rivanna River on what was then tidewater Virginia's western frontier. It was a frontier seething with new hopes, new aspirations, and new ventures. During the three years since his parents, John and Ann Rogers Clark, had established themselves there the Ohio Company had been formed, Thomas Walker and Christopher Gist had made their great land-seeking explorations, and the trickle of settlers into the Valley of Virginia had become a stream. The year of his birth the Boone family, including 18-year-old Daniel, was making the long trek by covered wagon from Pennsylvania to the Yadkin in North Carolina and the year after it the 21-year-old Washington was making his dedicated winter journey to confront the French on the distant borders of Lake Erie. The next year Washington's little army was fighting in the defiles of the mountain barrier, and the year Clark was three Braddock's disaster had laid open the Virginia frontier to Indian invasion. For Clark later Indian wars could present no terrors with which he had not been made familiar by the earliest impressions of his childhood.

He was not, however, destined to grow up among the deprivations and limitations of life in a frontier cabin. When he was five, the family moved east again to a small plantation in Caroline County inherited from an uncle. Here, though he could continue to satisfy a boy's natural appetite for riding, hunting, and fishing, he could also be subjected to a certain amount of schooling. This last was imperative since in the years ahead there would be need to prove himself more than the superlative woodsman. There would be the need also to handle the staff work of distant commands, to address assemblies, to correspond with governors, to draft dispatches announcing the conquest of provinces.

Undoubtedly, however, the greatest influence bearing upon his development was family associations. From the year of his first departure from home, his letters were filled with evidences of his devotion to those with whom he had been in such close communion until then. There is some justice in Clark's conviction that he came of most superior stock. The closely knit Clark-Rogers clan formed a loyal, vigorous, and enterprising unit which admitted dependence only on each other. His parents were individualists who impressed all who knew them by their force and character, and all of his brothers were distinguished by their readiness for public responsibilities. His mother was less concerned than proud to be able to say that five of her six sons were officers in the Revolutionary armies. Her youngest, William, failed to gain this distinction only because he was only twelve at the end of the Revolution, but before he was twenty-one he was in uniform. He served in the Ohio Indian wars with Hardin, Scott, and Wayne, commanded, with Meriwether Lewis, the prodigious exploring expedition to the Pacific, and through all his later years, as territorial governor and Indian Superintendent, served as guardian in chief of the nation's westernmost frontier on the Missouri. The range of the services of the Clark family has remained without parallel in their country's history. The two brothers, George and William, presided in turn over the west-ward movement from its inception on the upper Ohio until it had swept the entire breadth of the continent. George played a dom-inating role in the initial winning of the eastern Mississippi Valley. By the time William's services as Great Plains proconsul had ended with his death in 1838, the first American settlers were established in Oregon.

At school Clark was not a complete success. His masters found him often restless and inattentive. He was interested in geography and history but in little else that was to be found in books. Somehow he learned to write that vigorously expressive English that made his later reports and memoirs such a pleasure to read. Among his classmates were James Madison, future president of the United States, and John Tyler, future governor of Virginia, but for him law or politics had no appeal. His attention was already fixed on that distance beyond the Blue Ridge in the shadow of which he had been born. In his estimation the most important phase of his educa-tion came when he was taught surveying by his grandfather. Once that was mastered he was ready. In common with every Virginian familiar with the frontier all the members of the Clark family were intensely interested in western lands. George Rogers Clark, the second son of John and Ann, was delegated to be the clan's scout and forerunner in the search for the best available. The spring before he was twenty he set out. He was now six feet, straight, graceful, handsome, with sinews like whipcord, a thatch of red hair, and sparkling black eyes. No young man about to become a frontier hero could more perfectly have looked the part.

He crossed the mountains by the route made memorable by Nemacolin, Gist, Washington, and Braddock, by the repeated ebb and flow of Indian invasion, and more recently by the astounding post-Stanwix surge of westbound settlers toward the upper Ohio. By that spring of 1772 thousands had swarmed over the mountains, grasping at land to which none could hope to gain legal title. All of it was blanketed by the prior claims of immense land companies which were in the course of being blessed by cabinet sanction. More-over, with both Pennsylvania and Virginia claiming jurisdiction over the region, Pennsylvania and Virginia land seekers were almost as ready to fight each other as they were the Indians. This elbowing, brawling rush of settlers had come in such numbers that the game formerly so plentiful about the Forks of the Ohio had already been exterminated, and hundreds of families were starving while awaiting their first corn crop.

Clark did not linger long at Pittsburgh. He was excited by all the turmoil, but this was a frontier already three years old and he was more excited by what he might find on to the westward down the Ohio. His companions on the canoe trip well represented the diversity of types characteristic of this tumultuous border. One was David Owens, the ex-trader, ex-deserter, ex-squaw man, who during Pontiac's War had attracted wide attention even at a time when extremes of violence were little noted by bringing in the five scalps of his Indian wife and children to claim Pennsylvania's scalp bounty on them. Another was Reverend David Jones, the missionary to the Indians and later one of Washington's chaplains who wrote a journal of the voyage.

Clark paddled on southwestward, enjoying his first view of the noble river upon which he was to make so many other voyages, for which he was to fight so many battles, and on which he was to live for the rest of his days. The western Indians were still too confused by the great Iroquois betrayal at Stanwix to have reorganized their resistance, and that spring there were a few other ardent land seekers taking advantage of the lull by venturing as far as the mouth of the Kanawha. But it was an uneasy peace. Unexpected encounters in the wilderness more often than not resulted in shooting on sight.

Each race accused the other, with perhaps equal justice, of resort to ambush and assassination. Meanwhile the land seekers kept to the south bank. The north bank was still the "Indian side," as it was to remain for most of the next generation. And the infuriated Shawnee, the Indian most immediately affected by the sudden influx of white men, were beseeching support from other nations while gathering themselves to strike, alone if need be.

The next two years were marked, even for a man of Clark's inexhaustible energy, by an almost incredible activity. He pushed his inspection of the Ohio 300 miles down river. He blazed his claim to land on Fish Creek, built a cabin, and planted a corn crop. He made repeated trips back over the mountains to Virginia to report to the family on the results of his explorations and once brought his father out to see the Fish Creek claim. In a letter to Clark's brother, Jonathan, a friend accompanying the party reported it to be "a Bottom of fine land on the Ohio which would be Valuable were it not for it being so Surrounded with mountains surpassing anything you ever saw." It was here that Clark first became fascinated by the mystery of the Indian mounds which were so notable a feature of the central valley. It was an interest that became a lifelong speculation on their origin.*

The Fish Creek location, 130 miles down river from Pittsburgh, was far beyond the mountain crestline which for so long had seemed a permanent barrier to any possible further advance of the frontier. But already it seemed too near, too accessible, to be highly prized. Kentucky, waiting at a more glamorous distance, offered rich level land not constricted in narrow mountain valleys, land described by the few who had seen it as more beautiful than any other on earth. There had even been a species of legitimacy cast about the reach for this Kentucky land by the recent astonishing pronouncements of Lord Dunmore, the royal governor of Virginia, whose ordinary duty it was to discourage western settlement. The magic word Kentucky had suddenly become the one word most often on the lips of every truly dedicated land seeker. This spontaneous new excitement which had gripped the frontier was perhaps most strikingly expressed by Reverend John Brown in a letter to William Preston, the organizer of the Kentucky surveys: "What a Buzzel is amongst People about Kentucky, to hear people speak of it one Would think that it was a new found Paradise."

In the spring of 1774 Clark was on the Ohio at the mouth of the Little Kanawha as one of the leaders of a group of some 90 land seekers headed for Kentucky. It was a more or less chance assembly of venturers seeking the safety in numbers in event of a Shawnee

---

* He eventually concluded, as have most modern anthropologists, that they were raised by the immediate ancestors of the contemporary Indians.

attack en route. That same spring James Harrod, with a smaller but similar group, had gained an earlier start and was already well down river on his way to the establishment of Harrodsburg. Informed that the Shawnee appeared at last determined to resist the occupation of Kentucky, Clark's party returned to Wheeling to inquire how they might best serve the white cause. It was his first-hand knowledge of events at this juncture that enabled him later to testify that Michael Cresap had had nothing to do with the atrocious murder of the Logan family and had instead counseled against any aggressive move upon Logan's village. The outrage had in any event made certain that the impending war could no longer be postponed.

Clark was commissioned captain of militia and gained his first military experience with the two expeditions into the Indian country, commanded by Angus McDonald and Lord Dunmore. There was little hard fighting in either campaign. The issue of the war was determined in the one fierce battle down river at Point Pleasant between Andrew Lewis' Virginians and Cornstalk's Shawnee. But it was an immensely valuable experience, nevertheless. Among his companions were fellow frontiersmen who had already won or were destined soon to win some of the greatest names in frontier annals: Daniel Morgan, Simon Kenton, John Floyd, James Wood, Michael Cresap, Joseph Bowman, William Harrod, Thomas Nicholson, Jacob Drennon, Peter Parchment. There was one more of that company of heroes who then was among those most trusted and best liked: Simon Girty.

The outbreak of the Shawnee war had forced every white man to flee from Kentucky and the lower Ohio, but the Shawnee surrender after Point Pleasant reopened the way west. In the spring of 1775 all who had withdrawn rushed back, accompanied by a host of new land seekers. Clark had previously explored the river as far as the Falls and he now turned his attention to the interior of Kentucky. He had been engaged as deputy surveyor by the Ohio Company but his primary purpose was to find land for his family and himself. As further testimony to the extraordinary diversity of types among these men pushing eagerly hundreds of miles into the wilderness, among his companions on this 1775 journey was

James Nourse, a wealthy and cultured Englishman who had brought his wife and nine children to America and was now engaged in searching for a suitably wild and expansive estate upon which to establish them.

Clark took time off from his surveying duties to inspect all of central Kentucky and to visit Harrodsburg, Boonesborough, and Logan's Station in the first weeks of their existence. He was enchanted by the region, as was every other early viewer. He was writing his brother Jonathan, "a richer and more Beautiful Cuntry than this I believe has never been seen in America yet." If his father, he continued, "once see ye Cuntry he will never rest until he gets in it to live I am Ingrosing all ye Land I possibly Can expecting him."

This rich and beautiful land was being claimed by men who had every need for their boundless enthusiasm. No single one of them could feel that he had more than the faintest shadow of a legal right to the possession he was asserting. All had ventured so far and risked so much on the mere assumption that one way or another all would somehow work out well in the end. Most were never to succeed in justifying their hopes. Daniel Boone, for one notable example, was never able finally to establish a permanent legal title to a foot of Kentucky soil, and moved eventually to the Spanish side of the Mississippi. Each of these first Kentucky settlements or projected settlements based such claim as it could cite on a different theory of land rights. Each theory conflicted with provincial and English law and of necessity with that advanced by local rivals. The Ohio Company's claim to the tract Clark was surveying near what was later to become Leestown was based on the hope of gaining a royal grant which had already in fact been specifically disapproved. The Harrodsburg group of independent Pennsylvania settlers argued that all wild land had previously belonged to no company or state or Indian nation and therefore could become the property of the first man to take, use, and develop it. John Floyd and Benjamin Logan were erecting Logan's Station on land Floyd had surveyed by authority of William Preston, surveyor of Virginia's Fincastle County, whose authority to do so was far from clear inasmuch as by the English law on which his commission depended all settlement was forbidden west of the 1768 readjustment of the Proclamation Line. Boonesborough was being established on land purchased from the Cherokee, whose title to it the Cherokee themselves did not seriously assert, by Richard Henderson's Transylvania Land Company. All settlements were illegal under English law, but Henderson's claim was additionally clouded by the ringing denunciations of the governors of Virginia and North Carolina. As though this superfluity of disapproval were in itself sufficient reason to prefer it, the other settlers decided to pool all their claims under Henderson's dubious sponsorship. Representatives of all four settlements (Harrodsburg had already sprouted a short-lived offshoot at Boiling Spring), meeting in convention at Boonesborough, asserted their right to govern themselves, declared their fidelity to the King, and petitioned the Continental Congress for recognition as a separate province.

Important as was the question of title validity, the problem it presented was for the future. More immediate concerns were more pressing. None of these 350 men who had swarmed to Kentucky in the spring of 1775 was as yet a bona fide settler. Not one had brought his family with him. All so far were adventurers and gamblers, feverishly blazing trees to mark the boundaries of land that they felt there was a chance they might one day own, living in temporary huts, hunting to gain food from day to day. Essentially they were as much land speculators as were the great land companies. It was a speculation in which they had invested themselves, in lieu of money. The price offered was the risk of survival. The news of Concord and Lexington convinced many that the price was too high. The two major factors bearing on their situation combined to demonstrate how desperate were the odds. These were, first, that the two most belligerent of all Indian nations, the Shawnee and the Cherokee, were crouched on either flank and, second, that the only connection with possible support from the main frontier was the tenuous thread of a 200-mile-long mountain trail. To the majority of the adventurers it had become clear that their position was obviously indefensible. Most of them bolted. By mid-July not more than fifty men had remained in Kentucky. Again, as in 1774, the reach for the new promised land seemed to have been premature.

Then, in the first week of September, came the startling event that changed the whole aspect. Boone returned from a hasty trip back to his former home on the Clinch. With him were his wife and daughters. They were the first white women to stand on the banks of the Kentucky. With their coming what had been before a temporary camp of itinerant land seekers had made the vital transition to a permanent community of homemakers. Of all Boone's services to the foundation of Kentucky this moment, in which his wife, Jemima, shared, represented his greatest. Others had explored Kentucky long before him. There had been many other long hunters prior to his famous Kentucky hunt. The initiative in the establishment of Boonesborough had been taken by his land-company employer, Henderson. But indisputably Daniel Boone was Kentucky's first genuine settler.

In the course of that same week the women and children of the McGary, Denton, and Hogan families reached Harrodsburg. Unaccompanied men, accustomed to the forests and hardened to trail travel, had for years proved that they could venture widely and freely, knowing that with the threat of danger greater than they had foreseen they could swiftly escape. With whatever turn circumstance seemed to indicate, they could come and go and live to try again. But in bringing out their families this new breed of Kentuckians had made the final and fateful decision. They had come to stay. And it was a decision that they had made after they had been made fully aware that their frail, undermanned, and isolated stockades were about to be beset by all the shocks and terrors of a general Indian war.

That summer of 1775 the inhabitants of every one of the thirteen colonies were being required to make difficult decisions. But there could have been no choice inviting so grievous an ordeal as that made by these men and women inhabiting the farthest wilderness. Clark's personal decision was typical of a self-confidence so complete as to suggest a belief in his own destiny. He had been captivated by his first view of Kentucky. He had promptly decided to make it his home. The next conclusion was obvious. A home demanded defending. His was a temperament that welcomed responsibility. He accepted the survival of Kentucky as his. In any military sense the successful defense of a position so remote and feeble was utterly impossible. Forthwith he began to plan to achieve the impossible.

V

🎜

The Race for Indian Favor

THE SUCCESSION of great events in that summer of 1775 was like
one tremendous uninterrupted roll of thunder. The only English
army in the Americas was besieged in Boston by thousands of spon-
taneously assembled minutemen. Lexington and Concord were
followed by the sterner shock of Bunker Hill. Washington was
unanimously appointed commander in chief of the united forces of
what some were already beginning to call the United States. The
Continental Congress was daily making decisions leading unpre-
meditatedly yet inexorably to the Declaration of Independence. In
every city and hamlet people were being impelled to take sides and,
almost as irresistibly, to harass neighbors with whose opinions they
differed. Beatings, burnings, looting, rioting abounded. From every
quarter singing and cheering contingents of Patriot militia were
marching toward Boston. Through all the tumult throbbed the
ominous drumbeat of the Indian menace.

No one in Congress or out was able entirely to dismiss the thought
that beyond the country's western border were ranged half a hundred
Indian nations or that they were capable, if moved by any sudden
gust of passion, as in Pontiac's War, of dispatching thousands of
warriors in attacks excessively difficult to parry with so much of

the country's armed force already committed to engaging the English on the seaboard. Such an onslaught well might prove the determining factor in the struggle. Both parties to the conflict were conscious of this possibly decisive importance of the course the Indian might choose. Both were already anxiously maneuvering to gain Indian alliance or, at worst, neutrality. Ostensibly outraged by the Patriots having welcomed the services of Indians from the Stockbridge mission school in Massachusetts, Lord Dartmouth was on July 24th directing Guy Johnson: "It is, therefore, his Majesty's pleasure that you do lose no time in taking such steps as may induce them (the Iroquois) to take up the hatchet against his majesty's rebellious subjects in America." Congress would have been as ready to accept Indian military support, in any area where it might have proved useful, but realized that the recent westward leap of frontier settlement had so prejudiced the Indians that neutrality was the most that could be sought. On July 12th an American Indian Department was created, with Northern, Middle and Southern sections to deal respectively with the Indians of New York, of the Ohio, and of the region south of Virginia. The designated commissioners were furnished an address to the Indians of each area, impressing upon them that: "This is a family quarrel between us and Old England. You Indians are not concerned in it. We do not wish you to take up the hatchet against the King's troops. We desire you to remain at home, and not join either side."

Proposals that white men seek Indian allies against other white men, even though these included the women and children of a noncombatant border population, raised few moral issues immediately discernible in 1775. American denunciations of the practice only became clamorous later in the Revolution, and then largely as a propaganda device, after it had become apparent that the English had succeeded in enlisting most Indians in their service. Indian participation in the struggle had been expected from the start. Indians had taken part in every war on the continent since the foundation of Jamestown. Many had been localized eruptions forced on them by settlers' territorial encroachments, but they had been as ready to lend themselves to every reflection in America of the recurrent

European conflicts between France and England. It would have been impossible to have persuaded them to stand aside even had both powers so elected. The value Indian society set on personal valor compelled every warrior periodically to go to war. The superior loot and prestige to be gained by raiding white men's communities built every belligerent impulse toward a compulsion. Long familiarity with the evil had made people less sensitive to it. The existence of Indian nations on the continent had been necessarily accepted as a strategic factor as unavoidable as the location of its mountains and rivers. They were there and, whenever there was a war, they were certain sooner or later to be in it. Another generator of the insensitivity was the widespread realization that, of the brutalities associated with border warfare, the whites had seemed less guilty than the Indians only in so far as they had been denied the opportunity by being obliged to stand more often on the defensive. White men invading Indian country struck down women, children, and prisoners with as little hesitation as did Indian raiders among the settlements. Frontiersmen normally balked at burning captives at the stake or at the prolonged torments in which Indians delighted, but not at mutilation or scalp-taking and they revolted the Indian sense of decency by the frequency with which they murdered envoys and peace delegates. Each provincial assembly had repeatedly offered scalp bounties, including slightly smaller but still substantial payments for the scalps of women and children. Outrage fed upon itself on both sides of the frontier. The train of horrors that particularly distinguished the border warfare of the Revolution was appalling and yet essentially it was but another example of war's immemorial dictate that, once locked in conflict, either antagonist will grasp whatever weapon comes to hand.

The 1775 competition for Indian favor was most intense on the New York frontier where the historic military power of the Iroquois was the reward, and here also it first came to a crisis. Every surface factor appeared to serve the royal cause. Sir William Johnson had died the year before, but his former associates and the surviving members of his family were in control of all the official machinery of the imperial Indian Department with uninterrupted opportunity to use these familiar pressures on Iroquois opinion. His son, Sir John, had inherited the bulk of his enormous estate together with his private army of Highlander tenants and was able at Johnson Hall to dispense the same boundless hospitality to swarms of Indian guests and clients. His deputy and neighbor, John Butler, and his assistant and son-in-law, Daniel Claus, served in the same official capacity on the staff of the new Indian Superintendent, his nephew and son-in-law, Guy Johnson. All had every personal as well as public reason to continue staunchly loyalist. Moreover, New York as a province was more strongly Tory than any other. During the Revolution more New Yorkers served in the King's forces than in the American.

But there were other factors, less apparent at first, which delayed the decision. In New York, more than in any other province, the cleavage between rebels and loyalists followed class lines. The more prosperous and better educated tended to hold to the king, the poorer and less satisfied to welcome any change. In the increasingly envenomed disagreement rending each community that early summer, numbers counted. There were more common people than gentry. This was overwhelmingly so on the frontier. On the frontier also a large proportion of the actual settlers were Scotch-Irish or German. In neither racial strain had there been bred any innate sense of loyalty to England. On the white side of the frontier, therefore, the Johnsons were surrounded by a local population most of which was suspiciously watchful and definitely hostile to all traffic with Indians. Meanwhile, on the Indian side, the missionaries, whose original advent had been encouraged by Sir William himself, had proved to possess a totally unexpected influence. Most of them were Presbyterian, or at any rate non-Anglican, and inclined to harbor either Patriot or pacifist sentiments. They were able to gain and hold the attention of the nearer fringe of semi-Christianized Iroquois. Brant's onetime associate, Samuel Kirkland, even managed to keep the whole Oneida nation permanently out of the English camp.

In this frontier crisis, all realized how much depended on Brant. The services of his old friend and schoolmaster, Eleazer Wheelock, were enlisted. Brant was unresponsive to this earnest appeal to memories of his school days at Lebanon and his fellowship with the missionaries at Canajoharie. His conscience had been troubled by few doubts. As a Mohawk, he could have little sympathy with American settlers who had taken so much Mohawk land and were bent on taking more. As a man, all his sympathies were with the Johnson family of which he felt himself, in effect, a member. As a citizen, he considered himself an Englishman. In replying to Wheelock he pointedly wrote that one of the lessons he had learned at Lebanon was "to fear God and honor the King."

The news of Bunker Hill convinced Guy Johnson and Brant that a stubborn and possibly prolonged war had become a certainty. To stage at Johnstown the formal Indian conferences required to organize Iroquois participation was not possible without setting off an explosion of protest among the surrounding settlers. They therefore surreptitiously set off for Oswego, summoning the Iroquois to meet them there. In view of the prevailing tension and suspicion, this was a gesture so blatantly hostile that it amounted to a declaration of frontier war. John Butler, his son Walter, Daniel Claus, most of Brant's Mohawk, and a hundred of the more ardent frontier Tories accompanied them. Abraham Cuyler, mayor of Albany, attempted to follow with several boatloads of much needed supplies but was seized by Patriot militia before he reached the frontier. Sir John stubbornly refused to go. He was reluctant to leave his extensive possessions at the mercy of his Patriot neighbors and he feared for the health of his pregnant wife. His apprehension regarding the rigors of the wilderness journey were apparently justified. Guy's wife, Polly, died at the end of it.

The New York frontier was terrified by waves of rumors that Brant and Guy Johnson were already on the return march from Oswego with an army of Indian attackers. But the fears were premature. The nearly 1500 Iroquois who assembled for the Oswego Conference were received by nothing more provocative than long speeches urging devotion to the king. The loyalist leaders had at their disposal insufficient supplies even to entertain so many Indians, let alone enough to furnish a campaign. Guy Johnson and Brant went on to another conference at Montreal which was equally well attended, declamatory, and inconclusive. Governor Sir Guy Carleton of Canada directed the Indians, some 3000 of whom by now had tentatively offered their services, to hold themselves in readiness to support the king's arms but meanwhile to take no offensive action against the American frontier. He was advisedly apprehensive of an American invasion of Canada against which he could interpose only the feeblest defense, and he had no wish to feed the fires of American aggressiveness by a spate of border atrocities.

The bewildered and disgusted Iroquois drifted back to their towns. A few of them even attended a conference at Albany with the newly appointed American Indian commissioners. There they insisted that Carleton had likewise urged them to remain neutral and that this was the course that they themselves were only too happy to take. The New York frontier sighed with a relief that for a time appeared warranted. For more than a year the Iroquois continued to maintain this unanticipated and therefore doubly welcome neutrality. They returned to their normal seasonal routines of hunting, fishing, and cornplanting while they waited and watched to note, with that diplomatic sagacity which as a nation they had so long manifested, which of the two white combatants, the English or the Americans, appeared the stronger.

The frontier situation on the upper Ohio in the spring of 1775 was hopelessly confused by the dispute between Virginia and Pennsylvania which had reached the stage of jailing each other's magistrates. The defeat of the Shawnee the year before had persuaded most observers that the Indian threat was for the moment negligible. In March the Virginia convention, as reluctant to appropriate money for frontier defense as had been the House of Burgesses in the 1774 crisis, refused to provide for frontier garrisons. This suited Dunmore who had correctly estimated the imminence of armed rebellion and who promptly ordered Virginia militia withdrawn from the three forts at Pittsburgh, Wheeling, and Point Pleasant. He directed Dr. John Connolly, Virginia's foremost protagonist at Pittsburgh in the jurisdictional dispute, to devote his energies instead to preparing the Indians to support the loyalist cause. The news of Concord, Lexington, and Bunker Hill roused even tidewater Virginians to the potential Indian danger, and the House of Burgesses, without waiting upon congressional action, on the last day of its last session appointed George Washington, Andrew Lewis, Thomas Walker, Adam Stephen, John Walker, and James Wood commissioners to treat for Virginia with the Ohio Indians. Washington was called to broader duties, and the other commissioners selected Wood as their agent to proceed to the Indian country to invite the Indian nations of the region to attend a conference with the Americans at Pittsburgh in September at which Virginia's pacific intentions and the complexities of the sudden war between the colonies and England could be explained to them.

James Wood came from one of those extraordinary frontier families, such as the Clarks, the Prestons, or the Lewises, upon whose unstinted services the development of the frontier most depended. His father had served with Washington in the French War and had founded Winchester. He himself had served in the Shawnee War and was to become a brigadier general during the Revolution and in 1796 Governor of Virginia. He was twenty-five when he set out on his astonishing tour of the Indian country which, considering the personal perils and diplomatic uncertainties involved, was worthily reminiscent of Croghan's most illustrious ventures. His companion and interpreter who faithfully shared his every labor and risk was Simon Girty. Starting from Pittsburgh on July 18th, in the next 25 days Wood traveled through the wilderness nearly 800 miles and visited 15 towns in the course of delivering his urgent invitation to the Ohio nations to attend the projected American peace conference at Pittsburgh in September. Of the four principal nations he addressed only some of the Delaware, influenced by their singularly pro-American chief, White Eyes, by the Moravian missionaries at the three mission villages on the Tuscarawas, and by their anxiety to escape Iroquois domination,* were disposed to listen

* It was at the Pittsburgh conference that fall that White Eyes delivered his celebrated "petticoat speech." During the period a generation earlier when the Iroquois had been systematically selling to Pennsylvania the ancestral lands of the Delaware east of the mountains they had silenced the protests of the helpless Delaware with the humiliating rebuke that they were women not warriors. At this conference White Eyes astounded his Indian hearers by his brazen defiance of the mighty Iroquois in the course of an impassioned oration culminating in the cry: "The petticoat I have thrown away and I declare I am a man."

sympathetically to his message. The Shawnee had the year before suffered a humiliation in their bloody war with the Virginians which had left them with a burning desire for revenge. The Mingo harbored bitter memories of the brutal murder of the Logan family. The Wyandot were situated too far away to feel that the proffered American amity was of importance to them. All were subject to the anti-American agitation of French traders working in the English interest and of other emissaries circulating the warnings and promises of the English commander at Detroit.

Wood's journal is detailed and explicit about his itinerary and his official conversations but matter of fact about the daily dangers of his journey. Again and again there are references to the headlong pace which he maintained: "Set off very early in the morning . . . travelled very Constant . . . hired two fresh horses . . . travelled very fast and Constant . . . started before Sun rise . . . rode hard and constant . . . my horse failed." Only occasionally are there references to danger: "The Indians were very Angry Many of them Painted themselves Black . . . Waked and saw several Indians with Knives and Tomhawks . . . a Squaw informed us privately that they intended to kill us . . . the Indians were employed in Conjuring the whole night during which they kept up a Constant howling like Wolves till daylight."

Wood returned with the shrewd opinion that the Ohio Indians were attempting to perfect a confederation in preparation for a united attack upon the Virginia frontier but that they were not yet ready and would in the meantime undoubtedly attend the conference. His estimate was proved correct when their principal chiefs, accompanied by some hundreds of hungry attendants, turned up in Pittsburgh on schedule.

The conference which opened September 26, 1775, and continued to October 19 was one of the most significant in frontier history since it helped to delay the onset of war on the Ohio for more than a year and at the same time provided the central incentive for the succeeding twenty years of Indian war. The delegates representing all three parties were of unprecedented distinction. Among the Indian ambassadors were Cornstalk, who had commanded at Point

Pleasant, Custaloga, and Guyasuta, who had commanded at Bushy
Run, Shaganaba, son of Pontiac, and three of the most prominent
leaders of the wars to come, Wingenund, Half King, and Captain
Pipe. Among the congressional commissioners were Lewis Morris,
later a Signer of the Declaration of Independence, and James Wilson,
also later a Signer as well as a justice of the Supreme Court, and
among the Virginia commissioners were the two greatest of all
early frontier leaders, Andrew Lewis and Thomas Walker. Also
present and taking a leading, though anomalous, part was Alexander
McKee, the king's deputy Indian agent. His participation was
accepted as quite proper and natural. Independence was not yet a
serious prospect and the other commissioners represented shadow
governments not yet even provisional. He alone was clothed with
the unquestionable authority of having been constitutionally appointed to a constitutional office. Though his conduct throughout
the conference's deliberations was considered candid and honest by
the American commissioners, some of them entertained private
suspicions, later justified, that at preliminary conversations with
the Indians earlier in the summer he and Connolly had advised them
to remain neutral for the present in order more successfully to prepare for later hostilities.

The first American success of the conference was in the response
to the standardized request that the Indians return all white
captives, runaway slaves, and stolen horses. To this the Indians
gave at least a token assent.* The great achievement of the conference, however, was the exchange of an Indian pledge of neutrality
for an American pledge to recognize the Ohio River as the permanent
boundary between the Indian country and the area ever to be considered open to white settlement. This formal reaffirmation by the
Americans of the Proclamation Line, so often previously affirmed
and reaffirmed at English conferences, was to the Indians an
American pledge of sovereign significance. They were to fight for

---

* In the instance of returning Negro women they objected to including offspring
born to them during their Indian residence on the ground that it was not fitting to
subject children fathered by Indians to the slavery awaiting them on the white side
of the frontier.

the next twenty years to hold the Americans to this pledge, to be supported in their stand by England, France, and Spain, and not to relinquish their claim to the Ohio boundary until the Treaty of Greenville in 1795.

The insincerity of the pacific Indian professions at the Pittsburgh Conference remains apparent for all their having seized so seriously upon the American boundary pledge. After conversations the previous July with many of these same Indian delegates, Connolly had made his way east to consult with Dunmore, who had taken refuge in an English warship off the Virginia coast, and then with Gage, invested in Boston by Washington's siege lines. Both gave their enthusiastic approval to Connolly's elaborate project which involved his proceeding to Detroit to organize a general Indian-Tory attack on the Virginia frontier in the spring in conjunction with a fleet-supported landing by Dunmore on the Virginia coast.

The American invasion of Canada that fall and winter prevented Connolly's ascent of the St. Lawrence, and he was compelled to resort to an attempted overland passage to the Indian country. Alert Patriot militia arrested him near Hagerstown, Maryland. The invasion of Canada in 1775, painful as was the repulse of that gallant attempt at conquest of what it was hoped might become a fourteenth state, was of immensely greater service to the Revolutionary cause than in the mere confounding of the Connolly-Dunmore plot. For the nine precious months between September of 1775 and June of 1776 England was denied the use of the St. Lawrence, the sole transport route to the interior. The 1775 neutrality promises of the Iroquois and the Ohio Indians were as a result of necessity fulfilled for at least that period. Not until the English supply lines could be fully re-established in the spring of 1777 was there any possibility of organizing that combined Indian effort that had been contemplated from the first. By then the Ohio frontier settlements had become so accustomed to the prospect of Indian attack that they were largely immune to the panic which most certainly must have swept the inhabitants into general flight eastward had the Indian assault developed immediately after the outbreak of war.

Only in the south did English plans and preparations for the early employment of Indians mature on schedule. After escaping from the Patriots at Charleston and recovering from an illness at St. Augustine, John Stuart set up a supply base at Pensacola which until 1781 was kept safe from interference by English control of the sea. During the winter of 1775 when the Americans were besieging snowbound Quebec his deputies, Alexander Cameron, Henry Stuart, and James Colbert, were supervising the distribution among the eager Creek and Cherokee of some hundreds of horseloads of arms and ammunition.

In the fall of 1775 the American commissioners, both provincial and congressional, opened conversations with these two numerically most formidable of all Indian nations, each capable of mobilizing several times as many warriors as could any other, including the Iroquois. The Americans were appealing for Indian neutrality but had nothing to offer in return. They could not supply Indian needs with the trade goods which the Indians must otherwise continue to accept from the English. And they could not remove the Watauga and Nolichucky settlers who had infuriated the Cherokee by continuing for the past six years to occupy land well west of the Proclamation Line which by repeated orders and treaties had been pronounced indisputably Cherokee. However, the Indians found it expedient to listen inasmuch as Stuart, obedient to the instructions of his government, was also counseling them to remain quiet for the moment. The English high command wished to save the Indian effort until it could be deployed in conjunction with the forthcoming English invasion of Georgia and the Carolinas. But this tidy timetable miscarried when to the amazement of all beholders, including the defenders, the ambitious amphibious expedition under Sir Henry Clinton and Sir Peter Parker failed in one of the more decisive battles of the Revolution in its June 1776 assault on Charleston, and the projected invasion of the southern provinces was delayed for another four years.

Stuart still counseled patience, but the Cherokee had been aggravated beyond endurance by their land grievances. So intelligent and talented in many respects, they had an historic genius for choosing to rush righteously to war at what was manifestly the wrong time. From 1754 to 1758 they had actively assisted their natural enemies, the Virginians, against their traditional enemies, the Shawnee. In 1760 they had waited to make war upon the English until the complete defeat of their possible allies, the French, had freed the English to devote strong columns of veteran regular troops to the invasion of the Cherokee homeland. Now again they chose the wrong moment when in the first year of the Revolution the Americans, flushed with the enthusiasm characteristic of the early months of any war, stimulated by their surprising victory at Charleston, armed with many newly organized and still well supplied regiments of Patriot militia, were far stronger than they would prove ever again to be during the war.

According to Cherokee reasoning, however, they had little to fear from provincial militia. They remembered that in 1760 the provincial population had trembled in helpless terror until the English regulars had come hurrying to the rescue. This time there would need to be no concern for the regulars. When they appeared they would come marching this time as allies of the Indians. The Cherokee had even less respect for the fighting quality of the border settlers. In their experience settlers, so pushing and bold in peacetime, invariably fled in panic at the first threat of actual war. They had heard strange stories of the unaccountable fighting spirit recently demonstrated by Virginia's frontier levies at Point Pleasant, but these they discounted as manifestly incredible.

There was still a strong peace party in Cherokee councils, led by the older and more conservative chiefs, but the war faction, led by the violently aggressive Dragging Canoe, was more determined and more vociferous. New fuel was added to the blaze of war spirit by the arrival of a delegation of northern Indians that included representatives of the Shawnee, the Mohawk, and the Ottawa. These three were traditionally the most war wise as well as warlike of all Indian nations and to their spokesmen the Cherokee listened with the deepest respect. With the Mohawk and the Shawnee they had themselves been at war for generations. The realization that they were henceforth to be allies was exhilarating. The northerners explained that their truce with the Americans was only temporary. Every speech dwelt upon the happy prospect that all Indians were now to compose their every former difference and make instead a united assault upon their common white enemy. The northern delegation left on their long return journey, and the Cherokee resumed their grappling with their internal discord. The national decision became an expression of the simplest of democratic processes. The warriors who favored war flew to arms. The large majority still opposed remained at home.

In early July of 1776, Cherokee war parties, with some Creek support, attacked the whole arc of the white frontier extending from southern Virginia across the western Carolinas to northern Georgia. In a matter of days hundreds of homes were destroyed, and every settler fortunate enough to escape the first onset was forced to take refuge in stockades or to flee altogether from the border. As Stuart had feared, the blow fell as heavily on Tory settlers as on their Patriot neighbors. Indian aversion to white settlers took little account of political distinctions. The assumption that the ravagers were serving the English cause, the revelation that they were in several instances accompanied by Tory partisans stripped and painted like Indians, and the realization that the king's supporters were no safer from the insensate destruction than anyone else provided a series of cumulative shocks from which the loyalist movement in the south never fully recovered.

Dragging Canoe, burning to punish first of all the most flagrant trespassers on Cherokee land, chose to lead the strongest of the columns invading the Holston country. The settlers had had enough warning to race for the shelter of their stockades, but his approach was nevertheless so rapid that he surprised the local commander's wife and her sister bathing in the river. Concerned lest his warrior's rush for the fort be disordered if any paused to molest the bathers, he sternly directed that they be let alone, thus providing for the startled women one of the few recorded instances of Indian chivalry. The garrison, numbering 170, elected to come outside the walls to meet the advancing Indians. The two forces were about the same strength. This proffered test of racial prowess was welcomed by the exultant Indians. After an initial exchange of fire the white withdrawal to a more favorable position encouraged them to assume this was the anticipated rout. Their impetuous charge was met by a blast of aimed rifle fire from men who had more accurate weapons, were better marksmen, and were as able as they to take advantage of forest cover during battle. Thirteen Indians were killed in that first fire. Dragging Canoe was among the wounded. The Indians recoiled and broke off the action. They were not so much discouraged by their losses or the fall of their leader as they were astounded by the settlers' temerity in having been willing to exchange the security of their fort for the extreme hazards of a battle in the woods. The Cherokee were making the same discovery that the Shawnee had made at Point Pleasant. The day when the settlers could be considered easy prey had ended. This was indeed a new breed of frontiersmen.

Dragging Canoe took the lesson to heart. After the Battle of Island Flats he was never again to permit himself to become involved in a frontal clash between equal numbers. Through all his subsequent years of active campaigning he was to organize his forces as mobile parties devoted to raids, skirmishes, surprises, ambushes, and descents upon isolated farms, pack trains, travelers, salt camps. It was a tactic with which the frontier was to find it infinitely more difficult to cope.

That same morning another Cherokee column was closing in on Fort Caswell. Here, too, there had been sufficient warning for the inhabitants of the district to have assembled within the walls but here, too, the Indian approach was more swift than had been anticipated. The surprise produced one of the few pleasant anecdotes of that grisly summer. A number of the station's women were milking their cows in an adjacent meadow when the alarm was sounded. Among those running for the stockade was Catherine (Bonnie Kate) Sherrill, a young frontierswoman equally noted for her spirit and her beauty. The gates had been hastily closed against the onrushing Indians. John Sevier, already beginning to gain the reputation that was to make him the most admired of all southern frontier commanders, leaned down from the fire step with outstretched arms and cried: "Jump for me, Kate." She did. And later married him.

The garrison numbered only 40. The Indians pressed their attack with a vigor which caused the defenders a number of casualties. Several times they all but succeeded in setting the fort on fire, but after two weeks they became discouraged. Lacking cannon, Indians were seldom able to solve the tactical problems involved in storming a stockade that was resolutely defended by riflemen adequately supplied with ammunition. Their rare successes were almost invariably the result of having been enabled by surprise to rush in before the gates could be closed.

Meanwhile, numerous smaller bands of Cherokee were devastating the evacuated countryside from the Nolichucky to the headwaters of the Clinch and the Holston while the inhabitants enclosed in their stockades and blockhouses could only look on in grief and rage. Houses, cabins, barns, granaries, livestock, and crops that the settlers had been laboriously accumulating for years were swept away in a week. Not every inhabitant had gained in time the shelter of a stockade. Among the captives taken back to the Cherokee country were two whose fate attracted wide attention. The Cherokee, who had been much impressed by various white associations since the days of Attakullaculla's visit to London, Ludovic Grant's long residence, and John Stuart's captivity, prided themselves on having advanced beyond the savage stage of indulging in torture. But in two of their towns, at least, the excitements of war had stirred more primitive passions. In one, Samuel Moore, a youth of eighteen, was burned after having been subjected to more than usually revolting preliminary torment. Even the wildest Indians seldom burned women, but, in the other, Mrs. William Bean had been tied to a post and the wood piled about her had been ignited before she was dramatically saved. Nancy Ward, a Cherokee woman whose high rank authorized her to pronounce ritualistic pardons and whose faithful and long-suffering white sympathies were to make her a border legend, broke through the watching crowd, with her own hands threw aside the burning faggots, and cut the captive's bonds.

The so narrowly preserved Mrs. Bean was sentenced instead to teaching the Cherokee women to make butter and cheese.

Within a fortnight the Cherokee, with their Creek and Tory allies, had devastated a 300-mile stretch of the border from Virginia to Georgia. In more exposed areas even the stockades had been abandoned and everywhere along a belt 30 to 40 miles wide the inhabitants had gathered in the sanctuary of their community forts or fled eastward. Except for what little could be carried in the haste of their flight, everything they possessed had been left behind. On the Holston more than 3000 inhabitants had gathered in their widely separated and overcrowded stockades where they began soon to suffer from hunger and disease. An equal number were enduring the same penalties of concentration and confinement on the Carolina border. There was much discouraged talk of being compelled completely to abandon the whole border. People shut up in stockades for weeks on end, huddled in quarters as cramped and foul as in a slave ship, listening to the groans of the wounded and the mourning of bereaved families, seeing in the sky the smoke from their burning homes, sickened by filth, weakened by hunger, could not entirely resist a growing sense of helplessness and hopelessness.

But rescue and retribution were at hand. The newly established American governments of all four states involved moved with extraordinary rapidity and vigor. In each, militia had for months been organizing and drilling in preparation for calls to resist English invasion or to reinforce Washington's Continental Army. They were therefore ready for this nearer emergency. In Georgia, before the end of July, Colonel Samuel Jack with a hastily mustered and rapidly moving force of 200 militiamen drove the raiders from that border and burned two outlying Cherokee towns. In North Carolina, in August, General Griffith Rutherford with an army of 2400 militiamen scaled the mountain barrier at Swannanoa Gap and turned southward along the rugged route thereafter known as Rutherford's Trace to cut a swath of destruction through the most central and populous section of the Cherokee mountain homeland. There was little resistance for most Cherokee warriors were either absent on distant raids or guarding the natural invasion route by way of long-abandoned Fort Prince George, and Rutherford's surprise movement had been too rapid to give time to rally a sufficiently strong defensive force to oppose so formidable an army. In South Carolina, also in August, Colonel Andrew Williamson with 1100 militiamen, most of them embittered levies from frontier counties who had been further inspirited by the South Carolina assembly's offer of £75 for each Indian scalp, burned the lower Cherokee towns on the nearer slopes of the mountains, paused to recruit his force to 1800, and in September drove on into the higher mountains. He was following the historic route taken by Montgomery's and Grant's regulars in 1760 and 1761 when they had become involved in such difficulties with Cherokee resistance and the mountain terrain that they had been forced to turn back before reaching their objectives. Williamson encountered the same difficulties but he did not turn back. Tumultuous mountain rivers and narrow wooded gorges provided ideal sites for the most favored of all Indian types of attack. The slowly moving column, struggling to breast the waters of a ford or toiling along a rock-obstructed valley bottom, could be steadily fired upon from the forested heights. Twice Williamson's men recoiled from this bewildering punishment inflicted by invisible assailants, but each time the incipient panic was controlled and the advance continued. After taking a loss of 94 killed and wounded, a casualty rate comparable to those sustained by Montgomery and Grant, Williamson broke through the last rockbound pass to a junction with Rutherford. The two joined forces in the complete devastation of Middle Towns which had never before known so much as the approach of an invader. Every house was burned, every cornfield destroyed, every garden uprooted, every orchard cut down, and the homeless Cherokee driven in flight into the farthest recesses of their mountains. By now every inch of the Cherokee country had been devastated except that portion in the valley of the Tennessee west of the main mountain range. This was left to the care of the Virginians who could more easily reach it by marching down the river from the north.

Colonel William Christian's army of 1800 Virginians was later reaching the scene of operations because he had a greater distance

to cover. Pausing on the Holston to distribute food among the
starving inmates of the stockades, he began his march into the
Cherokee country on October 6th. The Cherokee offered no resistance beyond a little sporadic sniping. Both factions had been appalled by the unforeseen magnitude of the American reaction. The
peace party which had not wanted the war in the first place and
which at no stage had taken an active part in it, even in resisting
the American invasions, now resumed control of affairs in order
to offer peace on almost any terms. Christian's leniency offended
many of his followers. Five Overhill Towns were burned as a token
punishment, including Dragging Canoe's and the two to which
Mrs. Bean and the boy, Moore, had been taken. The Cherokee were
required to give up all captives and to attend a formal conference
the next summer in which they must agree to a land cession on the
Holston that included considerably more territory than had previously been disputed. On the march homeward many Virginians from
time to time broke ranks to mark sites to which they proposed to
lay claim. So soon were the afflictions of the summer forgotten.

Christian's moderation was undoubtedly well advised. Dragging
Canoe had refused to make peace on any terms and with a large
band of his more devoted followers had withdrawn southwestward
to a more inaccessible new location on Chickamauga Creek. From
this lair he was to continue to emerge to commit depredations
throughout the Revolution and for years thereafter. Had Christian's
terms been as harsh as his critics advocated, many more Cherokee
must have joined him to make the perpetual menace he represented
even more grievous.

The Cherokee offensive of 1776 was so ill-timed with relation to
any Indian or English interest that it was an enormous disservice
to both. Had the effort been withheld until it could have been exerted in conjunction with an English invasion of the southern
provinces, or with more massive Creek support after Stuart had
managed to end the long-standing war between them and the Choctaw, or with the next year's acceleration of Indian assaults in the
north, or even until there had developed a more united war policy
among the Cherokee themselves, it would have proved a vastly more

damaging blow to the American cause. Still, heartening to the frontier as were the invasion and devastation of the Cherokee country, the American victory was far from so conclusive as it appeared that fall of 1776. The Cherokee War had not been ended. It had only begun. The flames of their burning towns had fired fiercer Cherokee hatreds. From new and secret towns in more distant and less accessible fastnesses of their mountains, they were for the next eighteen years continuously to dispatch roving bands of raiders to infest the Wilderness Road and to haunt every outlying settlement south of the Ohio. It was a war in which the cost to the frontier people was to exceed by many hundreds of lives the Cherokee losses of 1776.

Meanwhile, the St. Lawrence was again open, and the English could resume their preparations to employ Indian assistance in the northern theater of operations where the major campaigns of the Revolution's next four years would be fought. The race for Indian favor was already over. As the dullest Indian could see, the English had everything to offer, the Americans much worse than nothing. The English could offer the guns and gunpowder the Indians required as much in peacetime as in war since they must live by hunting. The Americans could not, faced by the near certainty the weapons would be used in Indian opposition to settlement. The English could offer the surplus of food the Indians required if they were to take time off from hunting to participate in the war. The Americans could not, even as a reward for neutrality, for they already lacked enough to satisfy the hunger of their own armies and garrisons. The English could offer to guarantee permanent Indian title to the land that to all Indians was their birthright. The Americans could not, for they could not dispossess their own citizens who had everywhere along the frontier already occupied land claimed by Indians.

All that remained, then, was trial by battle—and by starvation, exposure, sickness, fear, grief, and the apparently perpetual deferment of hope.

VI

&

Clark 2

THE FEW YOUNG and unattached men left in Kentucky were continuing to leave that late summer of 1775. Apprehension of Indian descents upon the weak and isolated settlements was not alone responsible. Henderson's Transylvania Company, maintaining that the Cherokee purchase gave it claim to the whole region, was raising the price of land. Men who had come so far and risked so much were not content to contemplate the payment here of the same quitrents that might have been expected east of the mountains.

Clark was one of the young men leaving Kentucky that fall, but early the next spring he was back. "It was at this period that I first thought about concerning myself with the future of that country," was the way he later described his state of mind. During the winter in Virginia he had given much sober thought to the Kentucky problem and had been struck by the mixed opinions among influential Virginians with regard to the legitimacy of Henderson's operations. As a result of his thinking he had brought with him to Kentucky a fully considered, clear-cut program. His principal proposal was that conversations be opened with Virginia to explore the possibility of some form of political link between Williamsburg and Harrodsburg. Most of the settlers would have preferred to remain free, not only of the Transylvania Company but of any of the three nearer provinces from which practically all had come. But the circumstances of the growing Indian threat indicated a positive need for some kind of support from east of the mountains. Even that absolute necessity, gunpowder, was already in critical short supply. A population required to live largely by hunting spent powder sparingly even if steadily, but with war the need must increase tremendously. The first Indian attack on a stockade would oblige the defenders to use more in an hour than they might otherwise use in a year. The settlers were prepared, therefore, to give Clark an attentive hearing. In angling for their approval of his plan he could dangle a double bait. In addition to the possibility of some military support there was the possibility of Virginia sympathy with the settlers' resistance to Henderson's land exactions. Most of his fellow Kentuckians began soon to regard this Virginia connection as probably the least of the several evils with which they were confronted.

Meeting in convention at Harrodsburg June 6, 1776, the settlers in their impatience failed to leave the room for negotiation that Clark had advised. Instead, they impetuously elected him and John Gabriel Jones, a newly arrived young attorney, Kentucky's delegates to the Virginia assembly with instructions to proceed to Williamsburg and demand their seats. This application for acceptance as a Virginia county was in conformance with the process by which for generations newly settled counties had progressively been organized along Virginia's western border on the Atlantic side of the mountains. But Kentucky's distance, isolation, and disputed territorial status made the overture a long and important step toward future acceptance on a broader scale of the most consequential of all American governmental principles, the doctrine that new territories in the west were free to seek admission as new and equal members of the existing union of states.

Setting out over the notoriously difficult Wilderness Road, which for the next twenty years was to remain the same narrow pack trail climbing a succession of forested, rockbound ridges beyond each of which it dropped into another cane-choked gorge, the two candidates rode hard in the hope of reaching Williamsburg before the assembly's scheduled summer adjournment. This was Clark's first experience with the land route connecting Virginia and Kentucky and, as with every undertaking of his extravagantly active career, it was an eventful one. Jones' horse broke down. They were forced to walk and ride in turn. A four-day rain set in. Ordinarily, men who wore moccasins, a type of footgear notably porous, took extreme care to dry both moccasins and feet at the campfire each night. But they had now reached a stretch of the Wilderness Road which co-incided with the Great War Road, the heavily traveled north-south Indian route running from the Cherokee mountains to the Ohio. It was not a path near which two lone travelers could risk adver-tising their presence by lighting a fire. Both became afflicted with the wilderness voyager's worst nightmare, "scald feet." This was a violent inflammation caused by long continued friction between wet skin and wet leather. The effect was as painful as seriously burned feet. The one whose turn it was to walk was soon finding each step a torment.

Emerging from Cumberland Gap, they heard in the surrounding forest shots readily identifiable as Indian. In order to conserve powder Indians customarily used very light charges. Clark and Jones veered from the trail to travel in the cover of the adjoining woods, but with their blistered feet they found progress there so difficult that they were obliged to return to the open. They had anxiously anticipated succor at the first station in Powell Valley; to their dismay they discovered it abandoned and partly burned. They were entering a region which had that very week been de-populated by the sudden Cherokee outbreak. They struggled on, less able to walk with each increasingly painful step, to Martin's Station. This larger establishment they found had also been aban-doned, though so recently that Indians had not yet looted and burned it.

Clark realized that in their condition it was useless to attempt to keep on to the more populous settlements on the Clinch 60 miles beyond, and yet Indians could be expected to appear at any moment. "I found myself reduced to a perfect desperation," was his later estimate of their dilemma in his *Memoir*. But he soon had a plan to which Jones, the frontier neophyte, "was over Joyed" to accede. The inhabitants had in the haste of their departure left behind most of their property, including a drove of hogs and cribs filled with corn. Clark proposed that they occupy and provision one of the smaller cabins and there defend themselves. He assured Jones that, unless attacked by a pack of "more than 10 or 12 Indians," there was a reasonable chance that they could stand them off until their feet healed or until the arrival of a larger party of eastbound Kentuckians that could be expected within a week or ten days.

Clark selected a cabin with some open space around it to make it difficult for Indians to approach unobserved. It was locked, and among its other advantages the door was too stout to be easily broken open. He pulled himself to the roof. His feet were too sore to permit his climbing down the stick chimney. He tore away its upper portion until he could lower himself to the floor within. Once inside he cut the lock from the door, punched additional loopholes in the walls, and arranged on the table their combined armament of two rifles, a case of pistols, and their extra ammunition. Jones, whose feet were in slightly better shape, lured the hogs with corn, dispatched one with his sword, and hobbled back and forth until he had stocked their little fortress with the carcass, a keg of water, a sack of corn, and a supply of wood. They built a fire and Clark set about preparing an "oil and ouse" of oak bark with which to treat their crippled feet.

The eventuality for which they had prepared appeared to develop late that same evening. They heard the approach of horsemen and snatched up their weapons. The newcomers, having seen the smoke, encircled the cabin. It was already too dark to see much, but both belligerents realized in time that they were friends. The horsemen were settlers who had dashed back from the Clinch to collect more of their movable property.

The travelers resumed their journey with this escort. Being now mounted, their feet had recovered by the time they reached Botetourt County. Here, realizing they were too late for the assembly, they separated. Clark continued on eastward to appeal to Virginia authorities for the emergency supply of gunpowder so imperatively needed by the Kentucky settlers. Lawyer Jones, undismayed by his so recent and to him unfamiliar experiences with frontier perils, elected to return to the Holston to serve with the forces being raised to resist the Cherokee invasion.

Governor Patrick Henry was ill at his home in Hanover. From his bed he listened to Clark's account of conditions in Kentucky. The sick man was faced by the need to make a decision upon which hung consequences surpassed in importance by no other among the many great decisions being made that year. In 1775, the great issue confronting the American people was whether or not their initial insistence upon comparative freedom of action was to develop into that opportunity freely to express their native genius represented by total independence. Pursuit of this objective raised at once a second issue. Would the new nation prove to have seized in time the opportunity to gain west of the mountains the room for unlimited growth required *fully* to express that same native genius?

Many hundreds of thousands of Americans were deeply and desperately conscious of the first issue; all but a few were ignorant of or indifferent to the second. The inclination of their national leaders became therefore of vital importance. Upon their judgment, whether informed or not, depended to a large degree the new nation's inheriting a chance to grow along with the chance to live. Among these national leaders those who held three posts were in a position during the Revolution to exert the most critical influence: the commander in chief of the continental armies, who must determine the use made of the limited military force available; the ambassador to the court of France, the Revolution's prospective ally; and the governor of Virginia, the province with the longest and most exposed frontier. The first of these required to grapple with the problem was Patrick Henry, Virginia's first Revolutionary governor. Here again, as so often in our country's early history, sheer providence appeared to have taken a hand. He had been prepared to understand the nature of the problem by a phase of his personal experience in no way connected with his rise to political power.

He was a self-educated lawyer who had represented so many

humble clients that their votes could become more important to him than their fees. Few of the causes he had represented had enjoyed the favor of Virginia's ruling oligarchy of great landowners. He had been a spokesman for the landless. He had been a flagrant rebel while most of his fellow patriots were still fumbling with petitions and remonstrances. The arenas in which he had battled had been provided by the courtroom, the statehouse, and the platforms. Yet this radical eastern lawyer, all of whose foreground activities were connected with popular movements and class struggles in the east, was himself a great proprietor in the west. From the moment he first began to accumulate some capital and more political influence he had invested both in western lands. He had been associated with Dr. Thomas Walker, founder of the Loyal Company and first explorer of Kentucky, in his plans for opening to settlement hundreds of thousands of acres on Virginia's southwest frontier, and with William Fleming, hero of Point Pleasant, in his 1767 proposal to establish a colony at the mouth of the Ohio. His own land agent was Joseph Martin, already notable as the founder of the first station in Powell Valley. Though in 1775 he drove Dunmore, the last royal governor, from Virginia, he had only the year before warmly approved of Dunmore's expansionist activities. The Kentucky surveyors had taken the same care to designate superior tracts for him that they had for Washington. While remaining an easterner, he had identified himself with the westward movement. These western sympathies had been strengthened by family ties. His sister Anne married William Christian, the noted frontier colonel who commanded a regiment in the Point Pleasant campaign, and his sister Elizabeth married William Campbell, commander at King's Mountain, and then William Russell, the Clinch River colonizer. His long, if vicarious, experience with the frontier had therefore well prepared him to listen with sympathy and understanding to Clark's plan to save Kentucky.

He sent Clark on to the council at Williamsburg with his hearty endorsement. The council was less sympathetic. There was much doubt that the assembly would prove ready when it reassembled to accept responsibility for the security of Kentucky. Clark was offered the 500 pounds of gunpowder he had asserted was a minimum necessity, but only on condition he accept it as a loan for which he would be personally answerable. This Clark indignantly refused, declaring "if a country was not worth protecting it was not worth claiming" and intimating that Kentucky would look elsewhere for protection. The council yielded to his angry insistence and made arrangements to deposit the powder in Pittsburgh, subject to his demand. He wrote his friends in Kentucky advising them to send for it and waited to face the fall session of the assembly.

Jones returned from the Cherokee campaign and the two presented themselves and their petition on October 8th. They were not permitted to take seats as delegates but were invited to state their case. In the two months of debate that ensued the brilliant and experienced Henderson was their principal opponent. He was well aware that Virginia's acceptance of Kentucky threatened to destroy his company's whole pattern of asserted land rights. Other opposition to the Kentucky settlers' appeal was strong and came from many quarters. Of even those Virginians interested in western lands many were associated with Henderson or with Fincastle, until now Virginia's westernmost county and consequently jealous of its own land prerogatives. Most Virginians had no western land interests and were inclined to regard the distant Kentucky settlements as a dangerous liability certain to interfere with Virginia's nearer and far more important commitments in the expanding war. But there was some important support for the Kentucky petition. Patrick Henry, who had been a Henderson supporter in the days of the royal government, saw less need of his theory of land rights now that the king's jurisdiction over the west had been undermined by the Declaration of Independence, and Jefferson, without personal interests, was led by his general democratic principles plus his belief in the west's future to take a firm stand in favor of Kentucky's admission. The compelling persuasion, however, was Clark's central and unanswerable argument that the maintenance of the Kentucky settlements provided a buffer which, if abandoned, would open the way to more direct Indian assaults on Virginia's present frontiers. On December 7, 1776, the assembly voted to admit Kentucky as a Virginia county.

Hurrying westward, Clark met Jones at Pittsburgh. The powder was still there. Clark's letter having miscarried, the Kentuckians had naturally failed to send for it. He and Jones were therefore faced with the task of delivery. Other frontier news awaited them. The major Ohio Indian nations were still professing their former uneasy neutrality. But there were many portents that the mounting tension was soon to break. The English supply line was again open. Colonel John Butler was at Niagara assembling Tory refugees soon to be organized into a regiment of partisans widely and terribly known as Butler's Rangers. Lieutenant Governor Henry Hamilton, commanding at Detroit, was stocking his magazines with the food and ammunition required if the western Indians were to take an organized part in the general English war effort. Meanwhile, repeated incidents had kept the upper Ohio frontier in a state of concern at times bordering on panic. Occasional stray parties of Indians, too impatiently vindictive to wait for the planned campaigns of the future, were committing minor mischief calculated to provoke both sides to greater excesses. A number of whites had been killed or taken on the Ohio and in Kentucky. The most noted of these preliminary outrages had been the abduction of Boone's daughter, Jemima, and Elizabeth and Frances Calloway at Boonesborough, July 14th, by members of the northern delegation returning through Kentucky from the Cherokee conference. Boone had pressed his pursuit with such vigor that three days later he had rescued the girls unharmed and had killed two of their captors. But by far the most disturbing of these premonitory activities were the aggressions of Pluggy's band. Pluggy was a transplanted Mohawk who three years before had begun gathering about him in a camp at what is now Delaware, Ohio, a nondescript collection of Mingo and wanderers and renegades from half a dozen other nations. Neither subject to tribal discipline nor bound by national engagements to remain neutral, they had been free to commit whatever barbarity appealed to them. Pluggy was now ready for a more ambitious undertaking.

With his amazing talent for attracting volunteers no matter how desperate the venture, Clark found seven men willing to help man the little boat carrying the cargo of powder upon which the fate of Kentucky depended. The existence and importance of the powder supply were no secret on the Indian side of the frontier. Little that happened at Pittsburgh had escaped the attention either of the swarms of resident Tory spies or of the throngs of Indian delegates flocking there for the recurrent peace conferences. Pluggy took it upon himself to make certain the shipment did not reach Kentucky.

But in his 400-mile dash down the Ohio Clark managed to evade ambush and elude pursuit. At the mouth of Limestone Creek, now Maysville but then uninhabited though already the Ohio River gateway to Kentucky, he buried the powder in five different spots rather than attempt to pack it inland. Its weight was too great and its value too precious to be carried and protected by so few men with the Indians in such close and active pursuit. He went on down river a few miles, set the boat adrift further to mystify the pursuers, and started overland for Harrodsburg to get help.

Near McClelland's Station he left Jones and five of his exhausted men behind and pressed on toward Harrodsburg with the two most able to travel. Returning to McClelland's with James Harrod and a strong party he was met by heartbreaking tidings. After his departure, John Todd, one of the most prominent of Kentucky's first settlers, had appeared with a party of eight surveyors and had persuaded Jones to guide him to the hiding place of the powder instead of waiting for help from Harrodsburg. Proceeding along the great buffalo trace leading to the mouth of the Limestone, they had on Christmas Day encountered and been overwhelmed by Pluggy's advancing Indians. Of the little party of ten Jones and William Graden had been killed and four others taken captive. In Jones' short wilderness career he had experienced enough action and excitement to crowd a long and adventurous lifetime, but the gallant young attorney had so soon come to the end of it.

Harrod, fearing for his station, rushed back to defend it. Clark remained to help hold McClelland's which the Indians promptly and furiously attacked. In the violent assault both leaders, John McClelland and Pluggy, were among those killed. It was a battle so grueling as to lead both antagonists to recognize defeat. The Indians failed to take the fort and withdrew. The defenders, anticipating stronger attacks to come, decided to abandon the station and add their remaining manpower to the defenses of Harrodsburg.

Harrod had meanwhile been informed by his scouts, among whom were such superlative woodsmen as Simon Kenton, Samuel Moore, and Benjamin Linn, that Harrodsburg was not in immediate danger. Possession of the gunpowder was of such incomparable importance that in any event to secure it was considered worth any hazard. Leading a party of 30 determined men, Harrod made for the Limestone by a circuitous route, encountered no Indians, found the five caches of gunpowder undisturbed, and successfully returned with the great prize to Harrodsburg on January 2, 1777.

The settlements in Kentucky had by now been reduced to two stations, Harrodsburg and Boonesborough. But few as they were, the defenders of Kentucky could now face the future with new confidence. Thanks to Clark's initiative they had won an enormous advantage which formerly they had lacked. They were armed.

VII

ဢ

Brant 2

THE LOYALISTS who had struggled through the wilderness to Canada that summer and fall of 1775 were greeted there by many most painful disappointments. They had hoped, with English, Canadian, and Indian support, to be able soon to return sword in hand to redress their grievances and punish their oppressors. But none of these hopes had been realized. There were fewer than 800 English troops in all Canada, scattered among widely separated garrisons. The Canadians were first of all French and most were disinterested in this quarrel between their recent conquerors. As a final blow it soon became evident that in the place of any prospect of an avenging return there was every indication that Canada, too, was about to fall to their Patriot adversaries. Two American invading armies, under Brigadier General Richard Montgomery and Colonel Benedict Arnold, were converging in a great pincers movement upon the St. Lawrence. Montreal fell and Quebec appeared doomed. Imperial authority had apparently lost all control of the situation. Governor Carleton, attempting to get down river to Quebec, was forced to make his way alone, in disguise and by night. Lieutenant Governor Henry Hamilton, attempting to get up river en route to his command post at Detroit, was likewise compelled to skulk in disguise through American lines and past American patrols. The one faint gleam of consolation for the Tory refugees had been the chance capture of redoubtable Ethan Allen, rebel captor of Ticonderoga.

These desperate circumstances seemed to Brant, Guy Johnson, and Daniel Claus to provide more reason than ever for the prompt resort to the services of their ready and willing Indian allies. But John Butler argued that to employ Indians prematurely would merely result in a useless dissipation of their military power and that their value should be saved until they could be deployed as auxiliaries in strategic conjunction with future English offensive operations. Butler was Johnson's deputy but he was the only one of the four senior members of the Indian Department who had had extensive military experience. He had, for example, commanded the Iroquois under Johnson at the siege of Niagara. Governor Carleton strongly agreed with his views. Brant, Johnson, and Claus were bitterly dissatisfied with the ruling and, contrary to Carleton's wishes, determined to go together to England to appeal directly to the higher authority of the cabinet. They sailed from Quebec November 11th, two days before Arnold invested the city. Ethan Allen lay below decks in irons in the same ship.

Brant's former white associations which he had savored with so much relish in Johnson's household, at the Lebanon school, with the missionaries at Canajoharie, and with Prevost and Croghan at Otsego, where but a pale preliminary to the glow of gratification that awaited him in London. He was hailed by the press, the public, and society as the "King of the Indians." The government underwrote the cost of his maintenance and entertainment. Among the items on his expense account were lodging at the "Swan with Two Necks," travel to Windsor, apothecaries', jewelers', tailors', and gunsmiths' bills, luggage, presents, and delicacies for his return voyage. London has always had a weakness for exotic visitors from far corners of the empire, and Brant cut a fascinating figure, appearing one day dressed as an English gentleman and the next in all the barbaric regalia of a Mohawk chief. All doors, official and social, were open to him. James Boswell became his companion. He was sketched to illustrate a long account of his visit in the *London Magazine*. Romney painted his portrait, commissioned by the Earl of Warwick. There were invitations from more great houses than he could accept. Everywhere he was received with flattery and applause.

But all was not play, and neither he nor the cabinet lost sight of the serious purpose of his visit. Lord George Germain, Colonial Secretary, sought through him to make more certain of the Iroquois alliance, while Brant lost no opportunity to impress upon him the reality of Indian land grievances. What he particularly demanded was so positive a reaffirmation of the Proclamation Line that Indians might hope for permanent protection from settlers' encroachments. For all of his fascination with white society and the deepening of his impulse to consider himself a citizen of the empire, he was never again to forget his identity as an Indian. To strive to guard the Indian world against every threat, present or future, had become his central purpose. His strongest impression in England had been of the white race's enormous superiority in numbers and power over the relatively few Indians. Inevitably, he realized, the tide of white settlement must sweep on westward, dooming the Indian way of life with its dependence on space in which to live by hunting. The one Indian hope was to resist in time with enough determination to extract from the whites guarantees that they might retain enough of their ancestral land to provide them room to survive. His understanding with Germain became a simple bargain: protection of Indian land rights in the future in exchange for an Indian alliance in the present.

On account of the nature of his plans after disembarkation, the time and route of his return to America were shrouded in official secrecy. This was maintained so effectively that it confused most people then and many historians since. The New York frontier had remained largely unaware of his English tour, and every new rumor of the imminence of Indian attack had continued to ascribe to Brant the command of the expected invasion. At the Battle of the Cedars, near Montreal on May 20, 1776, which hastened the American retreat from Canada, he was named by the detailed, eyewitness testimony of American prisoners as the commander of the several hundred Seneca, Cayuga, and Canadian Indians whose presence on the field had been adroitly used to frighten American officers into a precipitate capitulation sharply criticized by Washington. This was the first time Indians in any number had taken an active part in an English operation, but it was not yet a presage of things to come. Carleton and Butler saw a distinction between using Indians aggressively against the American frontier and defensively against American field forces engaged in an invasion of Canada. In any event Brant could not very well have participated. On May 7th he was still in London at his last audience with Germain. He sailed from England late in May, landed on Staten Island, and lingered there long enough to observe with admiring interest Lord Howe's success in driving Washington from Long Island and the city of New York.

With English arms so evidently in the ascendent, the time had come for him to take his appropriate if unofficial place at the head of the Iroquois war effort. Among the Iroquois the political authority of sachems was inherited, but war chiefs gained rank by acclamation dependent upon their fellow warriors' estimate of their martial capacities. He had been recognized as Mohawk war chief and traditionally the Mohawk commander was accepted as ranking commander of all Iroquois, in so far as Indians ever accepted any command.

He set out from New York in disguise, passing through Washington's lines and on across the frontier to the Iroquois country. The New York frontier was seething with Patriot-Tory animosities more fierce than when he had left the year before. Local Tories were being subjected to ever-increasing pressures. With the English evacuation of Boston a number of detachments of New England militia had become available for service in New York to reinforce the dictates of Patriot committees as well as to help defend the frontier. Fort Stanwix, guarding the all-important portage linking the Hudson Valley with the Great Lakes, had been ordered repaired and garrisoned. Sir John Johnson had held on through the winter but on May 31st, aware of imminent arrest, had fled to Canada, narrowly escaping death by starvation in the intervening forest en route after abandoning Johnson Hall and his vast properties to be looted by the occupying militia. His Highlanders had been cowed or driven into the wilderness, eventually to join Butler's Rangers or Johnson's Greens and with them to return to ravage the frontier that had ejected them. Most active Tories had long since left for Canada, but now even those suspected of royal sympathies were being penalized. Their property was confiscated and they were being imprisoned, flogged, tarred and feathered, sometimes shot or hanged. Drumhead court-martials acted swiftly and harshly. Wives, children, and relatives of known Tories, including the wives of Johnson and Butler, were taken as hostages. Some hundreds of Tory suspects were condemned to confinement in the tunnels of an abandoned copper mine in Simsbury, Connecticut, where many of them died of malnutrition, exposure, and disease. The English military successes in the spring and summer of 1776 in both major campaigns had encouraged the New York loyalists to continue to resist, but at the same time hardened Patriot determination to break down their resistance. These fires of internal political dissension were being furiously and continuously stoked by zealots of both factions to a flame which was soon to scorch the entire New York frontier.

Gaining the Iroquois country, Brant traveled from town to town, even to those of the neutrally inclined Oneida and Tuscarora, preaching his doctrine that the time had come for the Indians to strike. He enlarged upon the recent English triumphs in capturing New York and expelling the American invaders of Canada. For this argument he found a ready audience. The Iroquois had been waiting to note whether the English or the Americans seemed the stronger, and their own long military history had prepared them astutely to assess military power. The westernmost nations, the Seneca and Cayuga, were eager for war, and the Onondaga were receptive. Brant could speak for his Mohawk, except for a small minority which had chosen to remain in their homes on the white side of the frontier. But the Oneida and Tuscarora clung to their pacifism. This presented a peculiarly Indian difficulty. One of the traditional elements of Iroquois power had always been that war as a united confederation was never embarked upon unless sanctioned by every one of its component nations. The opinion of the Tuscarora who had been admitted to the confederation so recently could be dismissed, but the veto of the recalcitrant Oneida was an impediment of the first importance. The obstacle was at length surmounted in Gordian knot fashion. The sacred council fire at Onondaga, symbol of Iroquois union, which had been kept burning for centuries was ceremonially extinguished. This was in effect to declare the traditions of the ancient confederation suspended and to assert the consequent freedom of each nation to make its own military decisions.

By December, Brant could feel assured that many hundreds of Iroquois were prepared to follow him against the white frontier in the spring. He was confronted, however, by the same practical difficulty with which Clark that same December was endeavoring to cope in his struggle to organize the defenses of Kentucky: Enough powder with which to hunt was not a hundredth enough with which to fight a war. This need led to a renewed collision with a familiar obstacle and one more stubborn even than the Oneida. John Butler was in charge of Indian relations at Niagara, the base from which supplies must be drawn, and he was still opposed to committing Iroquois to active service. Brant had been given an English captain's commission but Butler, a lieutenant colonel, far outranked him and was in official control of the magazines. Despite Brant's urgent and then increasingly angry demands, he refused to release the powder to implement Brant's planned attacks. And again Carleton firmly supported him.

In February of 1777 the frustrated Brant took matters into his own hands by appearing at Oghwaga, the ancient Mohawk hunting and trading town on the upper Susquehanna a few miles north of the present Pennsylvania state line. This had been the site of Sir William Johnson's first trading post and was the center of those Mohawk ancestral hunting grounds for the assured future possession of which Brant had bargained with Germain in London. Here he raised the English flag. Many Mohawk who had left the valley with him the year before had returned to these familiar surroundings.

Two or three hundred other Iroquois had joined them. Some scores of Tory partisans had also made their way through the wilderness from their refugee camps at Niagara and Oswego, anxious to succor or at least to communicate with the wives and children they had left behind them on the American side of the frontier. Many of these who had not been confined as hostages had been driven from their homes to inhabit fields and woods.

The inescapable limitation upon the effectiveness of this improvised force, as with every wilderness maneuver, was supply. There did not exist that surplus of rations and ammunition required if an extensive operation were to be undertaken. Natural conditions in the wilderness permitted a group of two or three or a dozen experienced men to live off the country indefinitely and with comparative ease, but for any larger congregation the food problem became at once critical and soon insoluble. Brant's followers were compelled to spend most of their time hunting ever more widely to provide enough to eat from day to day. Therefore, though he had the numbers with which to make a sudden hit-and-run raid of the most terrifying proportions, he was not in a position to launch the sustained offensive he had so long and so earnestly advocated.

The presence of Brant at Oghwaga, within 70 miles of the outlying Cherry Valley and Schoharie settlements, soon became known and sent a pulse of alarm along the frontier. Former rumors of impending Indian attack had proved unfounded, but of this sudden development there could seem no doubt. The New York legislature hastily considered a resolution to offer a reward for Brant's head, then on second thought decided instead to dispatch John Harper, who had been a schoolmate of Brant's at Lebanon, as an emissary to reason with him. Harper was a seasoned frontiersman, the founder of the Harpersfield settlement, a confirmed Patriot, and a man who knew Indians and who could speak Mohawk. He left his militia escort behind and went on with one white companion to Oghwaga where he was received amicably by the Indians. In order to accentuate the friendliness of his mission, he roasted an ox to entertain his hosts and himself donned Indian costume, painted his face, and danced with them. He returned with the temporarily reassuring report that

Brant had stated that, while he personally was for the king, the Indians as a people wished to take no part in the white man's war. What they did want, Brant had emphasized, was undisturbed possession of their tribal lands.

By now Brant's purpose in stationing himself at Oghwaga seemed somewhat less mystifying. He was there not to represent English interests but Indian interests. In London, he had gained an English guarantee of Indian land rights. He was now waiting to hear what the Americans might have to offer. When there were no further overtures after Harper's visit he began to press the matter. In May, he moved north along the Unadilla and began to requisition supplies among outlying settlements and to require isolated settlers to declare their sympathies with the English cause. A number of harassed Tories from more distant settlements fled their communities to join him.

The pressure of his cat-and-mouse approach to the frontier at last forced its defenders to take some sort of action. The first necessity was somehow to ascertain his actual intentions. Brigadier General Nicholas Herkimer, the much respected old German commander of the Tryon County militia who as a neighbor had long known Brant, crossed the frontier in June with a force of 380 militiamen and made a gingerly advance toward the Unadilla, sending word ahead that he was coming not to fight but to talk. Herkimer took great care to halt at the Proclamation Line which here ran along the Unadilla River, so that his movement could not possibly be construed as an invasion of the Indian country, and sent on another request that Brant meet him for a conference. After keeping him waiting more than a week, Brant appeared.

There was on both sides much suspicion that the other intended foul play. The two commanders met in an open field between their camps, each attended by presumably unarmed guards. As a peace conference the meeting was confused and inconclusive and with little gathered by either of the other's true intentions. Brant's demands for land-right assurances could not very well be satisfied by the leaders of this little army of local militia who represented a class long devoted to gaining possession of more Indian land. Herkimer

THE NEW YORK FRONTIER

was patient, Brant was sarcastic; some of Brant's Indian followers encamped nearby periodically fired in the air and raised war whoops, and some of Herkimer's associates could scarcely be restrained from making an attempt to seize Brant. Nothing came of the conference more favorable than that neither army actually attacked the other. Herkimer accepted Brant's professions of armed neutrality and marched back to the settlements, most of his officers and men muttering with dissatisfaction. Far more clearly than they did he foresee the consequences to the frontier were a general Indian war to be precipitated.

Twenty years later, while a guest in the house of Theodosia Burr in New York, Brant gave his version of his intentions that early summer of 1777 on the Susquehanna when it had not yet been too late to turn back from the horrors so soon to follow. Had the Continental Congress sent him accredited plenipotentiaries with authority to offer him assurances of American respect for the principle established by the Proclamation Line, recognizing the need of designating lands to be reserved for Indians, he said he would have engaged to hold the Iroquois neutral. Instead, he complained, the Americans sent Harper, a local frontiersman without official standing, and then a German militia general with a staff composed of frontier settlers whose past record of land grabbing had made them perpetually suspect to all Indians.

Whether or not Brant had been so exasperated by the constraints imposed on him by Carleton and Butler that he was actually ready to come to terms with the Americans, it appeared that Indian interests remained uppermost in his mind. In any event, the failure of Herkimer and Brant to achieve anything approaching a meaningful peace settlement at Unadilla had become anticlimactic before they met. In the distance more powerful figures and greater events were shaping the destinies of the New York frontier. Lieutenant General John Burgoyne had disembarked at Quebec on May 6th, armed with England's master plan for the prompt suppression of the rebellion. By marching from Canada down the Hudson to a junction with Howe's New York army, the colonies were to be cut in two and further struggle made to seem patently useless.

In addition to the unwelcome notification that he had been replaced as field commander in Canada by Burgoyne, Carleton had at the same time received orders reversing his Indian policy. The cabinet bluntly directed that Indians henceforth were to be recruited, supplied, organized, and employed in continuous attacks on the American frontier that might serve the more rapidly and effectively to discourage American resistance to the king's regular armies. They were to be supervised, wherever possible, by white officers and counseled to spare women and children, but in any event to be made a part of the general effort to suppress the rebellion. Adjustment to this directive was made easier for Carleton and Butler by the circumstance that the first such use of Indians would, in consonance with their own military theories, be in support of a formally organized English invasion. Burgoyne's main advance southward across Lake Champlain and Lake George in the direction of Albany and the lower Hudson was to be attended by the companion advance of a secondary force from Oswego to take the American defense in the flank. The principal Indian effort was to be exerted in support of this flank movement.

Lieutenant Colonel Barry St. Leger, raised to the temporary rank of brigadier general for the occasion, was assigned command of this Oswego force. Every outstanding Tory of northern New York, except Guy Johnson who was still attempting to administer Indian affairs from his Staten Island headquarters, gathered to serve with the expedition. Sir John Johnson, John Butler, Daniel Claus, and Walter Butler all had commands of varying importance. Brant, his ardor reanimated by word of the new dispensation, made an incredibly swift forced march from Oghwaga to arrive in time to take personal command of the army's Indian contingent. The Tory refugees, grimly jubilant that their hour of revenge seemed at last to have struck, feverishly planned and drilled. With an absence of delay rare in a military project so complicated, the whole English operation was developing on schedule. By the time St. Leger had arrived and issued the order forthwith to march from Oswego, Burgoyne had pushed a hundred miles southward to take Ticonderoga. St. Leger had some 650 white troops, regulars, Hessians, Canadians, Tories, and 800 Indians. His mission was to take Fort Stanwix and then to burst into the Mohawk Valley to demoralize the inhabitants, turn the left flank of the American army confronting Burgoyne, and finally to join Burgoyne, and presumably Howe, at Albany.

The garrison of historic Fort Stanwix (during the Revolution referred to as Fort Schuyler) numbered 550 New York and New England militiamen commanded by two uncommonly able young citizen soldiers, Colonel Peter Gansevoort, 28, and his second in command, Colonel Marinus Willett, 36. The post had not yet been completely repaired and was insufficiently supplied with food and ammunition to withstand a siege of more than a few days. Ganse-voort was aware of the assembly of the English invasion force at Oswego. The imminence of attack was further advertised by the number of Indians infesting the forest surrounding the fort. Several officers and men who, contrary to orders, had ventured outside the walls to hunt or fish were killed or captured. Though intelligence as usual greatly exaggerated the invaders' strength the confidence of the two young colonels remained unshaken. Congress had the previous June 14th adopted the stars and stripes and a homemade flag of the new design was here flown for the first time in the face of the enemy. General Philip Schuyler, commanding the American armies on the upper Hudson, appreciated the importance of the fort and, in the midst of all his own difficulties with Burgoyne's continued advance, sanctioned an effort to strengthen it. A reinforcement of 200 militia, convoying a six weeks' supply of food and small arms ammunition, reached Fort Stanwix on August 2nd, just hours before St. Leger's advance force of Indians and rangers under Brant and Lieutenant Henry Bird closed in. St. Leger was prevented from bringing up his heavier cannon by the obstructions the Americans had placed in Wood's Creek, but the next day he made the usual formal demand that the fort be surrendered to his obviously superior force, accompanied by the usual warning that it might become impossible to control the excesses of the Indians were it found necessary to take the place by storm. The defenders were not outwardly impressed. St. Leger's Indians and rangers completed the investment of the fort while his regulars continued their efforts to bring up his cannon.

Meanwhile, the New York frontier after so many former alarms had been finally swept by the realization that 800 Indians were within a day's march. Ever since Brant's appearance at Oghwaga fears had mounted. All through the spring and early summer local authorities had appealed frantically for assistance. Both Washington and Schuyler, respectively absorbed by their immediate responsibilities in their twin struggles with the two major English armies on the continent, were disturbed by doubts that the inhabitants would make any effective effort to defend their border. The large Tory minority on New York's frontier was emboldened by the prospect of rescue, and any number of ostensible Patriots could be expected to turn their coats in the face of the developing threat. The inhabitants, largely German, were not in any event considered endowed with the temperament of fighting men. Few were natural frontiersmen. None had ever experienced Indian war on this frontier that had enjoyed Indian peace for generations. Most were ordinary plodding farmers. Though many were prosperous enough to own firearms, few were skilled in their use.

All of these doubts were presently dissipated. Once the advance of St. Leger with his hordes of Indians and Tories had become unmistakable, the frontier threw off its former lethargy. In response to Herkimer's summons of "all men 16 to 60," 700 militamen rallied to his standard. Rather than await attack among their homes and families, it was determined to march into the wilderness to the relief of Fort Stanwix. Seldom had a more inexperienced and untrained army taken the field. The one department in which it was thoroughly prepared was its commissary. It was accompanied by 400 wagonloads of provisions. The creaking of axles rose above the excited chatter of the marching men to echo and re-echo through the forest.

On the evening of August 5th Herkimer camped on the bank of Oriskany Creek, some eight miles short of Fort Stanwix. His bivouac centered about the huts of a small Oneida village which had been hastily abandoned during the preceding week. The Oneida had not fled before the advancing Americans but from the anger of their fellow Seneca, Cayuga, and Mohawk with St. Leger. This anger had been intensified by the presumption of some 40 Oneida in offering their services to Herkimer. He depended upon them as a forward screen to guard his inexperienced army against ambush.

The old German farmer was not a professional soldier, but his battle plan was soundly based on simple arithmetic. The enemy toward which he was advancing outnumbered him two to one. Only by operating in conjunction with the garrison of Fort Stanwix could the American total begin to match the English. He therefore dispatched messengers to advise Gansevoort of his approach and to urge that the moment the battle developed the garrison make a sortie in force. With the intervening woods crawling with Brant's Indians there was every chance his couriers might not get through to the fort. An essential feature of his message, therefore, was his request that Ganesvoort signal its reception by firing three cannon.

The next morning, August 6th, Herkimer remained in camp, listening for the signal. The silence remained unbroken. Soon his equally inexperienced colonels became restive. When he continued stubbornly to decline to go forward, they began accusing him of cowardice with many pointed references to his avoidance of combat at Unadilla. The altercation progressed until Herkimer's loyalty, as well as his courage, was being questioned. This was an aspersion difficult to ignore. The Tory-Patriot cleavages splitting New York's Revolutionary frontier frequently divided families as sharply as communities. Herkimer had a brother, a brother-in-law, and a nephew enrolled in St. Leger's army. Unable longer to endure the taunts, Herkimer climbed on his big white horse and gave the order to march. The ponderous train of oxcarts trundled forward. The thick column of men and wagons stretched through the apparently empty forest for more than a mile. It was an excessively hot day. At each glimpse of brook or spring men broke from ranks to drink and then to rejoin whatever portion of the command seemed most convenient. Late in the forenoon the head of the column reached a deep and shadowy ravine some two miles west of Oriskany Creek.

St. Leger's scouts had kept him informed of Herkimer's movements. Though the only organized defenders of the frontier were thus placing themselves literally at the mercy of his superior force, he was at some loss how most successfully to take advantage of his opportunity. There was no room in the dense forests along the narrow cart path for ordinary troops to maneuver. Therefore, to the eagerly available Brant was delegated the initial responsibility for engaging the advancing Americans, while at the same time making certain that none escaped. With 400 Indians and 80 Tory rangers at his disposal, he prepared an ambush about the thicketed slopes of the ravine. The terrain provided an ideal site for the favorite form of Indian attack. There they waited and watched while the American column tramped stolidly on into the trap.

The Oneida, who in later campaigns were to prove of notable service to other American armies, were of no use to Herkimer that day. They gave no slightest warning of the mortal danger immediately ahead. They must at the last moment have made use of the forest's cover to escape the scene of action for no battle account mentions their later presence. The surprise must have been even more devastating had not, to Brant's enraged disgust, several of his waiting Indians meanwhile become so drunk that they prematurely opened fire. As it was, the forward two thirds of the closely crowded column became instantly the nearly helpless target of a converging fire from howling, invisible enemies surrounding them on all sides. It was a classic example of the Indian style of forest attack, comparable to its famous predecessor that had ruined Braddock or to the first day at Bushy Run. The victims here were doubly vulnerable. They were neither woodwise frontiersmen accustomed to bush fighting nor professional soldiers sustained by discipline.

Colonel Ebenezer Cox, commanding the advance guard, was killed at the outset. Colonel Isaac Paris, attempting to take over, was seized and dragged away to be soon thereafter murdered by his Indian captors. Of the company commanders, whose personal presence and example in battle is even more important to militia than to regulars, many were among the first to fall. Herkimer's horse was shot to death and he himself suffered a wound in his leg from which he was not to recover. The rear sections of the column which had not been encircled by the ambush at once broke into panic-stricken flight. This portion of the army suffered even more heavily than those who remained, for Indians took special delight in running down fugitives.

For the upwards of 500 men who had been surrounded annihilation seemed certain. Scattered without formation among the thickets and across the forested slopes bordering the cart path, they were taking casualties at the rate which must soon have broken the spirit of the most seasoned troops. Yet, after the first shock of surprise and terror had passed, they began to gather in stubborn little knots and circles for mutual protection and most unaccountably to continue to resist. Herkimer, his bleeding leg stretched out before him, his pipe clenched in his teeth, his unsheathed sword in hand, sat on his dismounted saddle, imperturbably surveying as much as he could see of the engagement. Amid so much confusion and so many limitations on visibility any attempt at over-all direction of the defense was useless, but his calm heartened those of his men who could see him.

After the initial slaughter accompanying the first shock of surprise, the surviving Americans became somewhat harder to kill Under the stress of necessity they began, awkwardly at first, to attempt to adapt to wilderness tactics, each seeking the shelter of a log or tree under cover of which to fire. But the Indians soon countered by taking advantage of their inexperience. They provoked a man into firing, then rushed forward to ax him while he was reloading, a complicated process requiring successive manipulations of powder horn, shot pouch, ramrod, and priming flask. Forest fighting was an involved and intricate technique, demanding a greater variety of skills and stratagems than could be learned in an hour. The Indians, conscious of their advantage, sensing that victory might be only moments away, pressed their attack with an unaccustomed disregard for their own losses. But their moment had not yet come. A suddenly breaking thunderstorm with an accompanying deluge of rain forced a lull. Men could not expose their powder to reload during the downpour. The Americans devoted the hour's surcease to tending their wounded, reforming their lines, and improving their dispositions.

As soon as the storm passed the attack was resumed. The Indians were still as certain of their prey. For generations the proud Iroquois had resented the white man's galling assumption of racial superiority. The fierce Indian love of violence was infused with a fiercer gratification inherent in this long awaited opportunity to kill so obnoxiously arrogant an enemy. But it continued to prove an opportunity that had still to be seized. The Americans had in the interval provided by the storm improvised one device that made their resistance more troublesome. They had placed two men at each tree or patch of cover. The Indian who dashed in for the kill after the first one had fired was met by the second man's shot.

Two more companies of Tory rangers came up. The battle now reached its climactic pitch of ferocity. The adversaries were neighbors, friends, relatives, men who all their lives had known one another well. It became more than the formalized effort of soldiers to gain a military advantage over nameless and faceless strangers who were antagonists only because they were wearing a different uniform under another flag. The antagonism here was personal and intimate and envenomed by the past two years of neighborhood contention. The Tories saw their opponents as traitors, robbers, molesters of women and children. To the Patriots their opponents were monsters who had crowned their betrayal of their country by committing the most abhorrent of all crimes, the loosing of savages upon fellow white men. Inflamed by such furies, the Tory onset became a hand-to-hand convulsion of bayonets, knives, hatchets, gunbutts, fists, and eye-gouging thumbs.

The Indians began to hang back, enthralled by this spectacle of white men at each other's throats. Their own impetuosity had appreciably ebbed. During the later stages of the battle they had been exchanging life for life. A parity of losses did not conform to the Indian theory of a sensible way to make war. Then both Indians and rangers were disconcerted by the sound of firing behind them in the direction of the fort. The Americans before them were continuing to resist as obstinately as ever. Gradually the attackers broke off the engagement. The battered defenders were left in possesssion of the field.

Herkimer's message had not reached Fort Stanwix before the ravine trap had been sprung. Before the sortie had been organized the storm had caused a further delay. But when Willett did sally forth with 250 men, he struck that portion of the besiegers' camp occupied by the Indians and Tories, most of whom were engaged in the battle at the ravine six miles away. Those who remained were taken so unawares by the swiftness of the thrust that they were driven headlong into the river without his suffering the loss of even a single man wounded. The attackers were able to loot the camp at their leisure. Their booty included Johnson's headquarters, important military stores, five English flags, and all of the Indians' personal property. As a bonus for enlistment, each Indian had at Oswego been given a suit of clothes, a gun, a brass kettle, a tomahawk, powder, and money. When leaving for the ravine ambush they had as usual stripped for action to breechclout and weapons, thus leaving in camp their recently acquired wealth which Willett's men carried off by some tens of wagonloads. St. Leger's regulars finally got across the river from their camp to attempt to intervene, but Willett, unlimbering his three small field pieces, was able to complete his unhurried withdrawal to the security of the fort, still without losing a man.

At the ravine the Americans were tending their wounded and counting their dead. Considering the number engaged they had fought the bloodiest battle of the Revolution. Of the little army of 700, nearly 200 had been killed and another 200 wounded or captured. There was no feeling that afternoon, however, that they had won a victory. They had held their ground and escaped annihilation, but obviously any further attempt at forcing their way past St. Leger to the relief of Fort Stanwix was out of the question. Fearing a resumption of the attack at any moment, the survivors loaded their wounded in their wagons and retreated hastily down the Mohawk. The reappearance of the remnant of the army, the word of its frightful losses, the conviction that it had suffered a disastrous defeat convulsed every frontier settlement with grief and consternation. It was taken for granted that St. Leger with his host of revenging Indians and Tories would erupt from the wilderness at any moment. With so many of their only defenders already fallen, nothing seemed to stand between them and this catastrophe.

But in the siege lines at Fort Stanwix the situation had a quite different aspect. Victory in the battle had brought St. Leger no nearer success in his campaign. As an orthodox soldier he could not bring himself to advance across the defenseless frontier until he had reduced the fort which threatened his line of communications. Yet the fort was stronger than he had been led to expect and, with so resolute a garrison, was proving most difficult to reduce. An even more dismal difficulty was the misbehavior of his Indians. The striking force of his invading army depended upon the Indian contingent which represented half his strength. But he was discovering, as had many abler commanders before him, that to depend upon Indian allies was to mortgage every power to make command decisions.

As day succeeded day with the garrison as defiant as ever, the Indians continued to melt away like snow in the spring. In their first jubilation over their success at the ravine hundreds had gone home to display their captives and loot. Those who remained had, on second thought, begun to brood. They had been incensed by the plunder of their property in Willett's sortie and then, upon further reflection, infuriated by their losses at the ravine which had so far exceeded those suffered by their white comrades. They had been led to accompany the expedition, they reminded St. Leger, by the proffered opportunity to observe and learn how white men fought. Instead they had been required to do all the fighting themselves. The more closely they contemplated this grievance the more intractable they became. They disregarded the orders even of their own leader, Brant, indulged in drunken orgies, murdered most of their captives, and flagrantly insulted any white officer who ventured to reason with them.

Deprived of dependence on his Indians, St. Leger's remaining effectives scarcely outnumbered the garrison. He was therefore thunderstruck to learn that a no less renowned commander than Benedict Arnold was advancing upon him with a corps of continentals. Actually Arnold was still at German Flats without the means or the men to make a serious effort but, by adroitly broadcasting exaggerated reports of his strength, he convinced St. Leger of the need to withdraw while there was still time. On August 23rd the siege of Fort Stanwix was raised and the bedraggled and by now thoroughly demoralized conglomeration of English regulars, Hessian mercenaries, Canadian partisans, and Tory rangers, together with a residue of Indians, which so recently had considered itself an army of invasion, floundered back toward its Oswego base. During the retreat the increasingly insubordinate Indians added to the depression of all concerned the final aggravation of pillaging the officers' baggage.

Thus what at first had seemed the stunning defeat at Oriskany soon began to appear in its truer aspect as one of the more decisive victories of the Revolution. The valiant stand of Herkimer's embattled farmers at the ravine had had the effect any commander most wishes to produce in the mind of his opponent. It had profoundly altered the thinking and the expectations not only of the Indians but of St. Leger himself. Had St. Leger instead felt free to debauch into the Mohawk Valley, his Indians spreading terror before him and his strength constantly increasing as Tory inhabitants flocked to join him, his advance could have had an incalculable influence upon the course of the Saratoga campaign.

But to whatever extent the sacrificial service of the frontier people at Oriskany may be said to have served the general Revolutionary cause, there can be no question that it served to bring upon their own heads measureless disaster. There were not again to be great formal invasions of the strategic scope of Burgoyne's and St. Leger's. There were, instead, to be a seemingly interminable succession of lesser incursions, infinitely more difficult to fend off, of Indians bent on avenging their original losses at Oriskany. Brant's Indians, assisted by Butler's Rangers and Johnson's Greens, were for the next four years to devastate the New York frontier until it was left blackened, bleeding, and all but lifeless.

VIII

The Year of the Three Sevens

PEOPLE INHABITING THE westward sweeping arc of the frontier from the Allegheny to the Kentucky to the Holston long identified 1777 as "The Year of the Three Sevens" or "The Bloody Year." It was the year in which the border war of the Revolution began in dreadful earnest. From then on the daily existence of every inhabitant was oppressed by the perpetual apprehension that there could at any moment be an Indian behind the woodpile or a hundred of them in the underbrush fringing the clearing. No man could hoe his corn, no woman could go to the spring, no child could play in the dooryard without continually straightening and turning to peer and listen. Through the depths of the wilderness encompassing every frontier station or cabin, Indians were able to approach with little chance of detection so that every family was condemned to live with the constant assumption that any hour might bring unspeakable disaster.

This sudden change for the worse was strikingly illustrated in Clark's Harrodsburg diary. For the whole month of February 1777 he set down but the one entry: "Nothing Remarkable done." But beginning with the first week in March the record was dotted with such notations as: "Thomas Shores & Wm Ray killed at the Shawnee Spring." "We had 4 Men wounded and some Cattle killed." "Indians killed & scalped Hugh Wilson." "Archibald McNeal died of his wounds." "Indians killed and scalped Garrett Pendergrest killed or took prisoner Peter Flin." "Indians killed and scalped Danl Goodman wounded Capt Boone Capt Todd, Hite & Stoner." "Indians attacked Logan's Fort killed & scalped Wm Hudson wounded Burr Harrison & Jno Kennedy." "Barney Stagner killed & beheaded ½ mile from the Fort." But perhaps even more indicative of the times and the people was the insertion among these somber entries of the first one for July: "Lieutenant Linn married. Great merriment."

The most advanced points of frontier resistance to this sudden wave of Indian incursions were the three surviving stations in Kentucky: Harrodsburg, Boonesborough, and Logan's; * and the four small, militia-garrisoned forts on the upper Ohio: the blockhouse at Kittanning, the partially rebuilt fort at Pittsburgh, and the two stockades at Wheeling and the mouth of the Kanawha, Fort Henry and Fort Randolph. These were few and widely separated posts to interfere even slightly with Indian access to the more than 1500 miles of otherwise unguarded frontier.

A more important element in frontier defense was the reservoir of seasoned border militia in the Valley of Virginia and on the Holston, capable of undertaking long marches to strike back, as against the Shawnee in 1774 and the Cherokee in 1776. The most important of all developed on March 5th at Harrodsburg when Clark was commissioned major of Virginia militia and made responsible for the defense of Kentucky. Though not yet twenty-five he was recognized by his fellow settlers, who constituted the only force at his disposal, as the one man most suited to command. His subordinate officers were as signally adapted to the kind of war that was beginning. The captains he appointed, Daniel Boone, Benjamin Logan, James Harrod, and John Todd, were men who had already won never to be forgotten reputations and the scouts (then they were usually called "spies") for whom he had such imperative need were

---

* Logan's had been evacuated for a time in midwinter 1776-77 but reoccupied in late February. The station was sometimes known as St. Asaph's.

incomparable woodsmen of the stature of Simon Kenton and
Michael Stoner, able to meet Indians in the most tangled thicket on
better than equal terms. A final element of frontier strength, and
one without which all others might have proved insufficient, was
the arrival at Wheeling May 2nd of Lieutenant William Linn with
98 barrels of gunpowder.

Linn's exploit was remarkable even in those years when the most
extraordinary ventures were considered commonplace. A more adequate supply of powder was an absolute necessity if the frontier were
to be defended. It could not be had in the east where there was not
sufficient for the demands of the Continental Army. The nearest
other possible supply source was New Orleans. Linn was sent there
to get some. With George Gibson and fifteen companions he had
started down the Ohio from Pittsburgh the previous July and was
lost to American view for the next nine months. At New Orleans
the officially neutral Spanish had been persuaded, with the aid of
local American merchants, to furnish the powder which was paid for
by a draft on Virginia, establishing a precedent of which Clark was
to take later advantage in maintaining his Illinois supply line. To
confuse English agents, Gibson was at his own suggestion ostenta-
tiously clapped into jail, charged with imposing on Spanish neutrality, while Linn on September 22nd slipped away up the river
with his invaluable cargo. He got past the English posts on the
lower Mississippi by pretending to be a Spanish convoy and then
settled down to deal with the daily labor of rowing upstream and
with the daily risk of attack by Indians who could have counted
no achievement more triumphant than the acquisition of five tons
of gunpowder. The last military force to make the same effort,
Major Arthur Loftus' 1764 expedition of 400 veteran English regulars, had been so impressed by the combined difficulty of fighting
the current while fighting off Indians that it had soon turned back.
Linn did not. When for many months nothing further was heard
of him, authorities at Williamsburg and Pittsburgh organized a
relief expedition. But he had not needed help. Working his way
slowly northward from one hidden encampment to the next, continuing to elude Indian observation, struggling day after day against

the high water of winter and spring, he completed his tremendous 2000-mile, up-river journey before his rescuers had sailed. His gunpowder arrived just in time to arm the frontier against the summer's hurricane of Indian attacks.

The initial Indian offensive in the early spring of 1777 was a spontaneous and unorganized expression of chronic Indian aversion to white settlers, an extemporaneous resumption of Pluggy's activities the winter before. The English commanders at Niagara, Detroit, and Pensacola were not yet ready to promote a general Indian effort as an adjunct to the general English war effort, and the major Indian nations nearest the critical Ohio-Holston frontier, the Cherokee, Shawnee, and Delaware, were still, after repeated conferences and in the case of the Cherokee of a military capitulation, ostensibly at peace with the Americans. But in each there existed an aggressive minority dedicated to the conviction that there could never be peace while settlers continued to claim more land. Each of these hostile minorities was headed by a war chief of commanding personality, the Cherokee by Dragging Canoe, the Shawnee by Blackfish, and the Delaware, a few months later, by Captain Pipe. Excited by Pluggy's midwinter campaign and too impatient to wait longer upon their English patrons, scores of intransigent young warriors representing these dissident groups embarked upon small independent raids or joined the larger war parties being dispatched by the openly hostile Mingo, Wyandot, Chippewa, and Ottawa. The confused origin and composition of these raiding parties placed an added burden on frontier defense. Even had sufficient force been available to mount retaliatory offensive action against the Indian towns from which they had come, this was precluded by the risk that the full strength of the three nearer nations might thereby be drawn into the war.

These early 1777 attacks, painful as they were to the settlements upon which they were inflicted, were directed at no essentially military objective. The Indians who participated were not consciously striving to serve the purposes of their nation, of their English allies, or even of the general Indian cause. They were primarily animated by the traditional attitude of the Indian warrior who regarded war as a species of supremely dangerous game in which he was able to demonstrate those qualities of courage and cunning which most became a man. Measured by this standard, the object was not the conquest of territory or the capture of places, nor was distinction to be gained by personal sacrifice. Death in battle represented not glory but an irretrievable personal failure. What the individual warrior did seek was first the opportunity to display his contempt for danger while proving the ability to terrify his victims and then the reward of being able to return to his town with horses, captives, and scalps as unmistakable tokens of his valor. These had been valued forfeits when won from rival Indians but had become far more highly prized when won at the expense of his most bitterly hated adversary, the white settler.

The snow had scarcely gone off before the raids began at the two ends of the frontier. There were attacks near Kittanning in February and soon at other points along the Pennsylvania border. On the Holston, Dragging Canoe's Cherokee emigrees—thereafter ordinarily known not as Cherokee but as Chickamauga, in recognition of their having established new towns on Chickamauga Creek—began their active raiding as early. The Holston people who conceived that they had won an overwhelming victory over the Cherokee only months before found themselves already obliged again to take refuge in their stockades. As always a number of people were killed before they could reach the gates. Among these was David Crockett, grandfather of Davy Crockett. But the principal pressure in March fell upon Kentucky. Its three isolated stations, separated by so great a distance from any hope of succor, represented an irresistible temptation to Indian bands bent on distressing as many frontier inhabitants as possible, as expediently as possible.

Most of the early invaders of Kentucky were Mingo, whose special hatred of whites stemmed from the murder of Logan's family in 1774 and had been further fired by the death of Pluggy in the assault on McClelland's the previous winter. Nevertheless, the chief who attracted the most white attention was Blackfish, the Shawnee, possibly partly in retrospect after he had gained wider notoriety the following year by the capture and adoption of Daniel Boone. The attackers swooped down upon all three stations, in every case cutting off several men who were caught outside the walls in the first rush.

The stockade at Harrodsburg had not been completed, that at Boonesborough was small, and the one at Logan's even smaller. The total number of defenders at all three fell short of 150 men. The presence of many women and children in each station was an added drain on the scant food supplies and intensified the anxieties of their menfolk. At Boonesborough, the defense was further handicapped by Boone himself having been one of the first to be wounded, though this may be said to have been balanced by the unexpected addition to the garrison of Simon Kenton after he had made a desperate run through the forest in the hope of bringing in time a warning of the Indian approach. Yet for all the obvious weakness of the three stations the Indians forebore to devote their advantage in numbers to an attempt to storm even the smallest. For them this was not so much war as sport, a hunt with white human beings their prey. Just as they considered a man who had embarked on a bear hunt should take some care, if he had sense, to come back alive, so their purpose was to inflict maximum injury at a minimum cost. Persistently the besiegers endeavored, by various strategems, feints, pretended withdrawals, and offers to parley, to lure defenders outside the walls or to contrive an opportunity to gain entrance. For weeks they kept the stations under fire, hoping that the long-continued strain might bring the exhausted defenders to consider surrender.

The feature of the Indian invasion that bore most heavily on the inhabitants was the duration of these attacks. From March through July they were kept cooped up in their overcrowded and fetid stockades where they were increasingly weakened by hunger and disease. The people of Kentucky had had none too much food to get through the winter. They had intended to depend largely on hunting to tide them over until the new season's corn and garden produce had ripened. But with Indians watching from the nearest woods, constantly ready to pounce, men could not venture from the stockade to plant. The few cattle that had not already been butchered for food could not be turned out to graze. Hunting was out of the question, except at uncertain intervals by such singular experts as a Kenton or a Stoner who were occasionally able to pass the Indian lines at night and to return with meat the following night. The defenders could only dole out their remaining scraps of food in ever smaller portions, attempt to reassure their women and children who, in the event the Indians broke in, would suffer as harshly as any of the men, and watch grimly from their palisades for the chance that one of their red tormentors might venture near enough to present a reasonable target.

Realizing that defense, no matter how determined, could not continue after hunger had become outright starvation, the Kentuckians felt compelled to call for help. Logan, aware that his small station was in particular jeopardy, started off alone on June 6th. To creep undetected past the Indians besieging his stockade was only the beginning of his extraordinary achievement. Through forests and canebrakes and over rivers and mountains, for the sake of speed crossing at known fords and taking open trails, he continued to elude Indians on the alert to intercept just such desperate messengers as he. He reached the Holston, reported Kentucky's danger, and got back to his station on June 23rd to encourage his people with word that help, sooner or later, would come. He had traveled alone through 400 miles of savage-infested wilderness in 17 days. Since there was so little assurance that any one man might get through, other couriers were dispatched from other stations. Hugh McGary and John Haggin set out for Pittsburgh, and William Smith for the Yadkin. All got through.

Congress had in early 1777 at last become impressed by the need to recognize the growing threat to the new nation's western frontier. On June 1st Brigadier General Edward Hand, an experienced and capable continental officer, arrived at Pittsburgh to take command of the defense of the upper Ohio, thought to be in possible danger of invasion by Hamilton from Detroit. Hand's efforts were limited to the supervision of the local militia since he had been furnished no regular troops. The demands on the major fronts in the east were too pressing to permit Washington's sending continentals over the mountains, let alone to the extreme distance of far-off Kentucky. But the Holston settlements, though themselves engaged in fighting off Chickamauga raids, accepted responsibility for their fellow Virginians and Carolinians in Kentucky. On August 1st Colonel John Bowman reached Harrodsburg with two militia companies numbering 100, and early in September Captain William Smith arrived with another 48.

This was not an overwhelming reinforcement but was nevertheless enough to make a substantial difference. No longer were the defenders obliged to remain continuously behind their palisades. They were now numerous enough to sortie into the surrounding woods and able occasionally to close with the wary invaders. There ensued a succession of small bush fights, in each of which there were two to a dozen casualties, as parties of Kentucky or Virginia militia, groping in the forest to locate their enemies, alternately ambushed or cut off parties of Indians or were themselves taken at a similar disadvantage. In late summer the Indian pressures on Kentucky began for a time to relax. This new aggressiveness of the defenders was in Indian estimation making the game so much harder to play that it had lost some of its attractiveness as a sport. But elsewhere along the border the pressures were at the same time building up. On the more populous Ohio and Holston frontiers, there were many more people, many of whom had not yet recognized the need to take refuge in the nearest community stockade.

At Pittsburgh the American Indian Agent, George Morgan, was still receiving assurances of continued neutrality from the Shawnee and Delaware, both of whom had been deeply impressed by the frontier's military energies in the recent Shawnee War. The Delaware were still under the influence of their pacific chief, White Eyes, and their Moravian missionaries. Cornstalk, with his vivid memories of the Virginians' prowess at Point Pleasant, was determined to hold his Shawnee out of the war. Morgan was naturally anxious to encourage these neutralistic tendencies of the "near" Indian nations. He pointed out that the many minor raids that were tormenting the frontier were being made by "far" Indians from the vicinity of Detroit. The situation was admittedly bad, he argued, but could be made much worse if the "near" Indians were also antagonized. Hand would have preferred offensive action to punish the Mingo and Wyandot in their sanctuary at Sandusky but was unable to gather the resources to mount such an expedition. Virginia urged an offensive, but Congress after some debate decided against one, and the Ohio frontier was left to endure the intermittent raids, each of which wiped out a family or two, with such patience as could be mustered.

In the south a delegation representing the outwardly pacific majority of the Cherokee came in July to Long Island on the Holston * to sign the formal peace treaty with the Virginians which they had promised in their capitulation at the end of their war the previous autumn. They painfully ceded more land, professed a determination to remain at peace, and maintained that they had no control over the marauding Chickamauga for whose excesses, therefore, they could not be held responsible.

Meanwhile, American efforts to keep as many Indians as possible out of the war had been countered by more direct English efforts to bring all of them into it. In June, the English commanders at Oswego, Niagara, and Detroit received the long-awaited order to develop Indian attacks against the American frontier on the widest possible scale. These, it was confidently expected, would serve sooner or later to discourage the American will to persevere in the war and in the meantime to distract the attention of the main American armies engaged in the east against Burgoyne and Howe.

At Oswego and Niagara the Iroquois were assembled to serve with St. Leger's formally organized army of invasion advancing upon formally garrisoned Fort Stanwix. But at Detroit Hamilton had no such conventional opportunity to employ Indians for orthodox military purposes. His garrison consisted of but 70 regulars. Of the 300 militiamen available to him most were French *habitants* of little military value. No more than Hand did he possess the resources

---

* On July 4th the conference was recessed for the purpose of celebrating the first anniversary of the Declaration of Independence. There were orations and cannon salutes and much festive eating and drinking. The at first astounded Indians soon began to participate with enthusiasm and even staged a warrior's dance as their contribution to the ceremonies.

to undertake an organized offensive operation. His one recourse, therefore, in endeavoring to obey his instructions, was to incite the Indians to undertake promiscuous raids among the American settlements. Upon this project he embarked with marked diligence and energy.

Inviting the Indians of Ohio and the Lakes to a series of conferences at Detroit in June, Hamilton welcomed all who attended, feasted, flattered, entertained, and armed them. As at Oswego, their avarice was encouraged by generous presents and their belligerency stimulated by liberal issues of rum. These gratifying advantages of English friendship were to continue were they to recognize their great opportunity. The moment had arrived, he declared, for Indians to right their many ancient wrongs. The Americans, particularly the Virginians who had been the most aggressive intruders, must now be driven from all Indian lands on the Indian side of the mountains which they had during the past seven years so unjustly occupied in flagrant violation of the wishes of the king, the English army, the Indian Department, and even of their own provincial governments.

In urging these assaults upon the civil population of the American frontier Hamilton took pains at the same time to endeavor "to teach them to spare Old Age Women and Children." He accompanied all of his exhortations with, in the language of his official report, "the strictest injunctions to discourage and restrain them from their usual barbarities." His insistence upon the earnestness of his effort to minimize or channelize the traditional brutalities of the savages he was recruiting must, in the light of all the circumstances, be presumed the baldest hypocrisy. He had been commanding at Detroit for twenty months and must by then have become too familiar with the normal Indian temperament to imagine that these remonstrances were more than the emptiest of forms. He knew as well as did the French and English traders who were his interpreters and advisors that in the excitement of combat a pack of Indians was little more likely to distinguish the age or sex of its victims than might a pack of wolves. Hamilton did bolster his injunctions by offering higher direct payments for captives than those paid indirectly for scalps.

The decision to employ Indians was attended—from Germain all the way down through the official hierarchy of Carleton, Hamilton, the Johnsons, and the Butlers to the individual Tory ranger delegated to accompany a war party—by this same pious assumption that Indians could be dissuaded from committing unnecessary cruelties. But there appears no escape from the conclusion that it was also attended by the full knowledge that universal outrages must nevertheless result. The central purpose of the decision was not so much to defeat American soldiers as to terrorize American border inhabitants. In any event, Hamilton was able to report in July that he had succeeded in dispatching 15 war parties and a few months later the return of Indians with 73 prisoners and 129 scalps.

The most notable single event resulting from these accelerated and, for the first time officially, promoted Indian attacks of the late summer of 1777 was the first siege of Wheeling. This was one of the older and better established settlements, having been founded in 1769 by one of the most famous of all frontier families, the Zanes. Its stockade, formerly known as Fort Fincastle but during the Revolution as Fort Henry, was garrisoned by a company of militia which was frequently changed in order to distribute more equably the task of defending the post. At sunrise on September 1st Indians appeared in the vicinity and killed a number of people who had not succeeded in gaining the stockade in time. Underestimating the number of Indians, Captain Samuel Mason with 24 militiamen rushed out to drive them away. The Indians were confidently expecting precisely such an impulsive sortie and had already made careful preparations to receive it. The militiamen plunged on into the trap to suffer a loss of 15 killed. Only five men regained the fort unhurt. The attacking force of some 200 Indians, most of them Mingo and Wyandot but including, as usual, a few Delaware and Shawnee, burned that portion of the settlement outside the fort and destroyed cattle and crops but made no serious assault on the fort. After two days they withdrew, apparently content with their success. Three weeks later Captain William Foreman's militia company assumed garrison duty at Wheeling. He and his men were from an interior district which had had little experience with Indians. On September 26th Foreman went on patrol with 34 men. Disregarding the advice of Captain William Linn, who with a smaller detachment kept to higher ground, Foreman entered the thicker woods of the river bottom where he was ambushed by Half King and a party of 40 Wyandot with a loss of 26 killed and one captured.

The 1777 siege of Wheeling and its accompanying double massacre gained a place in contemporary records on account of the number of casualties at one place and time. Of the many lesser attacks then and later most escaped such notice. There remain passing references in the correspondence of Hand and the commanders who succeeded him to some of them. Private letters, family legends, occasional contemporary items in eastern newspapers offer scraps and bits of information about others. Reports and rumors circulated by word of mouth exaggerated some episodes while overlooking others. Their number and similarity often made accounts seem merely repetitive. John Hayward, the tireless compiler of border annals, was able later to assemble a list of more than 400 separate attacks on the southern frontier alone. The Draper Collection and evidence accumulated in many university and historical society libraries have served to recover traces and hints of many others in every region. But most of the raids from July to November of this year, as in every other year of the Revolution's border war, remained unrecorded, the identities of the men, women, and children who perished unknown. The confusion of the times, the extreme isolation of most habitations, the circumstance that many families had so recently arrived that they were still strangers in their neighborhoods, the fact that all too often there had been no survivors to tell the story, the very multiplicity of horrors which made no one instance worth wide comment left most such local tragedies a presently forgotten mystery. Sooner or later a militia patrol ranging an area for Indian sign came upon another burned cabin. If there were bodies these were buried. If not there was often little clear indication whether the family had been carried off as captives or had fled in time.

Yet it was the sum total of these unrecorded family-size disasters and the readiness of other families to continue to brave the constant threat of a similar fate that was to decide the issue of the Revolution in the west. It was upon these bewildered and distraught families that ultimate victory or defeat entirely depended. The major Indian purpose was to make the settlers' existence unbearable in order to compel them to retreat back over the mountains. With this the English purpose coincided, chiefly on account of the added hope that the ensuing opportunity to spread the Indian terror east of the mountains might disrupt the main rebel war effort on the seaboard. Success for either objective depended upon breaking the will of the settlers and their families to stand their ground. In striving to achieve this result the primary weapon was the Indian raid.

In every Indian war of the long period of border wars from 1754 to 1794, this unique institution was the basic, essential, and invariable feature. Except under unusual circumstances, as when their supply had been organized and their operations directed by white allies, whether French or English, Indians were seldom able to take the field in aggregations of a size to be ordinarily considered armies. Much smaller groups were better able to live off the country while making the long marches required to advance from distant Indian towns to the border area to be attacked. Indian scorn of discipline made smaller units more congenial. The most ardently sought of all advantages, surprise, was the more readily gained the fewer the number of attackers. Literally every Indian preference in the whole range of possible methods of waging war was most suited to the small party and its concomitant freedom of action.

The technique of delivering such raids was capable of almost infinite variation. Sometimes, when the march to be made was not too long for each warrior to carry with him war rations to sustain him en route, a descent might be made on a major settlement by a party of as many as 150 or 200. Among the advantages of attacking in sufficient numbers to permit breaking into such a comparatively populous district were the near certainty of catching many more inhabitants before they could get to the stockade and the assurance of greater quantities of loot in their hastily abandoned homes. Ordinarily so large a party then broke up into many smaller packs to scour the surrounding area to ravage homesteads too distant from the settlement's center for their inhabitants to have had any chance to run for the stockade. At the other extreme from this oversize raiding party was the unit of as few as two or three warriors. They hid in the woods near some farm or settlement for days at a time, waiting for just the right chance to kill an unwary hunter or berry-picker or to steal a child or a horse. But the most common raiding party numbered 20 to 40 warriors, a force large enough to fight a respectable engagement if pressed, and yet small enough to move about with ease. The favorite objective was a one- or two-family farm or a community too small or too new to possess a stockade. Dependent upon the whim of the raiders, the target of their selection might be one of the districts near the outer fringe of the frontier or these might be passed by to strike at others far behind the frontier where the inhabitants might be expected to be less on guard. Always the great object was surprise. Always there was the swift and secret approach, the sudden, brief, incredibly violent eruption of death and devastation, and then the equally swift and secret withdrawal.

To the victims these descents seemed always to conform to the same horrible pattern, as stylized as the conventionalized movements of some macabre death dance. Usually the family suffering the blow had long endured the strain of fearing just such a visitation. In common with every other family of the vicinity, many weeks of the past months had usually been spent in the shelter of the stockade. A militia scouting patrol might have reported their untenanted home to be still intact. If the immediate neighborhood had remained quiet for a few successive days, confinement in the stockade had become more irksome, the prospect of a return home, if only for a few hours, more appealing. Perhaps they had intended to dash from the stockade only long enough to harvest their ripened corn or to search for a cow left to wander in the woods. Perhaps they had decided it was safe to venture again living at home, at least until there came another alarm. If the Indians did return to the area, it could after all be upon some other household that the lightning would first descend. When instead the descent was upon their own, they found that all their former fears had in no way prepared them.

It still came as a stunning surprise. Moreover, the reality was infinitely more horrifying than any threat that they had been able to imagine. The sudden demoniac materialization out of the previously silent and seemingly empty forest of a pack of howling savages, painted in grotesquely fearsome designs of red and black and green, appeared at first glance and from that first second an apparition too appalling to permit comprehension.

The composite family of this representative instance might have comprised a husband and wife, his mother, her brother, and six children ranging from an infant in arms to teenage boy and girl. The husband was shot as the Indians sprang from the woods before he could even reach for his rifle. The brother, seated on the ground against a stump while shaping a new hoe handle, crawled frantically into a nearby patch of weeds where in the attackers' extreme excitement he remained undiscovered. The lack of resistance failed to temper the initial ferocity of the Indian assault. The raiders appeared possessed by an insensate frenzy. The scalp was torn from the still living grandmother. The baby was snatched from its mother's arms and swung by its heels to crush its skull against a corner of the corncrib. The expiring head of the family was dismembered and his entrails festooned about the dooryard. His wife's breasts and unborn child were carved from her convulsed body and cast into the flames of the burning cabin. Every item of property too bulky to carry away was destroyed. After a brief consideration of their prospective abilities to keep pace on the return march the three younger children were dispatched, one casually axed, one tossed on the point of a spear, the third shot with arrows after being permitted to start running away. The scalps of all three children were removed with as much interest as had been their elders'. Their value at Detroit would equal that of any white adult's. The older boy and girl, selected to be carried off as captives, were not harmed. Aside from being beaten if they lagged they would be well enough treated on the way back. They, too, had a value. When they reached their captors' town they would be required to run the gauntlet, but thereafter their prospects would be subject to wide variations. Either or both might be burned for the stay-at-homes' edification, might be adopted into the tribe, or might be sold at Detroit at the going price of $100 in cash or trade for each prisoner. Paralyzed by horror, the brother watched from his hiding place until the Indians had disappeared into the forest as suddenly as they had emerged from it. A thousand times he had heard that such things happened. He had listened while remaining inwardly certain that misfortune so monstrous could only come to other people. He was still unable to believe that it had come to his own.

The incidents of every raid varied from this norm only in detail. Indians were notoriously capricious. Occasionally they were more methodical, seldom more restrained. More often they were even more obscenely maniacal. There were instances in which they debated and joked with their victims and others in which they could be so impressed by an unexpected display of individual spirit that they might spare a child or a cripple. At other times, infuriated by an unanticipated resistance, they lingered at the scene to devote ingenious devices to the prolongation of every dying agony. Never were they known to exhibit any tendency that could be identified as humane. Often kindly and generous at home, at war they were never compassionate.

The overmastering impulse of the Indian at war was to force his adversary to fear him. It was an impulse directed by reliance upon a kind of primitive magic. The sudden death of an enemy was not considered a sufficient testimony to his own superior prowess. An adequate response was only to be extorted when his enemy had been made fully conscious of that superiority by protracted terror. This basic Indian urge to inflict pain added a nightmarish dimension to every raid.

Yet the never-ceasing repetition of their occurrence clothed each successive disaster in a protective mantle of inevitability. Personal catastrophe became no longer novel. To the inhabitants of the frontier it had come to seem their common lot. The family stricken presented no startling exception. Its luck had merely run out. Tomorrow another's turn would come. The process was taken for granted as deplorable but unavoidable. Only when the occasion was attended by some uncommonly tragic circumstance or some peculiarly affecting sidelight was attention attracted. Occasionally, then, a contemporary letter or report or journal included an incidental reference that casts a revealing gleam among the shadows that shroud an era so nearly incomprehensible to us now.

Major John Taylor, a local commander on the Clinch, opened a letter to Colonel William Preston, dealing with routine militia affairs, with the laconic statement: "The 18th Instant the Indians was In this Neighborhood and Fell in at James Roark's where they scalped seven of his children And his wife."

Colonel John Floyd, one of the original surveyors of Kentucky and a cofounder of Logan's Station, in the course of a letter describing the serious prevalence of sickness among Kentuckians long confined in stockades, added as a reflective afterthought: "My uncle Davis & his son were both killed near Cumberland Mountain . . . There were four brothers of them who have all been murdered in the course of 7 or 8 years."

John Heckewelder, the Moravian missionary with the Delaware, making one of his customary circumstantial reports on Indian war parties passing his mission, either on their way to attack the settlements or on their return with captives, was for all his familiarity with misery touched by one incident: "They also brought off a sucking child, which always crying they killed by Little Beaver Creek."

But perhaps the veteran border commander, William Preston, whose own unparalleled experience had begun twenty-three years earlier with his miraculous survival at Ingles' Station in the first of all Indian raids on the transmountain frontier, most clearly revealed the stresses of his times: "I cannot express my Anxiety for the People in Greenbrier; I long ardently to hear from them, at the same time that I fear it."

While the practical and essentially military effect of the raids was most succinctly put by Colonel Archibald Lochry, Westmoreland's county lieutenant, with the grim report: "Harvast is now just at Hand, what few militia we are able to send is no more than able Keep our Forts & . . . I can see no way of saving any Grain on Our fruntears."

The Indian attacks may have been designed to demoralize the inhabitants and force the evacuation of the settlements, but a more immediate result was fiercely to intensify every already embittered interracial animosity. An implacable hatred of all Indians had been implanted in the frontier people during the terrible years of the French War and Pontiac's War. The 1777 raids raised this hatred to a new pitch of fury. It had become a loathing that drew no distinction among Indians. The survivors of the thousands of frontier families that had suffered by former Indian depredations could not be brought ever to admit that there might exist "good" Indians, or "tame" Indians, or "friendly" Indians, or innocent Indian women and children. The frontier militiaman who was reproved by an officer for striking down an Indian child during an assault on an Indian town gave exact and realistic voice to this view with his terse and endlessly quoted reply: "Nits make lice."

This frontier conviction that all Indians were subhuman monsters equally deserving of extermination had led in the past to premeditated and coldblooded white excesses as indefensible in their way as the worst of which the Indians were guilty. In 1763, frontiersmen had broken into the Lancaster jail to dismember and disembowel fourteen men, women, and children, the inoffensive remnant of the pacific Conestoga tribe who had been granted sanctuary in the jail by local authorities. In 1764, hundreds of enraged borderers had marched on Philadelphia determined to destroy 140 Moravian-mission Indian converts who had taken refuge there. In 1768, ten Indians, three of them women and three others children, had been axed, scalped, and burned while they were invited guests in a white man's home. In 1774, frontiersmen had murdered nine other unsuspecting Indian visitors, among them the mother, brother, sister, and several cousins of Logan, the Mingo chief whose faithful attachment to white government and the white race had been proved during two wars.

This torch of frontier hatred of everything Indian was handed on in 1777. The frontier people of this new generation were a new and more aggressive breed. They had been hardened and toughened by many troubled years. They were no longer disposed to take panic-stricken flight at the first Indian war whoop as had the less seasoned border population of 1755 or 1763. Instead, their first impulse was to strike back, to exchange blow for blow, outrage for outrage. Vengeance was a more common concern than security. The rawest and newest young militiaman had only to view the mangled corpses left in one raided farmyard to begin instantly and fully to share the fiercest resentments of his most experienced frontier neighbor. Inhabitants west of the mountains were committed to an existence too harsh to admit appreciation of niceties more easily observed in more civilized regions. Had they been more amenable, more reasonable, they might not have been there and they most certainly would not have remained there. But they were never amenable and they were deaf to reason. They had been possessed of a perpetual and uncontrollable rage which had left them little respect for prudence and less for authority. Timothy Pickering, visiting the frontier on a congressional inspection tour, characterized them in a letter to Washington with the pungent statement: "The inhabitants appear to be a wild ungovernable race, little less savage than their tawny neighbors."

From the beginning of the border wars it had been characteristic of the frontier people that the more they suffered from Indians the less they were ready to tolerate any approach to Indian peace. No matter how threatening the immediate crisis, they had clung stubbornly to the dogma that maintained there could be no justification under any circumstances whatsoever for any kind of traffic with Indians. Even during those earlier years when they had repeatedly demonstrated their utter inability to defend themselves, they had nevertheless as repeatedly opposed any form of appeasement. Government packtrains transporting official presents to peace conferences, arranged with a view to ending Indian attacks, had been waylaid by the inhabitants of the very areas under attack. Traders en route to the Indian country with promised goods to supply Indian needs which, if unsupplied, would have led to further hostilities had been pillaged. It was as though the most ignorant and uninformed frontiersman was as instinctively aware that between the races there could never be peace as was the most farseeing old chieftain whose horizon had been widened by attendance at a dozen international conferences. The injuries each had visited and were continuing to visit upon the other were too deep and too lasting to permit any possibility of moderation or accommodation. They were locked in a conflict which could only end in the extinction of one of them.

This historic and relentless frontier refusal to recognize any distinctions or graduations in Indian guilt proved in 1777 a fatal handicap to the desperate efforts of American authorities to preserve the neutrality of the nearer Indians. George Morgan was attempting to organize another peace conference at Pittsburgh as a counterbalance to the English conferences at Oswego and Detroit. This was a project that was receiving the earnest support of Brigadier General Edward Hand, the area's military commander, of the governors of Pennsylvania and Virginia, and of Washington and Congress. Yet the preliminary conversations were obstructed by continuous frontier efforts to assassinate the visiting members of Indian missions. Morgan and Hand were compelled to keep Indian emissaries concealed in their private quarters. Morgan had even persuaded a pacific faction of the notoriously bellicose and anti-American Seneca to send a delegation. Unknown white assailants ambushed the approaching ambassadors, killing several. This put a certain and abrupt end to the last hope of moderating Seneca hostility.

That same month of July, while there appeared still some chance of keeping a considerable segment of Indian military power out of the war, the same frontier repudiation of any approach to peaceful settlement was evident in the south. During an intermission in the sessions of the Long Island peace conference at which the Cherokee were making an almost abject submission, Big Bullet, a warrior accompanying their delegation, was shot while sitting on the river bank mending his moccasins. The embarrassed American commissioners were unable to apprehend the assassin but eventually persuaded the embittered Cherokee to resume the conference.

This frontier sabotage of every move toward interracial conciliation was to continue throughout the period of the Indian wars. The next year White Eyes, the patient and endlessly perservering advocate of a firm Delaware-American understanding, was assassinated while discussing arrangements for a new conference. The frantic American authorities successfully concealed the circumstances of his death by announcing that he had succumbed to smallpox. The conference was held, and the deceived Delaware renewed their pledges of friendship. White Eyes' equally deceived son held to his father's pro-American policy and for a time even attended Princeton. The next year the Delaware were still eager to remain friends and undertook to send a delegation to Philadelphia to appeal directly to Congress. The delegates were received there by the central government with many warm though vague expressions of esteem but were much more impressed by the difficulty with which they were able to evade the repeated frontier attempts to waylay them en route.

These frontier rejections of any form of Indian peace had meanwhile reached a climax in the sensational fate of Cornstalk. The Shawnee chief, the most widely known and respected Indian of his time, was still resolved to hold his people neutral, or at any rate as many of them as he could prevail upon to follow his counsel. As evidence of his good faith, in the late autumn of 1777, he visited Fort Randolph, built upon the very site of his great battle with the Virginians three years before, accompanied by only two attendants, to renew his professions of peaceful intent. Captain Matthew Arbuckle, commanding the militia garrison, had been impressed by reports of the number of Shawnee who had been listening instead to Hamilton at Detroit and decided to hold Cornstalk as a hostage for his nation's better behavior. A few days later Cornstalk's son, Elinisico, came to inquire about his father. He, too, was held. On November 10th several members of the garrison went outside the walls to hunt. One of them, Robert Gilmore, was shot from ambush by an Indian who was at the moment assumed to be a Shawnee, though some days later identified as a Mingo. Gilmore's companions, all of whom were his neighbors on the Valley of Virginia border from which the company had come, recalled that eighteen years before four members of the Gilmore family had been killed and four more carried off as captives by a Shawnee raiding party led by Cornstalk. Infuriated beyond endurance by the coincidence, they determined now to take retribution into their own hands. Arbuckle protested. He pointed out that Cornstalk's status as ambassador, hostage, and prisoner of war gave him triple immunity and reminded them that he had come to the fort of his own volition on a mission of peace. But he could gain no hearing. He had lost all control over his command. The irate militiamen broke into the cabin where the old Shawnee chief had been housed and, shooting, stabbing, clubbing, dispatched father and son and their two attendants.

The crime was condemned everywhere except along the frontier. Hand went to Fort Randolph to investigate, only to discover that the unrepentant frontier militiamen were no more ready to listen to him than they had been to Arbuckle. The governors of Virginia and Pennsylvania sent urgent messages to the Shawnee seeking to convince them of their deepest regrets. Congress framed an apology. Morgan transmitted the official American attitude by writing the Shawnee: "Brothers When I look toward you or at the Kenawa River I am ashamed of the Conduct of our young foolish Men. formerly I was ashamed of the Conduct of your young Men. Now I see there are foolish people among all Nations. Our Wise men are ashamed and sorry for what has happened and our Warriors declare themselves in like manner." Patrick Henry issued a proclamation denouncing the murders and demanding that those guilty be brought to justice. He remained so exercised and persisted so indignantly that four of the militiamen most directly involved were brought to trial the next spring in their home county of Rockbridge. No one could be found to testify against them, and the charge was dismissed for want of evidence, thus preserving the frontier tradition that no white man might ever be punished for any injury, however flagrant, done an Indian.

Henry further insisted that Preston and Fleming, as spokesmen for the frontier, lend their enormous influence to the attempt to mollify the Shawnee. The two veteran colonels who had commanded regiments in the Shawnee campaign of 1774 and had for years been among the most aggressive defenders of the frontier were themselves so aware of the critical consequences of the outrage that they humbly and with a certain eloquence jointly appealed to the Shawnee: "We love you because you are generous and sensible. We wish to be friends with you. We have no desire to injure or molest you. We covet nothing you have. All we desire is peace with you . . . Your People and Ours live in the same land, breath the same Air, and drink the same water. We ought to live in Peace like Friends & Brothers."

But all regrets, apologies, and appeals were useless and, in fact, already too late before the first of them had arrived. The Shawnee had suffered more by the advance of the white frontier than had any other nation. The murder of Cornstalk had convinced a people who had long seethed with resentment of the folly of further restraint. Usually Indians refrained from attacks during the winter when on the one hand they needed to hunt and on the other a raiding party was bound to leave glaring tracks in the snow. But this time they did not wait. Blackfish invaded Kentucky in midwinter and, in the teeth of a snowstorm on February 7, 1778, surprised and captured Daniel Boone and 26 companions in a temporary camp where they were engaged in salt-making. This was a fearful blow to the defenses of Kentucky for the prisoners represented more than a quarter of the men endeavoring to hold the three stations. This, however, was only the first item in the long reckoning demanded for the murder of Cornstalk. For the next 17 years the Shawnee remained the most aggressive and inveterate of all Indian enemies of the frontier. The militiamen at Fort Randolph, while themselves escaping punishment, had pronounced a death sentence on hundreds of their fellow settlers.

The stresses to which Indian and settler alike had for so many years been subjected appeared by the end of 1777 certain to have extinguished any last lingering hope that peace could ever be restored under any circumstances. The issue between the races seemed progressively more irreconcilable, the events of each successive day to make the prospect of peace less likely. Attack invited counterattack, white aggression was met by Indian atrocity, hatred bred fiercer hatred. Yet here and there were peacemakers who refused to abandon hope. They were confirmed realists who permitted no disappointment to move them from their conviction that any alternative to war must be preferable to such a war. These few amazing figures stood steadfast against the storm of horrors. They were men and women of either race who, undeterred by outrage and insult and the denunciation of their compatriots, continued to advocate forgiveness and conciliation.

Some of these dedicated peacemakers were missionaries. Samuel Kirkland gained by his long and devoted service such influence over the Oneida that he was able to restrain them from participating in the attacks of their fellow Iroquois on the American settlements. The Moravians, John Heckewelder and David Zeisberger, clinging to their wilderness mission on the Tuscarawas in the face of threats and harassments from both sides, strove to lighten the burdens of war by counseling all Indians who would listen to keep out of it, by alleviating the sufferings of captives, and by warning the settlements of prospective Indian attacks. Other conciliators were Indian chiefs. It required unusual resolution to preach peace to warriors burning for revenge upon their white enemies and unusual vision to persist in the face of continually renewed white aggressions. Yet there were chiefs sufficiently clearsighted to perceive this to be their duty. White Eyes, the Delaware, and Old Tassel, the Cherokee, for example, continued to counsel their people to abjure war through long lifetimes in every year of which they had suffered by new white insults and encroachments. Each persisted until each met death in the same manner. Each was murdered by whites while under a white safe conduct and embarked upon the discussion of a peace treaty. Other mediators were traders. John Gibson, whose Indian wife was Logan's sister, used his trading, family, and official connections on both sides to promote understanding between the races and devoted his wide acquaintance in the Indian country to the support of Morgan's neutrality policy.* Nathaniel Gist, long a

* It was Gibson who at the Camp Charlotte conference transcribed the original version of Logan's celebrated lament which was so widely circulated in 1774 and 1775 and later gained even wider circulation when incorporated in Thomas Jefferson's *Notes on Virginia*. If, as has often been asserted, Gibson's translation made him chiefly responsible for the oration's unique eloquence this becomes but a further tribute to his interracial sympathies.

The version of Logan's oration as presented by Jefferson:

"I appeal to any white man to say if he ever entered Logan's cabin hungry, and resident of the Cherokee country, whose wife, Wurteh, sister of Old Tassel, bore him an illustrious son, Sequoyah, the great Cherokee scholar, espoused the American cause, in contrast to most southern traders who were active Tories, yet worked diligently to re-establish peace. But of all the peacemakers who sought against seemingly impossible odds to find some basis for understanding the two most notable were Indian women.

The tremendous influence of Nancy Ward, the Cherokee chief-tainess, was due primarily to her character and personality, but also to the extraordinary range and ramification of her connections on both sides of the frontier. Her station in the Indian world was pre-eminent. She was the niece of Attakullaculla and the cousin of Dragging Canoe. Two of her sons became prominent chiefs and her first husband had been Kingfisher, a noted war chief. Her personal heroism in the Cherokee-Creek War of 1755, in which she fought, rifle in hand, side by side with warriors at the Battle of Taliwa, had led to her elevation to the highest rank among Cherokee women, Ghigan (a title with the connotation of both "Beloved Woman" and "Beautiful Woman"), with authority to speak in council and pronounce pardons. In the white world her prestige was comparable. Her father had been an English officer. Her second husband was Brian Ward, a much respected English trader. (When, after spending most of his life in the Cherokee country, Ward retired to live with his white family on the white side of the border, Nancy in her old age was a frequent, welcome, and honored guest in his home.) One of her daughters, Betsy, married General Joseph Martin, close associate of Thomas Walker and Patrick Henry, Virginia's first In-

---

he gave him not meat; if ever he came cold and naked, and he clothed him not. During the course of the last long and bloody war, Logan remained idle in his cabin, an advocate for peace. Such was my love for the whites that my countrymen pointed as they passed, and said: 'Logan is the friend of white men.' I had even thought to have lived with you, but for the injuries of one man. Colonel Cresap, the last spring, in cold blood, and unprovoked, murdered all the relations of Logan, not sparing even my women and children. There runs not a drop of my blood in the veins of any living creature. This called on me for revenge. I have sought it: I have killed many: I have fully glutted my vengeance. For my country, I rejoice at the beams of peace; but do not harbor a thought that mine is the joy of fear. Logan never felt fear. He will not turn on his heel to save his life. Who is there to mourn for Logan? Not one."

dian commissioner, and leading Holston pioneer. James Robertson described her as "queenly and commanding," and Martin, as "the most superior woman I ever saw." All this influence with both races she devoted to reducing the tensions between them. Constantly loyal to her own people, she as continuously manifested her friendliness to whites, saving their captives, warning them of coming attacks, and once even feeding their starving troops. The war between the Cherokee and the white frontier, continuing almost without interruption from 1776 to 1794, was peculiarly relentless and savage and marked by many outrages perpetrated by both antagonists. Yet at every interval she resumed her efforts to restore understanding. Her services to peace were epitomized at the Long Island Conference of 1781 by her statement of the Indian women's point of view in her passionate address to the white commissioners: "We are your mothers; you are our sons. Our cry is all for peace; let it continue. This peace must last forever. Let your women's sons be ours; our sons yours. Let your women hear our words."

The other Indian chieftainess whose devotion to peace remained unshaken through innumerable trials was a more stern and primitive figure. The rank of women was not as formally recognized by the Shawnee as by the Cherokee, but as sister of Cornstalk she early acquired wide influence in her nation and at the time of Bouquet's Muskingum campaign in 1764, when she first gained the notice of history, she was already in her own right the head of her own town. The only name by which she was known in contemporary records was "The Grenadier Squaw," in recognition of her unusual height and regally erect bearing. Her observation of Bouquet's invading army and her participation in the negotiations by which he dictated Shawnee submission convinced her of the absolute and inevitable superiority of white military power. From then on her central purpose was to persuade her people that their wisest course under whatever provocations was to keep the peace. She was not moved to swerve from this policy by the injuries done the Shawnee by the Treaty of Fort Stanwix in 1768, or by the ensuing rush of settlers into Shawnee lands, or by the war forced on them by the Virginians in 1774, or by Cornstalk's murder. Even this final catastrophe but confirmed her opinion that peace represented the sole Indian hope. When, after Cornstalk's death, the Shawnee appeared unanimously determined upon war, she demonstrated her continuing devotion to peace by exiling herself from her people and taking up her residence at Fort Randolph behind the very walls within which her brother had been slaughtered. Being a woman of great wealth as well as high rank, she brought with her when she crossed the river her personal herd of more than half a hundred cattle and horses.* When the Shawnee besieged the fort the next spring, she volunteered at great personal risk to serve as mediator between the contending forces. When there was need to send couriers to warn the Virginia frontier of a coming Shawnee attack, she and her daughter, called "Fawney" by the garrison, painted and disguised them as Indian warriors so that they might run less risk of Shawnee interception. She remained at Fort Randolph at the edge of the Shawnee country until it was abandoned by the Americans and burned by the Shawnee in the spring of 1779. In 1780 she performed new services to the American cause by accompanying Colonel Mottin de la Balme's French expedition, designed to employ the ancient French influence with Indians, in an attempt at winning them away from their more recent English attachments. The last recorded contemporary reference to this formidable champion of her own convictions placed her living in poverty in Pittsburgh in 1785 and making a vain appeal to Congress for the grant of sufficient land upon which to end her days in peace.

The efforts of the few peacemakers, however laudable, had little effect. Meanwhile, the efforts of the far more numerous warmakers had in 1777 little more. Neither side had been able to gain an appreciable advantage. The campaign designed to dislodge the settlements had made scant progress. Some hundreds of families had moved back over the mountains. Settlers north of Forbes' Road in the Pittsburgh area who had been most exposed to Seneca attack had abandoned their holdings, as had settlers along the river below

---

* Hand expressed a somewhat more cynical view of her motives. In his opinion her pro-American inclinations sprang less from devotion to peace than a jealous hatred of the Shawnee wife of the pro-English Alexander McKee.

Wheeling. But at the end of the year the upper Ohio frontier ran substantially as it had at the beginning. In the south there had been an actual advance. After the Treaty of Long Island there had been a rush of settlers down the Holston, seizing upon land many miles nearer the center of the Cherokee country. In Kentucky the three stations still held. When the Holston militia returned home that fall, the remaining defenders at Harrodsburg numbered only 65 men able to bear arms, at Boonesborough only 22, and at Logan's only 16. Of these 27 were lost at the salt encampment. But the stations still held.

If the English-Indian efforts to dislodge the settlers had failed, the frontier's response had been not much more successful. It had amounted to little more than a continuing stubborn endurance. The frontier aggressiveness so strikingly manifested in 1774 and 1776 had been nowhere evident. Much of this decline in frontier energy was due to the prevalence of Tory sympathies which led every man to suspect his neighbor. On the upper Ohio the Pennsylvania-Virginia territorial dispute was an added damper, frustrating every effort to co-ordinate military effort.

Hand's endeavors to mount some sort of a retaliatory expedition to discourage Indian attacks had continued, ineffectually, all through the autumn. The concluding campaign of 1777 therefore dragged on into 1778. Hearing in January of the establishment of an English base for Indian supply on Lake Erie at the mouth of the Cuyahoga River, Hand determined to destroy it by making a midwinter overland march. He set out with a force of 500 militia he had at last been able to muster. This was the first United States expedition into the Indian country and it proved in every respect an inglorious inauguration. The militia began at once demonstrating the two principal difficulties associated with any attempt to employ them in an organized military operation. They paid little or no attention to their officers. And their aversion to all Indians was so deepseated that they were more interested in haring off after the first stray Indians they encountered than in pressing on to come to grips with the main Indian enemy.

The army's route up the Beaver River valley stretched across the hunting grounds of the Delaware, who since 1764 had earnestly and at times almost desperately sought to keep the peace with the white frontier. A militia patrol coming upon a Delaware hunting camp occupied by a brother of the prominent Delaware chief, Captain Pipe, and a number of women and children, killed the man and one woman and wounded another woman, Captain Pipe's mother. Another militia patrol surprised a Delaware salt-making camp occupied by four women and a boy, and killed all except one of the women.

The expedition's progress was further impeded by a thaw which required much circling around the heads of flooded creek bottoms. The weather finally became so unfavorable that the advance was abandoned and all straggled back to Pittsburgh. Hand could barely control his rage and disgust and beseeched Washington to transfer him back to the Continental Army. On the border the undertaking was thereafter derisively known as the "Squaw Campaign."

It was with these dismal aftermaths, the Squaw Campaign and the capture of Boone's salt-makers, that the Year of the Three Sevens came to an overdue end.

IX

๛

Clark 3

ON MARCH 5, 1777, Clark held the first muster of Kentucky militia. The next day the first two settlers were killed in the opening action of the Indian invasion which continued throughout the summer to threaten Kentucky with extinction. Yet, in the midst of all his desperate concern with keeping the three little settlements alive, he was looking forward not so much to making a counterattack as to launching a counterconquest. On April 3rd he made his first considered move toward this objective by dispatching two young hunters, Samuel Moore and Benjamin Linn, as spies instructed to bring him a report on the state of enemy defenses in the Illinois.* Already fixed in his mind was the contemplation of a campaign destined to affect the future of his country more decisively than any other of the Revolution excepting only Saratoga and Yorktown. He was then twenty-four.

It was not chance or accident that had drawn his attention to the Illinois. No region in the west have ever or for so long held so glit-

---

* During the French, English, and early American period, the term applied to an expanse roughly corresponding to the present state, but with special reference to the Kaskaskia-Cahokia area bordering the Mississippi.

tering a place in frontier imagination. The mystery of distance had gilded its glamour. Illinois had been a familiar word long before the name Kentucky had ever been mentioned. The great French travelers of the past, Marquette, Hennepin, Lahontan, Charlevoix, whose accounts had been published in English almost as early as in French, all had devoted ecstatic descriptions to the Illinois. The little French towns that had existed for generations in the Illinois were reputed to occupy the richest land on the continent. Half a century before, credulous Europeans had lost millions in the fantastic Mississippi Bubble promotion promising limitless returns from the fabled gold and silver mines of the area. Fort Chartres, the great stone stronghold on the Mississippi, had been a bastion of French dominion exceeded in importance only by Louisburg and Quebec. The English army had struggled for ten years just to get to it during the French War and Pontiac's War. Traders had envisaged immense profits in the Illinois. Land companies had competed for preferment there. George Washington, Benjamin Franklin, and Patrick Henry had been actively interested in schemes for establishing colonies there. George Croghan, the frontier magnate, George Morgan, the present American Indian agent, and William Murray, the last English commandant at Fort Pitt, had devoted years to efforts to gain commercial advantage there. Every individual frontier land seeker had dreamed of the possibility of establishing himself there.

Clark, himself a confirmed land seeker, shared this general interest in Illinois opportunities, but his more immediate concern was with the strategic bearing of the Illinois on the defense of Kentucky. The French towns of Kaskaskia, Cahokia, and Prairie du Rocher were centers of influence over a large Indian population. Were the Illinois Indians to be persuaded by the English to join the Ohio Indians in their attacks on the American frontier, then Kentucky was surely doomed. On the other hand, a counterstroke in time might forestall this development and even turn the tables of military advantage. This was the essence of his plan.

His spies returned on June 22nd, having aroused no suspicion by their visit. Footloose American frontiersmen ranged so widely that they excited little surprise wherever they chanced to appear. Neither

Moore nor Linn nor any of Clark's fellow Kentuckians had any idea as yet of what was in his mind. Had they guessed they would have thought him mad. That summer there seemed too few defenders to hold Kentucky. Any thought of invading the faraway Illinois could only have been considered preposterous. The spies' report made continued secrecy the more imperative. The one chance of success for the project lay in no hint of warning being allowed to reach Hamilton in Detroit, for the young hunters had discovered the Illinois to be for the moment undefended by the English. Fort Chartres had been abandoned by the English army in 1772 as part of the general English policy of disentanglement from the wilderness that had led that same year to the abandonment of Fort Pitt. It could not now very well be reoccupied for a change in the course of the Mississippi was undermining the walls. Fort Gage, on the bluff opposite Kaskaskia, had burned in 1766. Captain Hugh Lord with the last vestige of English occupation troops had the year before been removed to Detroit from the makeshift fort in the center of the town. The Illinois now depended for defense upon local French militia under the command of Phillipe de Rocheblave, a former French officer now in the English service. With receipt of his spies' report Clark's notion became at once a firm intention. If he moved with sufficient stealth and speed, he foresaw the possibility of seizing the whole territory with an expedition numbering as few as 500 sufficiently resolute men. As was soon to become evident, he was determined to make the attempt with no matter how few.

Clark's responsibility for the defense of Kentucky held him there through the summer and into the fall. Then, as the second necessary step in the advancement of his great design, on October 1st he started for Virginia. His fellow Kentuckians regarded his departure with sadness and regret. They did not expect him to return, feeling it only natural that an unattached and ambitious young man might prefer the wider opportunities of service with the main Continental Army. With him on this second journey east over the mountains were 76 men and a number of women and children. Most of his companions were Holston militiamen returning home after their tour of Kentucky duty, but a few were settlers who had come to the

CLARK'S ADVANCE UPON VINCENNES

Clark left Harrodsburg October 1, 1777, set out from Williamsburg December 4, sailed from Redstone May 12, 1778, passed the Falls June 26, captured Kaskaskia July 4, marched from Kaskaskia February 5, 1779 and captured Vincennes February 25, having traveled more than 2500 miles over a period of 17 months to reach his objective.

Hamilton sailed from Detroit October 7, 1778, and occupied Vincennes December 17.

The other five English-Indian invasion attempts were launched in the early spring of 1779 but all were abandoned at the points indicated upon learning of Hamilton's disaster.

conclusion that Kentucky was not the most suitable of all places in which to attempt to raise a family.

Governor Patrick Henry had been given an outline of Clark's proposal in a preliminary letter. He had been nonplussed by the obvious hazards and difficulties involved. But he was converted by Clark's personal presentation of his plan and soon became as enthusiastic as he had formerly been dubious. Henry was naturally attracted by the prospect of striking so shrewd and unexpected a blow against the enemy, and his lifelong interest in western lands had prepared him to recognize the future value of establishing a solid American claim to the territory. There was still the same need to maintain complete secrecy. Only a very narrow circle of Virginia's most influential leaders, such as Thomas Jefferson and George Mason, were informed of what was afoot. All approved. Clark was commissioned lieutenant colonel, authorized to raise seven 50-man companies of militia by calling for volunteers in any county, and granted £1200 to meet the expedition's incidental expenses. His public orders directed him to devote this special force to the defense of Kentucky. His secret orders directed him to proceed with it against Kaskaskia.

Clark now had that freedom of action of which he so often was to prove abundantly able to take advantage. According to his carefully considered plan, he was to raise a portion of his force on the upper Ohio frontier and then, after descending the Ohio, to be joined at the mouth of the Kentucky by other contingents coming overland from the Holston and Kentucky. But when he arrived at Redstone on February 1, 1778, he was at once confronted by unforeseen recruiting difficulties. The depredations of 1777, the violence of the Shawnee hostility aroused by Cornstalk's murder, and the Squaw Campaign fiasco had combined to leave the frontier in no mood for distant ventures. The Pennsylvania-Virginia dispute made Pennsylvanians disinclined to support any Virginia enterprise and Virginians reluctant to offer the advantage of their absence to their Pennsylvania rivals. Widespread apprehension of Tory plots, highlighted in March by the flight of Alexander McKee, Matthew Elliott, and Simon Girty to the Indian country, persuaded many others of the need to stand guard at home. Had Clark been in a position to reveal his real intentions, he might have met with a more ready response. But not many were so eager to share the bleak and unrewarding trials of Kentucky's defense. People on the upper Ohio who had discovered the difficulty of holding a border as populous as their own were inclined to feel settlements as weak, exposed, and isolated as Kentucky's were better abandoned, thus sparing a drain on the resources needed to defend the main frontier.

Nevertheless, by persistent persuasion and unflagging spirit, with valuable recruiting help from William Harrod and boats and supplies furnished by Hand, Clark rounded up 150 volunteers and was able to sail from Redstone on May 12th. With him went 20 families of settlers who may only be regarded as truly indomitable. In spite of all they had heard of Kentucky's straits, they still wanted to get there and had been deterred only by the near certainty of being overwhelmed by Indian attack along the river en route. They were delighted by the opportunity of proceeding in the relative safety of so strong an escort. In his capacity as commander Clark considered their company a great nuisance, but as a Kentuckian he was forced to admit they would be regarded as a welcome addition to Kentucky's tiny population. He let them come. It was a fortunate decision. William Linn who had brought the 1777 powder shipment from New Orleans was head of one of the families. His younger brother, Benjamin, had been one of Clark's Kaskaskia spies, and William was presently to perform an even more important service to the enterprise.

The flotilla reached Fort Randolph at the mouth of the Kanawha the day after the Shawnee had raised their week-long siege of the place. There had been no assault but the attack had cost the garrison one killed, several wounded, and all of their cattle and horses. Having angrily rejected the Grenadier Squaw's delivery of the Preston-Fleming letter of conciliation but, at the same time, having been persuaded by her that the fort was invulnerable, the Shawnee had moved off up the Kanawha to ravage Virginia's Greenbrier frontier. Captain William McKee, acting commander, urged Clark to pursue and attack the Indians, believed to number 250 to 300, as a means of averting so serious a threat to the borders of his native state.* The appeal presented Clark with a difficult dilemma. He decided that his primary mission was too important to permit even so tempting a divergence. He argued that the couriers then being disguised by the Grenadier Squaw had a better than even chance to get through and that, if the Greenbrier inhabitants received the warning in time, they would prove amply able to defend themselves. His judgment was vindicated. The messengers did get through, and the outlying Greenbrier people gathered in time in Colonel Andrew Donnally's neighborhood blockhouse where they stood off the attackers in one of the hardest fought border engagements of the war.

At Fort Randolph, Clark's fleet of barges was joined by others commanded by Captain James O'Hara, also on his way down river. For Clark's, though by far the most important, was only one of three American expeditions proceeding westward that year. On January 10th, Captain James Willing, with 27 men in a small armed galley, had left Pittsburgh, dispatched by authority of Congress to raid the English posts and presumably Tory settlements on the lower Mississippi. O'Hara was on his way to support Willing who had meanwhile been enjoying successes in the Natchez area which the English bitterly described as more piratical than military. In June, the third expedition set out under the command of Colonel David Rogers who had been instructed by Virginia to establish commercial and other relations between Virginia and the Spanish authorities in New Orleans and then to return with a shipment of munitions.

Clark changed his rendezvous with the overland forces from the mouth of the Kentucky to the Falls of the Ohio, the latter being on a more natural route between the Kentucky settlements and the Illinois. There he pitched his camp on Corn Island, a seven-acre islet just above the rapids, selecting the midriver site as one from which desertions must prove more difficult as well as one more

---

* Most historians have questioned McKee's request. Clark later stated that it was made. McKee in his report to Hand made no mention of it. Considering the timeliness of Clark's arrival and the circumstance that a combination of Clark's, O'Hara's and McKee's forces would have more than matched the Indian strength, it would appear strange indeed had the local commander, responsible for the defense of the Virginia frontier, not made such a request.

defensible by the 20 settlers' families who were to be left here. The settlers promptly began to plant their corn and to build a blockhouse.

Having by now traveled more than 1800 miles since he had set out from Harrodsburg, over wild mountains and down wild rivers with much of the distance in country where Indian attack had been an hourly risk, he was met here by new difficulties which for a time appeared to have made the entire tremendous effort vain. Necessarily uninformed of the expedition's purpose, the initial Holston interest in the call for volunteers had soon dwindled. Less than half a company of the four expected from that usually aggressive frontier showed up at the Falls. Kentucky's contribution was even smaller. New Indian threats had kept most Kentuckians more inclined to look to the security of their own stockades. Most discouraging of all, when Clark could no longer delay telling his men what was really to be expected of them, a good many decided, with that complete freedom of individual option traditionally asserted by frontier militia, that in their personal judgment the odds against success were clearly too great. Some 50 deserted by wading the river through shallows Clark and his officers had not detected. They were vigorously pursued but only eight were overtaken. The rest scattered into the forest. Some starved or were taken by Indians, but most of them lived to regret through the rest of their lives the unhappy choice they had taken that day.

The many disappointments at the Falls were made the harder to bear by an excessive heat wave which aggravated the tempers of all concerned. Clark's situation had become one to dismay any commander. Judged by every military standard he was confronted by a totally unacceptable risk. He had based his original plan on the assumption that a force of 500 men was a minimum necessity. In Virginia the state's limited resources had required a reduction to 350. After recruiting failures and desertions he now had but 178. His so-called army of invasion would be outnumbered 5 to 1 by the resident militia of the region it was presuming to invade, and 25 to 1 by the surrounding Indians it was presumed to impress. Nevertheless, he determined to keep on. He later described his reasoning as: "The more I reflected on my weakness the more I was pleased with the Enterprise." He could, in any event, feel that his recruiting and desertion difficulties had by a process of eliminating the less fit and the less ready reduced his force to a hard core of followers upon whom he could rely, and he could know that he could rely on his four company commanders, William Harrod, Joseph Bowman, Leonard Helm, and John Montgomery.

On June 26th Clark embarked upon the last lap of his memorable venture. The final issue of his year-long struggle was now immediately before him. As the boats bounced through the rough water of the rapids, the day was darkened by a total eclipse of the sun. The timing of the phenomenon excited varied reactions among men who were accustomed to believe in signs and wonders and, above all, in luck. Some were much disturbed. Clark, always on the alert to take advantage of any opportunity to raise the spirits of all around him, proclaimed it a certain portent of the imminence of great events. His confidence in the omen soon appeared justified. Rowing night and day, the 425 miles to the mouth of the Tennessee were made in four days without mishap.

More luck ensued. A boatload of American buffalo hunters was captured. They were wanderers who had been in Kaskaskia eight days before. Their information was of inestimable value, for Clark had had no word of conditions in the Illinois since the return of his spies twelve months before. They said the region's sole defense still consisted of local French militiamen who remained unaware that an American invasion was in immediate prospect. They also said, however, that there was no chance that they would readily accept or even tolerate an American invasion but that, on the contrary, they were determined to resist with all their strength, inasmuch as they were convinced that all Americans, and particularly the Virginians, were barbarians. With his usual immediate impulse to see in each discovery of new difficulty a revelation of new advantage, Clark decided that "no part of their information pleased me more than that the Inhabitants viewed us as more savage than their Neighbors the Indians." The hunters supported the reliability of their report by readily volunteering to accompany the expedition.

Even better luck immediately followed. The flotilla was overtaken by a lone man in a canoe. He was William Linn who had remained at Corn Island with his family to help his fellow settlers hold the new post there. With him he had a letter for Clark from Colonel John Campbell in Pittsburgh, informing him that France had come to the aid of the American Revolution. The letter had arrived the day after Clark had left the Falls and, realizing its supreme importance, Linn had undertaken the extraordinary risk of coming on with the message. Clark could now hope that, when the Illinois French learned that their mother country had declared war on England, they might the more easily be persuaded to foresake their half-hearted attachment to their present English rulers.

He left his boats near the ruins of Fort Massac, the French post abandoned by them in 1758 and never occupied by the English. He proposed to march the last 125 miles overland through the wilderness. To have continued along the normal water route by way of the Mississippi would have denied him the complete surprise upon which all still depended. The onetime trail between Massac and Kaskaskia had been obliterated by the passage of time and in the intervening labyrinth of woods, marshes, and prairies his guide, John Saunders, one of the buffalo hunters, became confused while the army, proceeding in single file, was crossing a wide expanse of grassland. Suspecting treachery and realizing the hopelessness of his situation if the approach of his small force were discovered by the French and Indians, Clark flew into a rage. He ordered the man shot unless he proved promptly able to lead them on by the most direct route. The trembling woodsman desperately assembled his wits, peered toward the various wooded edges of the plain, appeared to have identified familiar landmarks, and the muttering men resumed their march. They had been unable to bring enough food to last. The final two days they marched hungry. At dusk on July 4th, 1778, the starving and exhausted Americans stood in the edge of the Kaskaskia clearings.

The surprise was total. After so long and agonizing an effort, the triumph when it came was complete and gained without the firing of a shot. In the night the invaders swooped silently upon the town in two divisions. The sleeping inhabitants were restrained within their houses. The gates of the fort were open and unguarded. The first Rocheblave knew of the attack was upon being awakened in his bed by Simon Kenton tapping him on the shoulder. It took a little time to get the commandant dressed and out on the parade ground to deliver in person his formal surrender for his summoners were routed from the bed chamber by Madame Rocheblave's shrewish cries of outraged modesty.

At daybreak the inhabitants peered fearfully from their doors and windows at the ragged, bearded, uncouth intruders patrolling their streets. Clark had established guard lines around the town to prevent the dispatch of messengers to summon assistance or spread the alarm and had instituted a search for and a confiscation of weapons. The strain and the suspense continued. Finally the priest, Father Pierre Gibault, approached Clark to beg for clemency. Having subjected the townspeople to hours of terror, Clark was suddenly overflowing with friendliness. He was astonished by the good father's alarm. The inhabitants' persons, property, and religion would of course be protected. The Americans had come not as enemies but as friends, saviors, and allies. He broke the sensational news that France had joined the United States in the war with England. The sudden relief from their fears swept the impressionable and volatile population to the other extreme of rejoicing. They rushed to the church to give thanks, danced in the streets, and took the barbarous invaders to their bosoms. Most of them readily subscribed to the oath of allegiance demanded by Clark. Cahokia fell as painlessly. The better part of the Illinois had been delivered into his hands literally for the asking.

So much had been achieved, but if possession were to be held, Vincennes, 180 miles away on the lower Wabash, a principal control post on the great portage route connecting the Mississippi with Detroit, the Lakes, and the St. Lawrence, must be secured. Simon Kenton with two companions was dispatched to spy out the situation there. He sent back word that Vincennes likewise had no English garrison. The English high command had entertained no thought that there could be the faintest possibility that the harassed American frontier could be capable of any sort of a counterstroke.

Father Gibault, by now an energetic American partisan, rushed to Vincennes to persuade the French militia and population there also to change sides. With a readiness as cheerful as that shown by Kaskaskia and Cahokia, a celerity which was becoming suspicious, they agreed. Leonard Helm with a single platoon was dispatched to take possession of Vincennes.

Kenton went on to Kentucky to report to Colonel John Bowman who, in turn, sent on to Patrick Henry the news of the extraordinary success of the Illinois invaders. Hearing that his friend Boone had escaped from his Shawnee captivity, the irrepressible Kenton promptly joined Boone in a scouting expedition devoted to the location of a strong Indian war party believed to be moving toward Boonesborough. Even such nearly superhuman experts were capable of occasional lapses. Kenton was taken as easily as could have been the rawest recruit by Indians who were overjoyed when they realized the identity of their victim. He was subjected to one of the most painful captivities, involving a succession of torments in one Indian town after another, any man was ever known to suffer and still be able to survive.

Clark, meanwhile, was riding out a crisis far more demanding than his initial invasion. The central purpose of his venture had been to seek an opportunity to impress the Indians of the region with a demonstration of American power. There was every danger that they might instead be brought to realize the extent of his actual weakness. No sooner had his first success been achieved than most of his Kentuckians became impatient to return to assist in the defense of their homes. By continued and urgent appeals Clark persuaded a hundred of his original army to re-enlist for eight months' service in his occupation force. The rest returned to Kentucky under the command of William Linn. Upon arrival at the Falls, Linn constructed a stockade on the south shore opposite Corn Island, about which the town of Louisville began to form.

Clark's was a meager force indeed with which to hope to maintain control over an area 600 miles from the slight help he could expect from Kentucky, 1000 miles from his nearest significant source of military support in Virginia, and 1300 miles from his only available source of supplies in New Orleans. Yet it was with the backing of only these 100 men scattered among the garrisons of four towns that he was undertaking to influence the inclination toward war or peace of surrounding Indian nations capable of placing 5750 warriors in the field, according to Croghan's authoritative Indian census of 1765.

He put up a bold front. He assured his already uneasy new French friends that they need feel no concern for the apparent weakness of his forces. His major army, he said, was at the Falls of the Ohio where it could be called upon whenever necessary. And he summoned the Indians to a general peace conference with all the insolence of a conqueror absolutely certain of his superiority. He advised them in his summons to "lay down their Tomahawk, and if they did not chuse it to behave like Men and fight for the English as they had done; but they would see their great father as they called him [Hamilton] given to the dogs to eat." In an aside to his confidants he explained that he "gave Harsh language to supply the want of Men; well knowing that it was a mistaken notion in many that soft speeches was best for Indians."

The Indians of the region had been astounded by the sudden appearance of armed Americans in the Illinois. This was country into which the English army at the peak of its power, after having so overwhelmingly manifested its might during the French War, had nevertheless been unable to penetrate during Pontiac's War. Only three years before there had been no Virginians within a thousand miles. Now they were here in the very heart of the Indian country. Indians swarmed to the proposed conference, indignant, suspicious, antagonistic, but burning with curiosity to see for themselves what manner of men these interloping strangers really were.

The Indians of the immediate Illinois area did not represent a serious threat. They had been weakened by the disease, indolence, and dissipation connected with their long association with their French neighbors, their tribal disciplines had been impaired by intermarriage with the French and with the Santa Domingo Negroes introduced in Mississippi Bubble days, and their military power had never recovered from the stresses of the Iroquois invasions of 1680 and 1684. But among the nations occupying the region's perimeter, the Miami, Ottawa, Potawatomi, Chippewa, Ojibwa, Kickapoo, Winnebago, Sauk, Fox, were included some of the most belligerent and dangerous on the continent. The number of their delegates to the conference at Cahokia far exceeded the number of Clark's soldiers.

An early incident of their assembling was an attempt by one Winnebago group to kidnap Clark for the sake of the English reward in prospect. Clark frustrated this maneuver and boldly placed the culprits in irons. How he then dealt with his central Indian problem is far better described in his own words in a letter to his old friend and advisor, George Mason:

"It was with astonishment that I viewed the Amazeing number of Savages that flocked into the Town. . . I must confess that I was under some apprehention among such a number of Devils . . . but I told the whole that I believed they were a set of Villians, that they had joined the Inglish and they were welcome to continue in the Cause they had espoused; that I was a Man and a Warrier: that I did not care who was my Friends or Foes; and had no more to say to them. Such conduct Alarmed the whole Town: but I was sensible that it would gain us no more Enemies than we had already. . . To shew the Indians that I disregarded them, I remained in my Lodging in the Town about one hundred Yards from the Fort seemingly without guard, but kept about fifty Men conceiled in a Parlour adjoining, and the Garrison under Arms; there was a great Counciling among the Savages dureing the Night; But to make them have a greater idea of my Indifferency about them; I assembled a Number of Gentlemen & Ladies, and danced nearly the whole Night. In the morning I summoned the different Nations to a grand Council . . . I produced a Bloody Belt of wampom and spoke to them in the following manner I told the Chief that was guilty that I was Sencible their Nation was engaged in favour of the English, and if they thought it right, I did not blame them for it, and exhorted them to behave like Men, and support the Cause they had undertaken; that I was Sensible that the English was weak and wanted help; that I scorned to take advantage of them by Persuading their friends to desert them ... that they were at their Liberty to do as they pleas'd ... that I should have them escorted safe out of the Village, and ... if they did not choose to return and fight me, they might find Americans enough by going further. . . Then told them . . . that I should give them Provisions & Rum while they staid ... and I did not care how soon they left me. . . I observed that their Countenances and attitude favoured my real design; the whole looked like a parcel of Criminals. . . I told them that I had instructions from the Great Man of the Big Knives [Virginians] not to ask Peace from any People but to offer Peace and War, and let them take their Choice. . . I presented them with a Peace & War Belt . . . they with a great deal of seeming Joy took the Belt of Peace. . . Our Influence now began to spread among the Nations even to the Border of the Lakes. . . I continued for about five weeks in the Town of Cohos; in which time I had settled a peace with ten or twelve different nations."

Themselves traditional virtuosos of eloquence and oratory, Indians were notoriously impressionable in council and not even Johnson or Croghan had been equipped with a presence and personality capable of more forcibly impressing them. The great achievement of Clark's 1778 campaign was not the uncontested occupation of the Illinois, but his success in neutralizing so considerable a segment of the Indian military power upon which English strategy had depended. The whole English program for the full employment of Indians against the American frontier was for months thrown off balance and off schedule.

As winter came on Clark could well feel a surge of satisfaction. He had apparently succeeded in all he had set out to achieve. Through the patriotic co-operation of the American merchant, Oliver Pollock, his New Orleans supply line was functioning. Though he had not yet heard from Virginia, he could be confident his services were appreciated by his own people. He had been informed of the projected advance of General Lachlan McIntosh from Pittsburgh and, as Christmas approached, he expected to hear any day of the fall of Detroit. There had been for him even the leisure for a romantic interlude. His courtship of Señorita Teresa de Leyba, sister of the

Spanish commandant at St. Louis, is not well documented but appears to have aroused much interest on both sides of the great river.*

Then the Illinois' midwinter merrymaking was disrupted by a thunderbolt. Instead of word of new American victories there burst upon the celebrants the worst of all possible news. Far from having been contained by McIntosh, Hamilton, breathing wrath and vengeance, was making a sudden advance upon the Illinois with an army of 600 regulars, militia, and Indians. He had already recaptured Vincennes, and advance parties of his counterinvasion force were in the woods within three miles of Kaskaskia.

The real battle for the Illinois was only now beginning.

* There is no direct evidence that after this winter Clark ever saw her again. He never married. She later entered a convent.

X

℘

Brant 3

Fᴏʀ ᴛʜᴇ ᴛᴏʀʏ ᴇxɪʟᴇs in Canada, the winter of 1777–78 had been more oppressive even than that of 1775–76 when their Patriot opponents had been actually invading their sanctuary. Hopes raised to heights by the Burgoyne-St.Leger offensive had been cast into corresponding depths by its ignominious failure. Lesser blows, each painful, had deepened their depression. More than 400 of their wives and children had been seized as hostages by Patriot authorities. Colonel Butler's impetuous son, Walter, had been captured while undertaking a reckless recruiting venture on the American side of the frontier. St.Leger's frustrated army which they had joined with so much anticipation had been dispersed, the regulars moved to Montreal and Butler's Rangers to Niagara. To the great dissatisfaction of their Indian allies the English supply base at Oswego had been left undefended. At Niagara sickness had reduced the effective strength of Butler's newly organized Rangers to 75 men able to walk. The Americans, realizing their enemies' demoralization, had renewed with considerable success their efforts to influence the Iroquois. A conference at Johnstown on March 9, 1778, at which the Marquis de Lafayette presided, was attended by 700 Oneida,

Tuscarora, and Onondaga who vowed, in the case of the Oneida with some sincerity, their loyalty to the United States.

In this dismal crisis in Tory affairs efforts to restore their prospects were hampered by personal jealousies and dissensions within the Indian Department. The Johnson-Claus faction continued to devote its more direct contacts with English commanders in America and influential officials in London to persistent attempts to undermine and disparage Butler's every undertaking. Past personal and family associations had inclined Brant to sympathize with the Johnsons but gradually he was beginning to realize that, while the Johnsons remained preoccupied with writing letters and whispering malice, the Butlers were in the field fighting the rebels. He had also begun to recognize that in the new English strategic conception of the war there was no longer concern for the Mohawk Valley. There were to be no more English regular armies of invasion from the north. The inference was clear that future fighting on the New York frontier was to be left to Butler's Rangers and to his Iroquois.

Accepting his share of this responsibility, Brant spent most of the winter in another tour of the Iroquois country, reanimating the Indian war spirit and recruiting warriors for the coming summer's campaigns. The Seneca, enraged by their losses at Oriskany, were ready for the opportunity to get at the American frontier which had been denied them the year before. In early spring Brant was back at Oghwaga. This time he had not come to temporize or to negotiate but to make war. His first task was to forage for supplies and to gather recruits in preparation for the arrival from Niagara of Butler with his main force of Rangers and Seneca. Along the nearer border, so far untouched by war, supplies were abundant and easily to be had by the use of requisitions which amounted to threats to take by force. Any number of recruits were already at hand. Scores of fugitive Tories had taken refuge on the upper Susquehanna, along with packs of runaway Negroes and several gangs of roving bandits as ready to prey upon one side of the frontier as the other. In late May Butler arrived, and the two commanders reached agreement on their co-ordinated campaign, Brant deferring to Butler's more extensive military experience. As a result Brant's function became the delivery of a vigorous covering attack to distract American attention from the major thrust at Wyoming to be commanded by Butler.

The Revolution was entering upon its fourth year. New York had been invaded thrice by English armies. The most important of the war's campaigns had been fought on New York soil. The one decisive American military success so far achieved had been gained at Saratoga. But, through all of these three years of the state's experience with the general war, its frontier had yet directly to suffer from the border war with which every other American frontier had long since been made so fearfully familiar. No single Indian raid had struck one of New York's settlements. No single New York settler had died in defense of his home. This prolonged immunity was about to end. And when now at last the first Indian onslaught came, it struck with a sustained rigor never evidenced elsewhere.

For weeks the Mohawk Valley had been agitated by reports and rumors of Brant's return. On the next to the last day of May he put an end to any remaining doubt. He emerged from the shadows of the wilderness on the crest of the ridge above the Schoharie, the scene of the young William Johnson's first acquaintance with the frontier exactly 40 years before. From his vantage point Brant could see out over the Mohawk ancestral homeland, toward Albany 37 miles to the east, toward Johnson Hall 30 miles to the northeast, and toward his own home, Canajoharie, 15 miles to the north. With him were some 300 Indians. Also with him were a number of Tory partisans, a number which fluctuated in the weeks to come as it was increased by volunteers rushing to join him from districts he invaded and reduced as he fed recruits back to Butler's forces assembling at Unadilla behind him.

Brant's first strike was at the hamlet of Cobleskill. His burning of it was interrupted by a body of Schoharie militia, supported by a company of continentals en route to garrison Fort Alden at Cherry Valley. The American attackers, unaware of his strength, were soon routed among the blazing houses with a loss of 20 killed. Ordinarily, after such a thrust an Indian raiding force retreated rapidly back into the wilderness, prompted by hunger or fear of pursuit. But this was a new kind of raiding which gave the afflicted border no such surcease. Brant was inviting pursuit and the rich farmlands of this border afforded ample food supplies for both his and Butler's growing forces. He withdrew only a few miles to rest his followers and to select his next target. For the next two months he continued to march and countermarch among the wooded hills separating the intricately interlaced watersheds of the Mohawk, the Susquehanna, and the Delaware. Upon every district along the New York frontier was imposed the dread that it might be the next to suffer. His movements were too swift, erratic, and elusive to give counterattacking forces opportunity to gather against him. The defense was forced instead to remain deployed among the garrisons of the many forts and stockades in a vain attempt to guard all points at once. From time to time he detached small parties to raid exposed farms and communities. At other times he struck with his full force at towns. His purposes were simple and direct. He sought by the maximum spread of terror along the frontier to confuse the attempts to organize its defense, to seize cattle and grain to stock his and Butler's commissaries, to destroy food and property that could not be carried off, to gather Tory recruits, to rescue Tory families, and to single out for punishment Patriot inhabitants who had been particularly active in the persecution of their Tory neighbors.

His next major stroke was at Springfield on June 18th. Here he burned houses and barns, even wagons, ploughs, and haycocks. More than 200 head of cattle and horses were driven down the Susquehanna to Butler's army. After Springfield he ravaged the settlements about Otsego Lake. If he was disturbed by memories of his onetime happy associations here, he did not permit the recollection to stay his hand. His devastations here were as rigorous as elsewhere.

The time had now come for Brant to turn over most of his force to Butler for the Wyoming campaign. Nevertheless, with a few selected followers he continued his covering and flanking operation. In early July he was confiscating cattle and grain far down the Delaware among the Minisink settlements within 35 miles of the headquarters Washington had established on the Passaic after the Battle of Monmouth. Two weeks later, on July 18th, he burst again from the wilderness 150 miles to the north to burn Andrustown. A hastily assembled detachment of local militiamen pursued his relatively small force but, failing to come up with him, solaced their disappointment by burning the houses of a number of their Tory neighbors.

His mission was now completed, his immediate objectives all attained. With Butler's advance upon and withdrawal from Wyoming there had at no time been the slightest threat of American interference. All attention had been centered on Brant's depredations. His success in maintaining a raiding force in continuous contact with the frontier over so long a period was without precedent. For two months he had kept 150 miles of border in turmoil, its inhabitants in flight to their forts, its military defenders confused and distracted. In his summary of the total operation he reported that he had killed or taken 294. All of those killed had been armed men met in action. Most prisoners he had released after lecturing them on their wickedness in rebelling against their king. There were no contemporary American complaints accusing him or his Indians of the indiscriminate murder or maltreatment of women and children or other noncombatants during this campaign. The strategic effect of his effort was to reduce materially an important American supply source. Washington's army depended to a considerable degree on beef and wheat from the Mohawk Valley. Brant's destruction of existing stores and interruption of current harvesting seriously impaired this supply pattern. The rigor of his devastations may be ascribed in part to the natural delight his Indians took in any form of destruction but also to his own emotional conviction that he was striving to recover the homes of his people and of his Tory companions in arms. This confidence in the righteousness of his cause was fortified by the fervor of his loyalist sentiments. As he expressed it in a letter written that spring: "I mean now to fight the cruel rebels as well as I can."

Colonel John Butler, organizing the main Indian-Tory army at Unadilla in June, was fifty-seven, fat, short of breath, and in uncertain health but bristling with determination. All dispossessed Tories burned with a perpetual flame of wrath and lived only for the moment they might visit it upon their former neighbors. He had selected a position in the apex of a wilderness salient from which he was enabled to strike at will either north, east, or south at the American frontier. For a number of reasons, in sum commanding, he elected to attack Wyoming, the narrow, fertile valley in northeastern Pennsylvania occupied by Connecticut settlers in defiance of Pennsylvania's objections. It was a prosperous community, promising rich loot, yet totally detached from its parent state, Connecticut. It was isolated, being separated from the nearest other settled portions of Pennsylvania or New Jersey by ranges of wooded hills. After the bitterness of the long land war with Pennsylvania, marked by sieges, pitched battles, and many casualties, the Pennsylvanians could not be expected to rush wholeheartedly to its defense. During its stormy history it had been destroyed by Indian as well as by Pennsylvania attacks for Indians also viewed the settlers as trespassers. At no point along the whole American frontier could they be expected to strike with more relish. As a final inducement, Butler's second in command, William Caldwell, a former Wyoming resident who had been expelled for his Tory activities, knew the ground well.

In late June Butler started down the Susquehanna by boat, canoe, and raft. That week's blistering heat wave was as oppressive there as elsewhere across the whole troubled expanse of country from the Hudson to the Mississippi. The sun's eclipse on June 24th, everywhere visible, caused a diverse multitude of sweltering and struggling people to pause to stare with renewed anxiety into the darkening sky. For the heat and the eclipse marked one of the more active weeks of the Revolution. Virginia settlers were fleeing to their stockades under threats of a new Indian invasion. The people of Boonesborough were bracing themselves for the renewed attacks of which warning had been brought by Boone, just escaped from his Shawnee captivity. Clark was running the rapids on his way to Kaskaskia. On the New York frontier the dusk of the eclipse was further darkened by the smoke of Brant's devastations. Congress was returning to the defiled State House after the English evacuation of Philadelphia. Washington's Continental Army, marching through suffocating clouds of red dust, was pursuing Clinton across New Jersey. All of this was taking place under the same somber sky, while

Butler was on his way to win the one strategically significant victory ever won by English-Indian border forces during the Revolution.

On June 30th he encamped on a hill overlooking Wyoming Valley. Contemporary estimates of his strength varied widely, ranging from the American assumption that it ran to 1100 to the assertion of Richard Cartwright, who was with him, that it was limited to 110 Rangers and 464 Indians. His own reports were unclear. Possibly the recruitment of volunteers and the detachment of raiding parties occasioned frequent variations in his available total. The weight of evidence would seem to indicate that his command consisted of around 200 Rangers and Tory partisans and 500 Indians. At any rate he regarded his strength as ample for his purpose. In appearing on the hilltop he had abandoned any attempt at surprise and elected instead to rely on the realization of his presence spreading fright among the defenders.

The Wyoming settlers, however, were not of a stock easily frightened. During the past 15 years of tumult, dissension, and violence connected first with Indian attacks and then with the land war, the settlements there had nevertheless continued to flourish until now the inhabitants, occupying the 25-mile long valley, numbered nearly 5000. They gathered in their many forts and stockades and prepared to resist. The major portion of their militia was concentrated in Forty Fort * in readiness to sortie when opportunity offered. Colonel Zebulon Butler, a continental officer whose considerable experience in the French War had included service at the siege of Havana, chanced to be in the valley on furlough. By popular acclaim he was elevated to share command with Colonel Nathan Dennison, in whose 24th Connecticut Regiment most of Wyoming's militia was incorporated. A garrison detachment of continentals was also available.

John Butler advanced slowly into the valley. The first two stockades he approached, Wintermoot's, held by a Tory clan, and Jenkin's, with a Patriot garrison, capitulated on demand. The main American force at Forty Fort became less content merely to look

---

* Situated near the junction of River Street and Fort Street in present Kingston, Pa.

on while the invaders proceeded with their depredations. Rage supported their assurance that they were more than a match for any such parcel of skulking Indians and Tory renegades. The impulse to march out and do battle became overwhelming. There was some basis for their assurance. As a result of their experiences in the land war, the Wyoming militia was better drilled and more accustomed to action than most local militia.

There were 450 angrily determined men in the column led out of the fort by the two colonels on July 3rd. John Butler had been delaying his advance in the hope of inviting just such a sortie and had made astute preparations to receive it. He set fire to the two captured forts and the Americans, assuming he must be retreating, rushed forward more confidently than ever. After a first exchange of volleys the Rangers fell back for more than a mile. The exultant Americans charged headlong into the trap. The Rangers turned to face them again behind a low breastwork of logs at the edge of a woods. The Americans recoiled. From their former concealment in a marsh hundreds of Iroquois sprang at that instant upon the American left flank and rear. This was in every particular an exact re-enactment of that other July day, 19 years before, when John Butler had led another hidden force of these same Iroquois under precisely the same circumstances in the rout of Aubry which had determined the fate of Niagara. The consequence now was the same utter disaster. The American formation broke, panic ensued, and the battle degenerated into flight and butchery. The Indians, never more ardent than when in hot pursuit, leaped among the fleeing militia with tomahawks, spears, war clubs, and knives, bringing them down by the hundred. Some estimates of the dead ranged to 400. John Butler reported a count of 227 scalps and 5 prisoners. Dennison reported his losses as 1 lieutenant colonel, 2 majors, 7 captains, 13 lieutenants, 11 ensigns, and 268 men. One Indian and 2 Rangers were killed, and 8 Indians were wounded.

Zebulon Butler escaped from the field and did not pause in his flight until he had escaped also from the valley. Dennison also escaped the battle but, with more regard for his command responsibilities, took his stand in Forty Fort with the remnant of his regiment. The next day, July 4th, the disheartened defenders, including the survivors of the battle, the garrison, and a large aggregation of settlers' families who had taken refuge in the fort, surrendered. The essential feature of the capitulation from the American point of view was that after laying down their arms every inmate of the fort was to be permitted to march away unharmed, and from the Indian and Tory point of view that the soldiers being set free were giving their parole to engage in no further hostilities during the war.

There was no testimony by anyone present that any American man, woman, or child was killed after the surrender. A Tory deserter, identified among the prisoners, was ordered shot by Butler, many of the American prisoners were robbed, some even of their clothing, by the Indians, but no Americans died at Forty Fort after the gates were opened. Dennison himself remarked in his report on the extraordinary exertions of Butler while managing to maintain control over his Indians and to insure respect for the terms of the capitulation.

Meanwhile, thousands of settlers and their women and children were streaming over the hills into the more populous sections of Pennsylvania. Everywhere they carried frantic stories of disaster, murder, rapine, and outrage which became more horrifying with each retelling. The actual battle was largely overlooked. The impression became fixed that Wyoming had been the scene not of a battle and a surrender but of a prolonged and peculiarly hideous welter of Indian atrocities. Instead of providing one of the few instances in which Indians at war had ever been kept under approximate control, it came to be regarded as the supreme example of Indian excess. It was never referred to as the Wyoming campaign, or battle, or attack, or invasion, but always as the Wyoming Massacre. A whole literature grew up around the subject. Instead of gaining credit for a significant victory, John Butler became the target even in his own country of personal aspersions on his honor as a soldier from which his reputation never recovered. Brant, who was 70 miles away, was likewise charged with participation in the monstrous barbarities always associated in American public opinion with Wyoming.

The military significance of the victory was soon apparent, with consequences that rolled explosively a thousand miles westward along the frontier. On June 18th, Congress had directed Brigadier General Lachlan McIntosh, Hand's successor at Pittsburgh, to undertake an advance upon Detroit and had authorized an army of 3000 to implement the design. But Butler's massive Indian-Tory strike to a point within 75 miles of Philadelphia impressed the startled lawmakers with the need to guard first against threats so much nearer. Continental troops which had been assigned to Mc-Intosh were withheld to cope with Butler. On July 25th, Congress directed McIntosh to abandon the Detroit expedition and reduced his authorized strength to 1500. Instead of advancing upon the western center of English-Indian power at Detroit, he was able only to push into the edge of the Delaware country and there establish largely useless Fort Laurens. Relieved of their former apprehension of Mc-Intosh's intentions, the Shawnee were enabled to undertake their sensational second siege of Boonesborough in September while throughout Kentucky Indian attackers swarmed in greater numbers than in 1777. Hamilton who had been frantically strengthening Detroit's defenses was able after the effects of Wyoming became evident to dismiss his fears for Detroit and to embark instead upon his autumn invasion of the Illinois.

Butler fell ill during his withdrawal from Wyoming and left Caldwell in command on the Susquehanna. He kept on to Niagara with a portion of his forces, his slow march burdened by plunder and rescued Tory families. Caldwell joined Brant who, with his command now enlarged to nearly 500 Indians and Tories, aimed another blow at the American frontier. The most productive section of the Mohawk Valley was the fertile riverside plain known as German Flats. It was upon this major Patriot granary that he advanced. His approach was detected by a party of four scouts. Three were caught and killed but the fourth, John Helmer, after a desperate run of many hours outdistanced his Indian pursuers to reach German Flats with a warning. The inhabitants of the district gathered in their two forts, Herkimer and Dayton, from which at dawn on September 17th they watched in helpless rage the burning of their homes and the destruction of their property. The devastation was methodical and merciless. Colonel Peter Bellinger, local militia commander, reported that the raiders burned 63 houses, 57 barns, 3 grist mills, 1 sawmill and carried off or killed 235 horses, 229 cattle, 269 sheep, and an undeclared number of hogs. Due to Helmer's memorable run the loss of life was limited to 2 white men and 1 Negro. More damaging to public morale than the material loss was the realization that the local militia regiment had felt obliged to remain supinely behind the walls of their forts while Brant's Indians and Tories unhurriedly laid waste the whole region.

Four months of uninterrupted disaster along the New York and Pennsylvania frontier had demonstrated again and again the validity of the fundamental tenet of border warfare which proclaimed a passive defense against Indian raids to be impossible. The assailants were always able to select their targets, to strike by surprise and with local superiority, and then to withdraw before a sufficient countering force could be assembled. The one effective defense, according to long-established frontier military doctrine, was to ignore any defense and to devote all available strength to a strike at the sources from which the attacks came. By early fall the slow-moving American authorities at last contrived to mount two such countermeasures. Colonel Thomas Hartley with a regiment of continentals made a cautious advance northward from Wyoming, burned several small Indian villages around Tioga, and withdrew somewhat more hastily after a rearguard action in which he suffered a loss of 15. In New York, Colonel William Butler assembled another expedition of continentals which included a detachment of no less distinction than 4 companies of Morgan's Rifles and, in the first week of October, struck hard at the Indian towns and Tory settlements on the upper Susquehanna. The weight of the blow fell upon empty air for there was no opposition to the attack. Most of the male inhabitants were absent, either following Hartley or engaged at a distance in raids of their own. Unadilla and Oghwaga and all lesser communities along the river were burned, and a quantity of cattle and other loot formerly taken on the American side of the frontier was recovered. The success of the undertaking was clouded by various excesses, including the mass rapes of a number of cap-

tured Indian women. Indians were curiously shocked by sexual outrages. Among all the atrocities of which they were capable this was
the one from which they almost invariably refrained. Tories and
Indians were to cite these offenses during William Butler's raid to
excuse the increased brutalities exhibited in their own later New
York raids.

The first snows of winter were beginning to fall and the 1778
campaign was presumably ended. Everywhere it had been a dis-
maying year for the frontier. New York and Pennsylvania had not
suffered alone. The borders of Georgia, the Carolinas, Virginia, and
Kentucky had been tormented by successive waves of Indian raids,
each less extensive than the more organized ones in the north, but
each also more murderously unrestrained in execution. American
countermeasures had been everywhere ineffectual. The importance
of Clark's uncontested seizure of the Illinois was not yet apparent.
McIntosh's advance to Fort Laurens had proved but little more
effective than the Squaw Campaign. The Hartley and William
Butler expeditions had served more to arouse than to discourage
the Indians against whom they had been directed. Meanwhile, the
New York frontier, strategically the most important to the general
conduct of the war, had been ravaged literally from end to end.
Indian and Tory forces, unaided this year by English regular armies,
had succeeded in implementing the basic English war plan which
contemplated striking at the American frontier so severely that the
general American war effort would be impeded thereby. Stores of
critically needed foodstuffs had been destroyed and thousands of
soldiers, continentals as well as militiamen, who might have strengthened Washington's army had been necessarily devoted instead to
frontier defense where most had remained relatively unused. After
Wyoming, defense forces tended to remain in their forts, as at
German Flats, and thus for all practical purposes out of action. Con-
gressman James Duane, writing Governor Clinton that summer,
complained of "the unmanly dread which our militia entertain of
these savages." Yet, for all the vigor with which the New York frontier had been devastated, there had in that theater still been no
instances of indiscriminate killing of noncombatants which always

before had invariably been associated with Indians at war. Brant and the Tory commanders had so far kept their Indian followers in hand. The attacks had not been made by the small packs characteristic of ordinary Indian raids but by large and organized military commands in which many white men were mingled with warriors who tended to ape the conduct of their white comrades. Among all the hundreds of letters and reports exchanged that summer by American commanders and authorities, there was no single charge of promiscuous murder. However, this commendable record was not to endure. Indians could not indefinitely be held in check. Inseparable from the decision to resort to the use of Indians was the decision likewise to accept the constant risk that they might at any moment return to their normal savagery. It was this constant risk that was about to produce the historic eruption of calamity and horror at Cherry Valley.

Walter Butler was a young man in a very great and bitter hurry. After his escape from American imprisonment on April 21st and the recovery of his health, he had arrived in October on the Susquehanna to take command in the place of his sick father. He had been busy with Hartley during William Butler's Unadilla raid, and the combination of the two American strokes determined him, in spite of the lateness of the season, to strike a retaliatory blow before returning to winter in Niagara. Contemporary commentators maintained that he was chiefly motivated by a wish to be revenged for his sufferings during his imprisonment. If so, he elected to seek it by an attack on the strongest point on the New York border rather than to vent his spite on the inhabitants of some more vulnerable district. Tactically, Fort Alden in Cherry Valley was more important than Fort Stanwix and represented in every respect a legitimate military objective. It had been ordered strengthened and garrisoned by Lafayette the previous spring. He had realized that Fort Stanwix, formerly considered the principal frontier bulwark, was ineffective in barring the inroads of Indians who no longer came by the Oswego-Mohawk portage route but from Niagara by way of the Genesee and the Susquehanna. Colonel Ichabod Alden had been placed in command of the post with a garrison of 300 Massachusetts continentals and 150 local militia.

Brant had been campaigning without rest or relief for seven months. He and his Indians were more than ready for retirement to winter quarters. He was also asserted by American report to have disapproved of Butler's intention to attack Cherry Valley and to have been reluctant to serve under Butler's command. Whether or not this was true, it must have been largely by his influence that so many Indians could be persuaded to accompany the expedition so late in the year. By immemorial custom Indians were always bent on getting home by the first snowfall in order to get on with their winter hunting. Butler later said that the Indians were made more willing to go with him by their rage at the excesses committed by the Americans at Unadilla and Oghwaga.

Whatever the mood in which the command set out, their spirits were sadly dampened by the weather en route. During the 150-mile march from Chemung to the pine-clad slopes above Cherry Valley, there were alternating storms of snow, sleet, and rain. This was young Walter Butler's first independent command, and to have been able to keep his men going on in the face of conditions so unfavorable as those marking every aspect of his undertaking suggests either a personality forceful enough to impress his unruly followers or devoted support from his more experienced lieutenants, Brant and Caldwell. With him were 200 Rangers, 50 regulars of the 8th or King's Regiment with four regular officers, and 400 Indians. Success hinged on taking Cherry Valley by surprise and thereafter getting quickly away, for in adjoining districts there were a thousand additional American troops within a day's march. Hopes of surprise were raised by the taking of an American scouting party, curled up for the night around their campfire. The scouts had taken it for granted that nobody, least of all Indians, would be moving about in such weather.

Butler halted at nightfall, November 10th, six miles from Cherry Valley, planning to march on later in the night in order to make his attack at dawn. But the snow again turned to rain, and the increasingly disgruntled Indian refused to wade through the slush.

He was unable therefore to make his actual assault until nearly noon on the 11th. As a last frustration, complete surprise was lost by Indian heedlessness in shooting down two woodcutters, thus giving the garrison and inhabitants at least some minutes of warning.

But these difficulties which dogged Butler's approach were more than matched by the total ineptitude of the defense. On November 8th, an express from Fort Stanwix had brought a warning gained from friendly Oneida sources that an attack on Cherry Valley was imminent. Alden was not impressed. Hand, who had been transferred from the frying pan of command at Pittsburgh to the fire of command at Albany and who was present in the valley on an inspection tour, took the report more seriously. On his way back to Albany he ordered Colonel Jacob Klock, commanding the 2nd Tryon militia regiment, to reinforce Cherry Valley. Klock had been directed to arrive November 9th, but on the day of the attack was still 20 miles away and took care not to arrive until two days later. Meanwhile, Alden and his principal officers, together with part of a headquarters company, continued to live outside the walls in the more comfortable Wells house, 400 yards from the fort. After the Oneida warning many of the inhabitants had wished to take refuge in the fort, but Alden had refused them permission.

When the attackers burst from the woods to rush down the slopes through the freezing rain, Alden, together with a number of his officers and soldiers, ran from the Wells house toward the fort. Alden was killed and Lieutenant Colonel William Stacey captured in these first moments of action. Butler's primary objective was the fort which he had hoped to take by storm in his first onset or, at the worst, immediately to invest so strongly that a capitulation might ensue, as at Wyoming. But almost at once he lost control over his own command. Most of the Indians, particularly the wilder Seneca, swung away from the fort and scattered to seek easier prey among the private habitations in the valley. Freed of the restraint of their white officers, though accompanied by a number of Tory partisans fully as savage as any Indian, they for the first time inflicted upon New York settlers the unbridled murderousness which elsewhere had always accompanied every Indian attack. In this pillaging of homes and farms and indiscriminate slaughter of noncombatants, the most brazen ringleader was gigantic Hiokatoo,* the veteran Seneca war chief, long famous for his feats in the Catawba and Cherokee wars, at Braddock's Field, and in Pontiac's War and celebrated even among his fierce fellow Seneca for his unparalleled ferocity and cruelty.

The most notorious single outrage of that afternoon of horror was the Indian assault on the Wells family during which they killed Wells, his mother, his wife, his brother, his sister, three sons, his daughter, and three servants. Robert Wells was a prominent pioneer, much respected by both parties, who had been a valued friend of Sir William Johnson, John Butler, and Brant. John Butler wrote from his Niagara sickbed, "I would have gone miles on my hands and knees to have saved that family and why my son did not do so God only knows." Brant said that the Wells family had been as dear to him as his own. Many other unarmed men and women and children were killed during the hours of burning and looting that swept the valley. The total mounted to 31 (some accounts say 32). A few inhabitants escaped through the rain into the surrounding woods, but the Indians rounded up 71 prisoners.

Butler's attack plan was totally disrupted by his having so completely lost control over his Indians. After the majority of the Seneca and Cayuga had rushed off to pursue their own macabre devices, the force remaining to him to conduct his investment of Fort Alden, consisting of the regular detachment, most of his Rangers, and most of Brant's Mohawk, was actually outnumbered by the garrison that he was presuming to besiege. He abandoned the investment, gathered this residue of his army on an adjoining hilltop, and there prepared to resist the sortie in force which he took for granted the garrison

* Second Indian husband of Mary Jemison, subject of one of the more noteworthy published captivities. She was born on shipboard en route to America, taken captive at the age of 13 in a raid in which her father, mother, two brothers, and a sister were killed, was adopted first by Delaware and then by Seneca, bore seven children to two Indian husbands, and continued to reside among Indians to her death at the age of 91 in 1833. In the *Life of Mary Jemison* by James E. Seaver she says of Hiokatoo "during the nearly fifty years that I lived with him he uniformly treated me with tenderness, kindness and attention."

would undertake. But the garrison, though most of them were continentals, made no move. They continued to watch the appalling desolation of the valley from the security of the fort. They had undoubtedly been dismayed by the loss of all their senior officers. During the attempted dash of the headquarters detachment from the Wells house to the fort in which their commander had been killed, three other officers had been captured. In that same tragically ludicrous race for life which marked the opening phase of a battle which failed thereafter to remain a battle, 12 soldiers had been killed and 12 others captured.

Gradually, late in the afternoon, the ravage of the valley was completed and the Indians began to reassemble, yelling their delight in their booty and prisoners and brandishing their still dripping scalps. Butler, supported by Brant, attempted to admonish them for their disorder which had defeated the major purpose of the campaign and then to persuade them to realease their captives who could not be expected to survive the 300-mile march through the snow to Niagara. The Indians were bitterly and resentfully impenitent. They argued that it had been a great mistake to have freed the prisoners at Wyoming, for most had promptly violated their paroles, including even Colonel Dennison who had accompanied Hartley. They pointed out that after Wyoming where they had shown restraint they had nevertheless been accused of every enormity. They cited the American excesses at Unadilla and Oghwaga. Butler and Brant, however, eventually prevailed. Most of the captives were released during the next 48 hours. By Butler's direct order, however, Colonel Samuel Campbell's wife and four children and James Moore's wife and three daughters were retained. He sent word to Governor Clinton that he was holding them as hostages for the exchange of members of his family and of the families of other ranking Tories held in American confinement.

Butler remained in the valley most of the next day but, realizing the low morale of his forces, made no further serious effort against the fort. It was snowing again, and by the time he got under way two feet of snow added to the hardships of his followers and his

captives on the long march back.* Colonel Jacob Klock arrived in
the valley the next day and after a few hours marched home again
without even attempting to relieve the sufferings of the remaining
inhabitants. Other American forces arrived the following day but
because of the depth of the snow likewise undertook no pursuit.

Accounts of the Cherry Valley massacre gripped and shocked
public attention. Occurring at the very end of the campaign season,
without a succession of other striking events to overlay the impression, people had time to dwell on it. The prominence in New York
of the Butler and Wells families and the participation of so notable a
figure as Brant contributed dramatic undertones and overtones. Elsewhere on the frontier hundreds of families had died obscurely in
the flames of their isolated cabins without attracting marked notice.
Cherry Valley was nearer, more comprehensible, and reported in
infinite detail by hundreds of eyewitnesses. Public revulsion against
resort to a form of warfare so manifestly barbarous spread to
England as well. Burke and Fox were supplied with fresh ammunition for their attacks in parliament upon the government's conduct
of the war.

Walter Butler defended his behavior strenuously, citing his efforts
to restrain the Indians and his success in persuading them to release
most of their captives. But there could be no adequate defense to
mitigate his basic guilt, any more than the guilt of every other English authority in the chain of command reaching up to the prime
minister. Having accepted responsibility for the command of Indians
being led in an assault upon a civilized community, there could be
no later escape from responsibility for the nearly certain consequences.

Moral concerns, however, could not disguise the brutal military
facts. In 1777 and 1778 that important phase of English strategy
involved in the employment of Indians had met with a very
considerable degree of success. The total American war effort was
being critically distracted and impeded by the incessant attacks
on the American border. Thousands of men who might otherwise

* All the captives survived. In Niagara that winter one of the Moore girls married a Ranger officer with whom she had become acquainted during the march.

have strengthened Washington's Continental Army had been absorbed instead by border defense needs. Meanwhile, thousands of American families along the whole frontier from New York to Georgia were subjected to what increasingly seemed unendurable agonies.

XI

ဢ

Frontier Tories

WITH THE OUTBREAK of the Revolution thousands of Americans who opposed the majority's decision to rebel were obliged to abandon their homes, their property, and their entire way of life. Many collected in seaport cities held by English troops or took refuge in the Bahamas, Florida, or Nova Scotia. Others escaped to Canada where the more pugnacious enlisted in Butler's Rangers or Johnson's Greens or to Pensacola where two regiments of Tory partisans were organized. But many more, after dispossession by local Patriot pressures, fled westward to the frontier where the suspicions they aroused, the conspiracies in which they engaged, the relations they established with invaders, the organizations for mutual protection they attempted to set up, and even their mere presence enormously confused the already so nearly insurmountable problem of frontier defense.

In 1775 and 1776 local Patriots had everywhere gained the upper hand and had taken stern advantage of their supremacy. In New York the numerous and powerful frontier Tories had been disarmed, dislodged, dispossessed, and driven into exile. In Pennsylvania the Connolly conspiracy had been frustrated and Connolly himself imprisoned. In Virginia frontier leaders of the stature of William Preston, James Robertson, and John Selby had taken a firm hand in enforcing the assembly's statute providing a fine of £20,000 and five years' imprisonment for anyone openly maintaining and defending the authority of the king or parliament. In the Carolinas the same burst of energy which was soon to crush the Cherokee had been equally successful in crushing the Tories. When Josiah Martin, royal governor of North Carolina, anticipating the first English attempt on Charleston, had prematurely assembled a Tory army, it had been routed February 27, 1776, at the Battle of Moore's Creek with a loss of over 900 killed and captured.

Continued adversities in the older centers of population, nevertheless, continued to accelerate the flow of Tory refugees to the frontier. Many hoped to find there a degree of anonymity. Pending the moment they could gain support from fellow fugitives or resident sympathizers, they were often able, if they chose, temporarily to conceal their political sentiments. Most border communities were so new that inhabitants were unfamiliar with one another's backgrounds. The newly arrived Tories had the added hope that they had less to fear from Indian inroads than might their Patriot neighbors. Both hopes, however, were disappointed. The Indian menace had sharpened Patriot vigilance. Newcomers were fiercely scrutinized and older residents whose attitude appeared questionable as fiercely catechized. The Patriot settler was infuriated by the thought that on account of his principles he and his family might stand in greater danger of Indian attack. In practice Indians usually fell upon their victims without concern for their politics, while any settler whose place chanced to be spared was as a result so strongly suspected that his enraged neighbors themselves often burned it.

The effect of this Tory influx and the consequent intensification of community suspicion and dissension first became critical on the upper Ohio. John Connolly had planned a combined operation involving the Ohio Indians, English forces from Detroit, and frontier Tories. This was confounded by the St. Lawrence blockade, but in 1777 Hamilton revived the undertaking. Every Indian raiding party dispatched that summer scattered in its wake copies of his proclamation, reading in part:

"By virtue of the power and authority to me given by his Excellency Sir Guy Carlton, Knight of the Bath, Governor of the Province of Canada, Quebec, General and Commander in Chief . . . I assure all such as are inclined to withdraw themselves from the Tyranny and oppression of the rebel committees and take refuge in this Settlement or any of the posts commanded by his Majesty's Officers shall be humanely treated, shall be lodged and victualled, and such as are off in arms and shall use them in defense of his majesty against rebels and Traitors till the Extinction of this rebellion, shall receive pay adequate to their former stations in the rebel service, and all common men who shall serve during that period shall receive his majesty's bounty of two hundred Acres of Land."

The proclamation produced no immediate or general uprising of Tories, but Patriot settlers were outraged by these handbills broadcast by packs of marauding Indians and every man's suspicions of his neighbors were redoubled. Hamilton's agents circulated through the area, impressing upon the inhabitants the appeals and promises cited in the proclamation. Many confused settlers, fearing Indian attack, English invasion, or seizure of power by Tories and, meanwhile, increasingly uncertain of protection from Virginia, Pennsylvania, or Congress, desperately took oaths of renewed allegiance to the king. Public excitement became intense and bordered on panic. Statements in letters that summer from militia commanders to Hand indicated how real the danger was considered. Colonel Thomas Gaddis: "The tories have joined themselves together for to cut off the inhabitants and we know not what hour they will rise." Colonel Thomas Brown: "From different accounts it appears the Tories are determined to stand battle." Colonel Zackwell Morgan: "We have taken numbers who confess that they have sworn allegiance to the King of Great Britain & that some of the leading men at Fort Pitt are to be their rulers and heads."

Under circumstances so tense suspicion became universal. George Morgan, still striving to maintain peace with the Shawnee and Delaware, was accused of pro-English sympathies and placed under arrest before being finally cleared. Hand himself was not spared. His inability to mount an offensive against the Indians and his reluctance to accept unproven charges against suspected Tories led to his own loyalty being questioned. Governor Patrick Henry revealed his alarm over the presumed extent of the Tory conspiracy by arguing that a blow to the Patriot cause so damaging as the murder of Cornstalk could only have been the work of Tories. The Virginia assembly appointed a commission to investigate the Ohio frontier conspiracy. Congress, also, on November 20, 1777, dispatched a commission to investigate and to report what action seemed necessary.

Similar fears of Tory disaffection were entertained everywhere along the frontier. On December 2, 1777, William Preston was writing, "Captain Burke & his whole Company except for four or five & forty of my Neighbors have Positively refused the Oath of Allegiance to the States." Neighbor's suspicion of neighbor everywhere distracted efforts to organize defense against Indian attacks. Some of the frontier's most firmly established reputations were not immune to this tidal wave of doubt. Upon his escape from captivity, Daniel Boone was tried by court-martial by his fellow militia officers on charges preferred by his son-in-law, Colonel Richard Callaway. Boone was charged with having betrayed the salt-makers' camp to the Shawnee, with having while at Detroit given Hamilton information on the state of Kentucky defenses, and with having attempted to surrender Boonesborough. He was acquitted but a number of his accusers who had been his oldest friends and closest associates remained unconvinced of his innocence. Another outstanding frontiersman indicted by his neighbors was William Ingles, who had been a leader in frontier defense longer than any other man and whose family had suffered from Indians more than had any other. On the court which tried him sat four of his lifelong friends, each likewise a renowned frontier colonel, William Preston, William Christian, James Robertson, and William Campbell. The evidence against him was ruled inconclusive, but he was held under bond and never cleared of the inference that he had indulged in Tory activities.

The efforts of Patriot settlers to detect, suppress, and punish their Tory neighbors continued throughout the war and progressively became more rigorous. On the Holston, Colonel Thomas Lynch's energetic application to the task of identifying Tories and his impatience of legal formalities in dealing with those suspected resulted in adding the word "lynch" to the language. When Jefferson became governor of Virginia, Tory conspiracies on the Holston were still a threatening problem. He was writing William Preston: "I am sorry to hear that there are persons in your quarter so far discontented with the present government as to combine with its enemies to destroy it . . . It will probably be better to seek the insurgents & suppress them in their own settlements than to await their coming, as time and space to move in will perhaps increase their numbers."

The deadly seriousness of the frontier's Tory problem was appallingly demonstrated in the spring of 1778 by Alexander McKee's cruelly delayed public espousal of the royal cause. No other instance of Tory disaffection during the Revolution produced consequences so catastrophic. He exerted an influence over Indians more enduring and effective than any ever wielded by another white man, including Johnson and Butler, and all of it he devoted with tireless determination to the overthrow of the frontier. No Indian could have been more fanatically bent upon driving the last settler from the borders of the Indian country.

Alexander McKee was in every respect a true and completely developed representative of the wilderness. A product of that strange, shadowed, perilous borderland between the white and Indian worlds, he was as much at home in a wigwam, at a council fire, or on the warpath as he was at a trading post, in a block house, or on a parade ground. For the terrible role he was to play in the history of the Pennsylvania-Virginia-Kentucky frontier he had been fully prepared by birth, background, and forty years of wilderness experience which had included official service of the most critical importance during the French War and Pontiac's War.

His father was Thomas McKee, one of the first and most important of Pennsylvania traders, who had spent his life in isolated trading posts or in excursions in the Indian country. His mother was reported by most contemporary observers to have been a Shawnee though others asserted that she had been a white captive taken in childhood by Shawnee in Carolina. In either case his father had married her after she had assisted him in an escape from an Indian town in which he was about to be killed. The question of his mother's race was perhaps made the more debatable by the circumstance that visitors to Thomas McKee's trading-post home during later years noted that her manner remained Indian and that she spoke little or no English. Alexander McKee was described by Simon Kenton, a notably keen observer, as looking "as if of Indian descent." In following his father's occupation as trader McKee's dealings were primarily with the Shawnee, the nation of which his mother, whether by birth or adoption, had been a member. When his own time came to marry he chose a Shawnee bride. Several of his sons became Shawnee chiefs or officers in the English service.

He had scarcely turned twenty when Croghan made him his assistant at Pittsburgh. In recommending him to Johnson, Croghan referred to him as a "modest young man," but no one was better fitted than Croghan to estimate the value to the Indian Department of McKee's intimate acquaintance with Indians. During Croghan's many long absences on his tremendous journeys McKee was in full charge of Indian affairs at Pittsburgh and, after Croghan's resignation in 1772, he was appointed Deputy Agent in his place.

At the outbreak of the Revolution McKee was therefore the only important English official on the Ohio frontier. Everything in his background, his Indian connections, his long and responsible employment in the royal service, and his private interests as a trader, could only have been regarded as certain to incline him strongly to the loyalist side. Yet his conduct remained so circumspect, he appeared so earnestly to devote his great influence with the Shawnee to holding them neutral, and he was held in such general respect, that public opinion tended to reserve judgment. The Indian attacks of 1777 and the circulation of Hamilton's proclamation, however, sharpened everybody's suspicions of everybody. But Hand was not even convinced by the Grenadier Squaw's circumstantial accusation that McKee had been regularly exchanging messages with Detroit.

Yielding at length to popular pressure Hand ordered him under house arrest. When Congress directed that McKee be sent east of the mountains for safer keeping, Hand delayed compliance, acquiescing weakly in McKee's plea of ill health.

Then, in the spring of 1778, came the bombshell. Hand was compelled to begin his report to Major General Horatio Gates, President of the Board of War, with the remorseful words, "I have the mortification to report that last Saturday night Alexr. McKee made his escape from this place." On the night of March 28th, McKee had slipped from his unguarded house and in violation of his parole crossed the frontier to place his extraordinary Indian influence at the disposal of the English command at Detroit. He was received there with welcoming acclaim, commissioned captain and then colonel, reappointed Deputy Indian Agent, and assigned chief responsibility for organizing the Indian effort against the American frontier, a task to which he applied himself with relentless energy. His flight had been a carefully deliberated move. With him had gone Matthew Elliott, Simon Girty, McKee's cousin, Robert Surphlitt, his white servant, John Higgins, and two Negroes. His brother, James, remained behind, holding to his American allegiance.

At the time, Simon Girty's defection was a greater sensation than McKee's. McKee had been a royal official whose resort to the royal standard was regarded as no more than natural. But Simon Girty had been a border hero. Among many distinctions which had elevated him in frontier estimation were the circumstances that his father had been a settler so early that his cabin had been burned by Pennsylvania authorities eager to placate Indians and had eventually been killed by an Indian in a drunken brawl, that his stepfather had been burned at the stake, that in his boyhood he himself, together with his mother and brothers, had spent three years in captivity, that he was fluent in at least three Indian languages, that he had been the original translator of Logan's famous speech, that he had been guide and interpreter upon historic occasions for Lord Dunmore, James Wood, and Hand, but most of all that as woodsman and bushranger he was the equal of his best friend, Simon Kenton. His sacrifice of the trust and respect in which he formerly had been held led to a complete revulsion of feeling. His presumed malignity became a border legend. To him was thereafter ascribed a principal part in every horror that was perpetrated. He was even charged with having led the Indians at Point Pleasant and at the first siege of Wheeling, events occurring long before his defection. His sole American defender was Kenton. The latter had some reason. Among Girty's first actions after his flight to the Indian country was the saving of Kenton from the stake at a moment Kenton was already so blackened that Girty did not at first recognize him.

For McKee, the break from Pittsburgh to Detroit was not so much a break with old associations as a pursuit of them. As a trader, as a friend and relative of Indians, as an imperial official, Detroit was the center toward which sooner or later he must gravitate. For a while his superiors had apparently presumed him to be of more service on the American side of the frontier. But circumstances had changed. The St. Lawrence supply route had been reopened. After Cornstalk's murder the Shawnee were committed to war. The time had come for McKee to take his place in the field. The final trigger appeared to be word brought by Matthew Elliott upon his return to Pittsburgh. Elliott was a Pennsylvania trader who had been captured by Wyandot and delivered to Detroit as an American prisoner. After examination by English authorities there and in Quebec, he was paroled, made his way back to Pittsburgh, presumably brought McKee instructions from Carleton and Hamilton, and then himself joined in the break.

The action of such noted border figures as McKee, Elliott, and Girty stirred lesser Tories to follow their example. The disaffection spread even to Hand's garrison. Fourteen deserters joined a Tory party headed for the Muskingum. A pursuing expedition captured a portion of the deserters, and the ringleaders were executed at Pittsburgh. Another group of Tories attempting to gain the Indian country encountered a Seneca raiding party and was attacked and scattered before the Seneca realized their identity and intention. Hand began increasingly to fear that he was fast losing all control of the situation. He expressed the view to General Horatio Gates that unless continentals were "put here immediately to encourage the timorous, tho' well affected, and overawe the Tory faction, this whole country will be abandoned or overcome by the enemy in a short time." In another letter to Gates he lamented, "I believe the Devil has possessed both the country and the garrison." The most experienced of all frontier authorities, Andrew Lewis, dispatched by Virginia to estimate conditions in the Pittsburgh area, was reporting: "I am sorry to have to tell you that there are no force at this place equale to acting . . . to afford the necessary protection to ye settlements . . . I dread ye consequences will prove fatal . . . I would not stay at this place one day longer were it not somewhat probable that in some way or other in the confution that things are in I may be of service."

McKee's flight caused public consternation from the Mohawk to the Holston. It was widely felt that his calculated move indicated preparations were under way to institute far more formidable Indian attacks. How well founded were these apprehensions was soon to be demonstrated. He was to become instrumental in activating and maintaining Indian hostility during the next sixteen years of Indian war which cost the lives of thousands of American settlers and led to the repeated and disastrous defeats not only of armies of American militia but of armies of United States regulars. No other Tory leader during the Revolution found an outlet for his services so injurious to the American cause. For him, and as a result for the frontier, the Revolution did not end west of the mountains until Anthony Wayne's ultimate victory at Fallen Timbers in 1794.

XII

༄

Vincennes

N O COMMANDER COULD HAVE BEEN animated by higher hopes, firmer determination, or more ambitious plans than Hamilton when he set out from Detroit on October 7, 1778. He contemplated no less than the conquest of the third of a continent. His recent concern for the safety of Detroit had been relieved by the construction of a new and stronger fort and the arrival of reinforcements under Captain Henry Bird, a fellow regular officer whose experience with frontier warfare had been broadened at Oriskany. Detailed and accurate intelligence from Hamilton's many agents in the Pittsburgh area had made it clear that there was no longer anything to fear from McIntosh's stumbling advance into the edge of the Indian country. He had long chafed under the conditions of his Detroit command which had condemned him to the irritating supervision of an irresponsible French population and the inglorious organization of Indian raiding parties. Before him now there loomed instead the dramatic opportunity to achieve a personal triumph reminiscent of a Clive's empire-building feats. His immediate objective was the reconquest of the Illinois and the establishment of forts to control the mouths of the Ohio and Missouri, and as a consequence the trade and navigation of the entire Mississippi. But his attention was fixed upon a wider vista. He had sent messages to Stuart urging him to raise the southern Indians to act in conjunction with the thousands of northern Indians already being rallied to follow his own advance across the Ohio. He foresaw as his campaign developed, support from English troops at Pensacola. On his horizon gleamed the prospect of restoring the whole vast region west of the mountains to English dominion.

With him in the boats and canoes in which he embarked at Detroit were 60 English regulars, 115 French militia, and 60 Indians. This was but the advance guard of the army that was soon to be, but he had no occasion to doubt that it was ample for his preliminary purpose, the reconquest of the Illinois. As he progressed from one Indian town to the next along the main water route connecting Lake Erie with the Wabash, he could be sure that he would be joined by hundreds of Indians. When in the spring he resumed his advance from his base in the Illinois, many more wild legions already in the process of enlistment among nations as distant as the fabled Sioux would swarm to augment his invading horde.

At the outset all proceeded as he had foreseen except the weather. Indians, always eager to add strength to strength, joined him at each town until his force exceeded 600. The weather, however, remained unprecedentedly bad. After a prolonged drought the streams were so low that his boats persistently grounded. Encumbered by stores and cannon, he could only make headway by releasing temporary gushes of water from beaver dams or by building and broaching dams of his own. When the weather did break into a succession of rain and snowstorms, the same desperate weather through which Walter Butler and Brant were marching upon Cherry Valley, it turned bitterly cold. As the streams refilled, the ice became so thick rowing became all but impossible. He had expected to reach Kaskaskia by late November. Instead, his floundering and frost-bitten army was 71 struggling days making the 600 miles between Detroit and Vincennes even though he had kept driving his men on in the face of whatever hardship and difficulty. The magnitude of the design upon which he had embarked had made no effort seem to him too painful.

His final approach to Vincennes was a soldierly masterpiece in which he provided for every contingency which could occur to a commander. He surprised and captured the scout patrols sent out by Captain Leonard Helm, the American commander. He threw out a net of his own patrols to make certain Helm could not get off a warning to Kaskaskia or Kentucky. He dispatched stronger patrols to watch the mouths of the Wabash and the Tennessee. In August, when first report of Kaskaskia's fall had reached Detroit, he had assumed James Willing to have been the captor. Not until he reached Vincennes did he for the first time hear the name George Rogers Clark, a name that was so soon to be spelled out for him by gun flashes in the night, and thereafter to haunt him to the end of his life. His first impulse was disdain. He got off a party of 40 Indians and French partisans with instructions to take the backwoodsman alive, feeling certain, with some reason, that in midwinter the Americans in the Illinois would be off guard.

Hamilton's entrance into Vincennes, December 17, 1778, was unopposed. The French population accepted the return of the English as cheerfully as they had recently accepted the intrusion of the Americans. The French militia as readily turned their coats again. Deserted by his French allies, Helm's garrison had dwindled to one American and he had no alternative to the surrender of the fort on demand. Hamilton ran up the English flag and changed the fort's name from Patrick Henry back to Sackville. His prisoner, Helm, made himself the hero of countless frontier anecdotes by soon becoming his confidant and card-playing crony in the course of teaching him to like corn whisky.

The continuing heavy rains had flooded the valley of the Wabash for tens of miles around the town. Surveying the preposterous terrain with the judgment of a professional soldier, Hamilton came to what seemed to him the only possible conclusion: To attempt this late in the winter to continue his advance to Kaskaskia was totally inadvisable; no army could conceivably make such a march. Nothing, in any event, was to be lost by a pause at Vincennes until the

weather improved. Clark was too remote to receive American reinforcement in the meantime, while the delay synchronized with
Hamilton's over-all plan. The great rendezvous of his northern Indians with Stuart's southern Indians on the Tennessee was not
scheduled until spring. He could easily deal with Clark and Kaskaskia en route to it with the overwhelming northern force he would
then have at his disposal.

In Kaskaskia, Clark was estimating the bearing upon his situation
of the same conditions. He had heard through his French agents of
Hamilton's departure from Detroit, but had at first assumed he
must be moving to resist McIntosh. Late in December he learned
through the apprehension of an English spy in Cahokia that McIntosh had turned back long before he had posed any slightest threat to
Detroit. This unwelcome revelation raised at once the suspicion
that Hamilton might instead be advancing upon the Illinois. Clark
had had no word from Vincennes for weeks, suggesting the possibility that it could already have fallen. The same practical considerations that had so impressed Hamilton led him, however, to doubt
any threat of an immediate attack on Kaskaskia. The excessively
inclement weather, the long-recognized difficulty of persuading Indians to campaign in midwinter, the flooding of every stream in the
intervening 200 miles of wilderness, all indicated that even were
Hamilton at Vincennes he would hold there. Nevertheless, Clark
ordered out scouts to watch every trail to the east.

Clark was en route to Cahokia to confer with Joseph Bowman,
commanding the town's garrison, when the chaise of one of his
French companions became mired. All members of the convivial
party were much diverted by the predicament during the hour or
more required to extricate and right the chaise. None was then
aware that in a thicket a few yards away seven Indians of Hamilton's kidnaping patrol, stationed to watch the road for Clark's expected passing, were fingering their rifles while debating whether
or not to open fire. Recalling Hamilton's instructions to take Clark
alive, they refrained. Since Clark's party was judged too numerous
to close with hand to hand, the Indians remained hidden. The
chaise was pulled free and Clark rode on, unaware that he had just

enjoyed another of the innumerable narrow escapes from death that marked his career.

At Prairie du Rocher the arrival of Clark's party promptly stirred the pleasure-loving inhabitants to stage a ball to celebrate the occasion. Toward midnight the merrymaking was suddenly stilled by the entrance of a haggard express from Kaskaskia with the announcement that Hamilton was in the outskirts with an army of 800 soldiers and Indians, prepared to attack at dawn. Clark, as always when to any other man his situation would have appeared hopeless, maintained his confident composure. He directed the music resumed and continued to dance while his horses were being saddled.

Riding through a snowstorm, he regained the fort at Kaskaskia and braced his American garrison of less than 70 men for its defense. Much depended upon the townspeople making at least some show of resistance, but he knew that their alarm would degenerate into panic were he to betray any sign of uncertainty. He rebuffed their self-conscious protestations of loyalty with the cold assertion that he had no need of their help. Even the few bolder French militiamen who professed readiness to aid in holding the fort were turned out into the street, while Clark began to burn some of the nearer houses of the town in order to clear the fort's field of fire. The inhabitants, oppressed on the one hand by Clark's destruction of their property and scorn of their fighting value and on the other by their dread of the momentary descent of Hamilton's Indians, were in a tumult of despair. Not until Clark's garrison had been strengthened by the arrival of Bowman's Cahokia company did he relent enough to listen to their renewed offers of support. By then they had been so impressed by his self-assurance that they were genuinely prepared to take their stand with him.

Within a few hours the first great alarm was proved premature. Scouts determined that the enemy encamped in an adjacent woods had been not Hamilton's main army but only a large patrol. Unable to conceal their presence after the snowfall had commenced, the intruders were already in hasty retreat to the Wabash.

It was now obvious that Hamilton was in possession of Vincennes.

But his strength or intentions remained an enigma. Clark dispatched new messengers and spies toward Vincennes. Not one returned. The suspense continued for weeks. Finally, on January 29th, it was ended by Francis Vigo's appearance at Kaskaskia. Vigo was an Italian trader of St. Louis who had been captured by one of Hamilton's patrols near Vincennes. After an interrogation Hamilton had released him on his undertaking to transmit no information to Kaskaskia. Presumably, Hamilton assumed that whatever Vigo's story it could be expected to increase the alarm of the Illinois French and further undermine Clark's position. Vigo was actually a business partner of the Spanish commander, de Leyba, Clark's friend and Teresa's brother, and he did come to Clark with his story, though without producing the effect Hamilton may have hoped. Vigo's information was complete, detailed, and accurate. He said that Hamilton had taken Vincennes with an army of 600 soldiers and Indians, that to conserve his supplies he had returned most of his Detroit militia to winter in Detroit, that most of the Indians who had not been released for their winter hunting had been dispatched on various raids, that he was holding Fort Sackville with a garrison of 80 soldiers supported by artillery, that to his reassembling army in the spring were to be added not only many more hundreds of Indians from the north but 500 from the south, and that he proposed to resume his advance as early in the spring as weather permitted.

The suspense had ended but very much for the worse. To Hamilton's coming invasion from so near a base with so overwhelming a force there could be no adequate resistance. It was already too late to hope for any assistance from faraway Virginia, from which Clark had had no word since he had crossed the mountains more than a year before. More than the Illinois must fall. Kentucky, too, was doomed; possibly even the Pittsburgh area. To Clark the situation was so desperate that all was very simple. Since to wait for Hamilton to reassemble his main army in the spring was to invite certain destruction, the one alternative was to attack him at once. The chance that with his fort surrounded by miles of seemingly impassable flood water Hamilton might be off guard offered a possible opportunity for surprise which provided the project's sole hope of success. As Clark so clearly put it in his letter to George Mason: "I saw the only possibility of our maintaining the Country was to take advantage of his present weakness, perhaps we might be fortunate." He consulted his officers. All stoutly agreed.

His campaign plan contemplated an attack by water as well as by land. He armed a large oared barge with 2 cannon and 4 swivels, manned her with a crew of 40 under the command of his cousin, Lieutenant John Rogers, and named the so hastily commissioned warship *Willing*. The galley was to sail by way of the Mississippi, the Ohio, and the Wabash and, upon approaching Vincennes, to co-operate with his land force in any way that then seemed indicated.

After manning the galley, there remained to Clark fewer than 90 Americans for his overland expedition. These were manifestly too few for the venture, even for a commander of Clark's temerity, and he was driven to the expedient of calling for French volunteers. So far in the Revolution the French had proved of little fighting value to either side. This had not been due to the inherent indolence, worthlessness, and timidity so often ascribed to them by their scornful American frontier neighbors. In the fur trade, the most arduous of all occupations, the wilderness French had demonstrated for generations, and were to continue to demonstrate for generations to come, a hardihood unequaled by men of any other race or breed. Throughout the period of French dominion they had been capable of prodigies of endurance and valor. But in this war they were largely indifferent to the successes or failures of either of the English-speaking contestants. What was required to capture their interest was a sufficiently dramatic appeal to their imagination and the appearance of a leader with a personality capable of arousing their enthusiasm. Clark furnished both these elements. His accomplishment of the near miracle is again better explained in his own words: "I conducted myself as though I was sure of taking Mr. Hamilton, instructed my officers to observe the same Rule. In a day or two the Country seemed to believe it, many anctious to retrieve their Characters turned out, the Ladies also began to be spirited and interest themselves in the Expedition, which had great Effect on the Young men ... We set out on a Forlorn hope indeed ... I cannot account for it but I still had inward assurance of success; and never could when weighing every Circumstance doubt it."

Clark had pressed his preparations so vigorously that on the seventh day after receipt of Vigo's report on Hamilton he had equipped and dispatched his navy and was marching eastward from Kaskaskia at the head of his army. Various accounts have estimated his force at as few as 130, but according to the testimony of both Clark and his second in command, Joseph Bowman, it numbered 170. Roughly half were hard-bitten American frontiersmen most of whom had been with him since passage of the Ohio rapids, but the other half were so far untried French volunteers. The moccasined and leather-shirted column, winding in single file off into the storm-beaten wilderness, was less an army than a band of adventurers whose one element of military cohesion was their instinctive reliance upon a great commander.

The icy rains continued. All the lower Illinois was a wind-whipped morass. They waded in water that was by turns ankle deep, knee deep, and waist deep. At night they built scaffolds upon which to place their baggage and especially their scant reserve store of powder, while they slept on the ground in the slush and mud. During the first week they passed among herds of buffalo, providing them with at least the one comfort of all the meat that they could eat in camp at the end of each exhausting day. But after that there was only an occasional coon or opossum marooned by the rising flood water. Once they brought down a fox that had most unnaturally taken refuge in a tree. It clearly was weather fit for neither man nor beast. They had been unable to transport enough food and were presently weakened by hunger. The farther they marched the deeper became the water. As they approached the Wabash, the flooded earth had become an inland sea across which they could barely distinguish the tops of the submerged trees on the farther side. As Clark well said: "This would have been enough to have stop'd any set of men that was not in the same temper that we was."

The wilderness Frenchman was a born boatman. Clark set his Frenchmen to contriving makeshift canoes and rafts. The first raft was used to look for land on the eastern shore and the first canoe was sent down river to look for *Willing,* for which they had now such desperate need. But the galley had been delayed by the difficulty of making headway against the sweep of flood waters and, to the vast mortification of the crew, eventually proved unable to reach Vincennes until the second day after Clark arrived. He could not wait. His men were starving and each hour's delay reduced the chance of the surprise upon which the whole enterprise depended. They were already so near Vincennes that they could hear the thud of the morning and evening gun at the English fort. With the completion of a second canoe he began ferrying his army by driblets to the eastern shore. A canoe with five Frenchmen appeared. The astonished hunters were swiftly taken. Their canoe was a godsend and their information even more welcome. They said Vincennes was still unaware of Clark's approach.

Yet Hamilton had not been altogether off guard. He had patrols out at the moment, commanded by two of his most experienced French partisans, Francis Maisonville * and Guillaume La Mothe. Maisonville had cruised as far as the mouth of the Ohio but had turned back too soon to sight *Willing.* He had even from a distance noted the fires of one of Clark's encampments but had supposed them Indian. The one great advantage of the flood from Clark's point of view was that it effectually concealed the tracks of his army.

He got his men across the Wabash on February 21st. They landed on a knoll locally known as La Mamelle. The wilderness French were romantically fond of attaching the name *mamelle* oi *téton* to any natural protuberance, from hillock to mountain, with contours even faintly supporting the pleasing allusion. About this one the flood swirled and eddied with new warnings and threats. For the last 16 days Clark and his dogged followers had been marching through a flooded wilderness, sleeping in ice-crusted mud, never dry, never warm, exposed to midwinter cold, increasingly hungry. They were now within seven miles of Vincennes but what still lay

---

* Maisonville's first notable English service had been as guide to Lieutenant Alexander Fraser in that young officer's adventurous descent of the Ohio in 1765 to demand the surrender of Fort Chartres.

before them was worse than all that had gone before. The eastern shore of the Wabash was more deeply inundated than had been the west. The five captured Frenchmen who knew the country were certain that in the intervening lowlands the water was too deep for men to get to Vincennes on foot. Clark decided, nonetheless, that either resort to continued ferrying in the two canoes or delay while more were constructed was bound to make their approach too slow to preserve the essential element of surprise. As had been his custom throughout the march when the going was exceptionally difficult, he set off at the head of the long column of men plodding on through the water in single file. The most ordinary men, no matter how weary or discouraged, are prone to follow such a leader. But these were not ordinary men. By now their exertions and sufferings had transfixed them with a fanatical resolution to get on to the end of this fearful march.

There was an attendant hazard in following in Clark's footsteps. He was six feet. When he strode on into water until it rose to his chin it was over the head of many of those behind attempting to keep up. The two canoes paddled back and forth, helping shorter men to keep their heads above water and rescuing others who were at the point of collapse. They were all day the 22nd making the next three miles. That night they spent on a half-acre patch of slightly higher ground on a maple knoll where there had been a sugar camp. The weather turned colder, so benumbing many of the more exhausted men that the next morning they were only able to get to their feet when lifted by their companions.

On this last day of the march Clark was obliged continually to break the half-inch crust of ice with a stick as he pushed on through the water. So many men had reached the absolute limit of their endurance that these early hours of the 23rd were the most harrowing of the whole march. Clark had blackened his face to demonstrate his confidence that they were at last on the verge of making their so long anticipated attack. He started songs, yelled ribald nonsense, repeatedly called back the phrase "land ahead" which to his floundering followers had long since become the grimmest of all jokes. While heartening his men by every device that occurred to him, he also stationed Bowman at the rear of the column with orders to shoot any who turned back. Toward noon they came out on a slight rise which Clark termed "a delightfull Dry Spot of ground." The sun had also come out, and he afterwards referred to the 23rd as that "delightful Day." A passing squaw in a canoe was captured. She had with her a half quarter of buffalo. There was enough broth to provide every man a swallow.

The last lap became suddenly the easiest. There was a lake too deep to be waded, but so narrow that all could be ferried across in the three canoes. Early in the afternoon the starving, half-drowned, and utterly exhausted army of conquest staggered and crawled up among the trees of a low eminence known as Warrior's Island. From it they could see, two miles away across a rolling pond-dotted meadow, the town of Vincennes and, just above it, Fort Sackville. As Clark put it, "we ware now in the situation that I had Laboured to get ourselves in."

In the partially flooded meadow were a number of Frenchmen hunting ducks on horseback. One of them was captured. He said nobody in Vincennes even yet suspected the American approach. Clark studied his goal, the town and the fort now so near. He later wrote Mason, "A thousand Ideas flashed in my head at this moment." These led him to a daring decision. If Hamilton was still unaware of his danger, it was now too late for him to summon assistance. After having struggled so desperately to achieve surprise, Clark determined to relinquish that tactical advantage for the sake of the psychological advantage of advertising his confidence in his own complete superiority. He was not so much concerned with Hamilton's garrison as he was with the nearly 700 French inhabitants and with the hundreds of Indians in nearby Indian towns. A few of the French were pro-American, others had enlisted in the English service, most were resolutely neutral, but all had intimate relations with the Indians. Were his actual weakness suspected, he could be soon overwhelmed by any combination of the two. Taking care that the duck hunter learned nothing of his numbers, though informing him that this was an invading army not from the Illinois but from Kentucky, Clark dispatched by him a written message to the townspeople. In it he advised them that he was attacking at once, that those who favored the English should take refuge in the fort, that all others should remain in their homes, and that all found in the streets would be treated as enemies.

In late evening, a few minutes after the town had been stunned by his sensational message, Clark marched. His company flags and standards were attached to the tops of long poles. While moving obliquely across the rolling prairie, his men were hidden by the intervening low rises and only the raised flags were visible to indicate the size of his force. The French volunteers were partial to flags, each little group had its own, and the two dozen emblems waving in the gathering dusk suggested a very considerable army. The stratagem was a complete success so far as the townspeople were concerned. They were so impressed by the arrogance of his message and the array of banners that there was no thought of resistance or of appealing to Hamilton for advice. For fear of offending Clark no one from the town even informed Hamilton of Clark's message. Clark's devices to magnify the ostensible size of his army were wasted on Fort Sackville, however, for there all its inmates still remained incredibly oblivious. The garrison had that day completed the restoration of the fort, had celebrated the achievement with games and an extra issue of rum, and retired early. Sentries on the walls attached no importance to the sudden stir of excitement in the town and were prevented by an intervening wooded height from seeing the parade of battle flags in the meadow.

At nightfall Clark entered the town, unopposed. Preoccupied with assuring secure possession, seizing the principal structures, confiscating the inhabitants' arms, and making sure of their behavior, he at first sent only one platoon to open fire on the fort. This initial fusillade gave rise to the most relished of all contemporary anecdotes connected with the campaign. Hamilton was said to have been at that moment engaged in a game of cards with his prisoner, Helm. The first shots showered soot from the chimney into his toddy, warming on the hearth. According to Hamilton's official report, he for a moment thought the shooting to be by drunken Indians or French townsmen. According to the anecdote, he started up angrily, exclaiming, "What's the meaning of this?" Helm was then supposed to have replied, "It means *you* are now *my* prisoner."

Clark's occupation of the town was accomplished without difficutly. The inhabitants were delighted to find so many of their Illinois friends and relatives among the invaders. Many local militiamen joined his ranks, changing sides for the third time in hardly more than as many months. A secret store of gunpowder was disclosed and turned over to him. Food was urged upon his starving men. The investment of the fort was meanwhile completed and every loophole and gun port kept under persistent rifle fire. Hamilton replied with artillery salvos, damaging a number of houses in the town, including the church. In this exchange Hamilton's fire was more thunderous but less effective. No Americans were injured, while so expert was their marksmanship that a number of gunners were hit during the recurring intervals when a port was open to aim and fire a cannon.

The most eventful episode of the night attack was the attempted return of Hamilton's two patrols. Maisonville was captured, his hiding place betrayed by his neighbors. As a known partisan leader of Indian raiding parties, he was treated most unceremoniously by his American captors. A token nick was cut from his scalp and he was for a time tied to a post in the siege lines where he was used as a shield by riflemen firing on the fort. La Mothe's larger patrol broke through and scaled the walls. Clark had purposely withdrawn his lines enough to give him that opportunity, much preferring to have the French partisans inside the fort than scattering among Indian towns where they might rally Indians to Hamilton's support.

At nine the next morning Clark suspended firing and demanded the fort's surrender, accompanying the summons with the threat invariably made in wilderness warfare that he could not vouch for the conduct of his men were he obliged to take the place by storm. He was in unmistakable grim earnest with his declaration that he would welcome an excuse to exterminate white men who had been guilty of leading Indians against frontier inhabitants. As he phrased it in his written summons to Hamilton, "you may depend upon such Treatment justly due to a Murderer." Hamilton stiffly refused with the retort that he and his garrison were not "to be awed into any action Unworthy of British subjects."

The firing resumed. Clark was well enough aware that his position was not so superior as he was endeavoring to indicate. Until *Willing* arrived with artillery to breach the walls, he had too few men to attempt to storm a fort defended by so strong a garrison. Meanwhile, an English supply party from Detroit was approaching from the north which, if diligently directed, could speedily raise a swarm of Indian allies. Hamilton, for his part, was dwelling morosely only upon his own disadvantages. Though he could rely on his English regulars, the French half of his garrison was becoming increasingly nervous. His principal weakness, however, was the most enervating that can afflict a commander. He had permitted his thinking to be dominated by the bewildering initiative of his bolder and more aggressive opponent.

As the firing continued, several more of the garrison were wounded and one American finally was hit. Hamilton was still unable to adjust to the sudden, monstrous alteration in his situation. Yesterday he had considered himself a commander on the verge of a conquest of limitless extent. Today he was shut up in one little backwoods fort. Unable to endure his own uncertainty, he requested another parley for the sake of inquiring what terms Clark proposed to impose. Clark, as usual pressing every slightest suggestion of an advantage, refused to consider anything but unconditional surrender. Hamilton declined but asked for a three-day truce. Clark refused. The exchanges of views and arguments continued, Helm acting part of the time as go-between. Clark finally and grudgingly agreed to a meeting with Hamilton on the parade ground in front of the gate.

At this juncture there developed a bizarre interruption which for sheer timeliness at a critical moment in a campaign can surely never have been excelled. From the nearby forest burst an Indian war party, just returned from raiding Kentucky, whooping and firing their guns in the air to announce to their patrons in the fort the good news of their success in having taken prisoners and scalps. The Americans could for a moment scarcely credit the full breathtaking extent of their miraculous good fortune. Not in their fondest dreams had any of them ever imagined an opportunity of such consummately rounded perfection as to be in a position to preside over the homecoming festivities of a pack of red-handed Indian raiders. Clark sent Captain John Williams' company out to welcome their howling guests. The advancing Americans waved, beat their own breasts, echoed the wild scalp hallos, and made all the standard congratulatory gestures appropriate to the occasion. All men in buckskin look alike at fifty paces. The Indians took it for granted that this was the usual welcoming committee sent out by Hamilton and rushed literally into its disillusioning embrace. Even Clark admitted a twinge of harsh sympathy: "The Poor Devils never discovered their mistake until it was too late." Seven of the Indians were seized, five were shot down, and only one escaped. The two white captives were released and the captured Indians brought into town.

Clark ordered them tomahawked in the street in full view of the garrison. They were forced to sit in a circle with bowed heads while awaiting the death stroke. Some accounts maintain that Clark himself performed the hatcheting, others that an American sergeant, estimated to have lost more relatives to Indians than had any of his companions, was granted the coveted privilege. Several perplexities briefly delayed the executions. Two of the condemned were discovered to be Frenchmen who, while accompanying the raiding party, had been painted and accoutered to give them the appearance of Indians. One of these was suddenly recognized as his son by a French lieutenant in Clark's army and the other turned out to have relatives in Vincennes. Clark reluctantly spared both. Then Captain Richard McCarty of the Cahokia company learned that one of the genuine Indians was the 18-year-old son of Pontiac and interceded for his life on the plea that his own life had once been saved by Pontiac. Clark spared him, too. The other four Indians were axed.

Clark then walked toward the fort to meet Hamilton. If he had not himself wielded the tomahawk, he had stood so near the proceedings that blood had splattered on his face and hands. While Hamilton stared, he paused to wash his face and hands in a pool of rainwater that had accumulated in a beached canoe. He straight-ened and the two adversaries stood face to face. The English commander made no effort to conceal his disgust with the American's barbarous violence, and yet could not conceal his own secret agitation. His every impression since Clark had so incredibly materialized out of flood and darkness had forced him to realize his opponent's terrifying aggressiveness. The angry debate between the two continued on into the afternoon. Hamilton kept reiterating his determination never to surrender unconditionally, and Clark kept re-emphasizing his preference for a resumption of the assault to provide an opportunity sufficiently to punish white men who lent themselves to the ignominy of setting Indians on fellow white men. Each kept characterizing the other as a "Murderer." Again and again Hamilton furiously turned away, but each time he turned back. Once he re-entered the fort to consult his officers. This served only to remind him that, while the English portion of his garrison remained steadfast, the demoralization of the French half had been completed by the execution of the Indian raiders. Finally Clark sensed that his prey was ready for the kill. He offered at least the shadow of terms, permitting the defenders to march out before laying down their arms. Hamilton grasped at the straw of this small indulgence and surrendered. On the morning of February 25, 1779, the Americans took formal possession, and the fort became again Fort Patrick Henry. The ceremony of firing a cannon salute to commemorate the victory was marred by the explosion of a powder cask, seriously burning a number of the celebrants and providing the only significant American casualties of the campaign.

The victory had been a frontier triumph achieved by frontiersmen. They had taken more than an English fort, a garrison of English regulars, and an English lieutenant governor. They had had the deeper and even more rewarding satisfaction of inflicting a public, ritualistic punishment upon representative Indian raiders and of inflicting humiliation upon Hamilton, Maisonville, La Mothe, and Jehu Hay, until then the most noted of all promoters, organizers, and partisan leaders of Indian outrage in the west. To this cake of exultation was now added the ultimate frosting. At the head of a strong party, the just released Helm surprised and captured the approaching supply convoy, seizing, in addition to large military stores, $50,000 worth of Indian trade goods. Clark distributed the loot among his followers, making each impoverished young frontiersman "almost rich."

He paroled most of the surrendered garrison, but sent Hamilton, Maisonville, La Mothe, Hay, four other officers and 18 English regulars back to Virginia as prisoners of war. Their route extended for hundreds of miles along the Kentucky and Holston frontiers and imposed upon Hamilton an impenitent pilgrim's progress of prolonged mortification. Public indignation against him had been further stirred by the circumstance that, with so little snow, Indian raids had not ceased, as usual, during the winter and were still continuing while he was passing from station to station.* Hamilton's guards occasionally had difficulty protecting him from the infuriated inhabitants. The frontier, with some reason, held English policy largely responsible for Indian outrages and, as English commander in the west, Hamilton was universally execrated as "the Hairbuyer." To his indignant denials that he had ever paid for scalps no credence was given.† His tribulations did not diminish when he finally reached the presumably more civilized seaboard. Jefferson, aroused by his western sympathies and his severe moral principles, indignantly refused to consider Hamilton an ordinary prisoner of war. He kept him in a common jail, loaded with irons and on short rations, under sanitary conditions so primitive that his health was affected. In spite of English official protests and intercession by various Americans ranging from Daniel Boone to Washington, Jefferson declined to

* In one raid Logan had been wounded shortly before being obliged to give Hamilton overnight lodging in his station, and in another William Myers, Clark's devoted express messenger who had just completed one round trip to Virginia with the announcement of the capture of Kaskaskia and now was en route with dispatches announcing the capture of Vincennes, was killed.

† A number of American states offered bounties for Indian scalps during the Revolution, but there was no English bounty for white scalps. There seems little evidence that English commanders at Detroit or Niagara ever even privately offered payments for scalps. Large payments for captives were regularly disbursed, a practice defended on the grounds that it persuaded Indians to spare the lives of their victims. But even if no direct payment for scalps was made, the organization of the Indian supply system encouraged their taking. Indians who returned with scalps to prove their recent success were rewarded by issues of gunpowder, weapons, clothing, food, and rum in the hope of inspiring them to resume their attacks on the frontier.

permit his exchange until March of 1781. Of the other prisoners, Hay was exchanged with Hamilton, La Mothe paroled, Lieutenant Jacob Schieffelin and Rocheblave escaped, and Maisonville committed suicide in jail.

Clark saw the capture of Vincennes as only a prelude to the far more important capture of Detroit. Though without formal military training, his sense of strategic values was nevertheless so well developed that he clearly comprehended that only by reduction of the English base at Detroit could the Indian threat to the frontier be suppressed and the war in the west ever be brought to a successful conclusion. Many ensuing years of disaster were to demonstrate the soundness of this judgment, but never during those years was the capture of Detroit to prove again to be as nearly within reach as on the morrow of the capture of Vincennes.

For a few days Clark contemplated an immediate advance upon Detroit with the limited force of 200 men already at his disposal. There was at least a possibility that the same headlong boldness that had achieved Hamilton's downfall might prove again successful. The large French population of Detroit was on the verge of open rebellion and the English commander, Captain Richard Lernoult, dismayed by the Vincennes catastrophe, was desperately appealing to Governor Frederick Haldimand, Carleton's successor, for succor. But Clark for once permitted himself to be guided by the reasoning of a more orthodox commander. Dispatches from Virginia had assured him that Colonel John Montgomery was on his way to join him with a regiment of 500 Virginians. There was also the prospect of Colonel John Bowman joining him with a muster of 300 Kentuckians. Clark decided to wait until with these notable reinforcements he could be made certain of success. The opportunity passed, never to return.

Montgomery was delayed by participation in Evan Shelby's attack on the Chickamauga towns and, when he did arrive, proved to have brought with him only 150 men. Bowman, accused by some of his contemporaries of command jealousies, instead of joining Clark devoted his Kentucky force to an attack on Chilicothe, a principal Shawnee town from which so many attacks on Kentucky had been launched. He destroyed a portion of the town but was forced to withdraw after an inconclusive campaign in which his only perceptible success had been the fall of the noted Shawnee chief, Blackfish, during the engagement. With their command of lake navigation, the English had meanwhile improved their position at Detroit, while Clark was but little stronger in June than he had been in March. He was left stranded and frustrated, to lament: "Never was a person more mortified than I was at this time. . . Detroit lost for the want of a few men." Though not immediately apparent, except possibly to Clark, the tide of American victory in the west had already reached its crest at Vincennes. By midsummer, American power north of the Ohio was beginning to recede and, within but little more than another year, the entire region had escaped American control.

The temporary nature of Clark's Illinois conquest has led many historians to argue that it could have had little bearing on the eventual cession of the northwest to the United States by England at the peace table. But the significance of a victory may usually be most clearly identified by considering the contrary consequences had it not been won. Had Clark not taken the English lieutenant governor at Vincennes, the massive English-Indian invasion already under way could have been expected to gather a momentum certain to carry every American settlement west of the mountains and to have left to the peace commissioners no basis for discussion of a more favorable western boundary than the original Proclamation Line.

The English commanders in the west had reacted swiftly and diligently during the winter of 1778–79 to repair the disarray into which their Indian program had been thrown by Clark's insolent conferences at Cahokia after his occupation of Kaskaskia. In reestablishing English prestige they had relied heavily on the support of the wilderness French in the more northern areas as yet unaffected by Clark's advances. Many of these traders, voyageurs and former French officials, whose influence over Indians had been developed during the generations they had lived among them, were willing to employ this in the English interest in return for various forms of privilege and pay. By early spring of 1779, five expeditions in which

Indians of more than a dozen nations had been incorporated were en route to the projected rendezvous with Hamilton in the Illinois. Each as it progressed from one Indian center to the next was gathering recruits by the scores and hundreds. Three of them had been organized by Captain Arent de Peyster, commandant at Mackinac, that great junction of wilderness water routes and chief focal point of Indian population and trade. One, under Charles Langlade, a veteran of wilderness warfare the first of whose countless exploits had been the celebrated capture of Pickawillany in 1752, was skirting the western shore of Lake Michigan, gathering in Chippewa, Menominee, and Winnebago recruits. Langlade's nephew, Charles Gautier, was heading southward by way of the Wisconsin and the Mississippi, recruiting Sauk, Outgami, Sioux, and Iowa. Lieutenant Thomas Bennet, his less familiar repute supported by an initial force of 20 soldiers and 60 militiamen, was proceeding down the eastern shore of Lake Michigan, picking up northern Ottawa and Chippewa recruits, with the intention of uniting with Langlade at the foot of the lake. Working out of Detroit, McKee was assembling a rapidly accumulating force of Shawnee, Potowatami, Kickapoo, and southern Chippewa and Ottawa that had reached a total of 600. At Sandusky, Henry Bird, with assistance from Simon Girty, was rallying Wyandot and Mingo who had already evidenced their readiness to fight by keeping the starving American garrison at Fort Laurens in a state of siege since January.

This whole imposing effort, so instinct with menace to the American frontier, was disrupted by the electrifying news of the capture of its commander in chief. By calculated English policy, Hamilton had been elevated in Indian estimation to a height upon which his person represented English power in the wilderness. His sudden descent from the role of prospective conqueror to that of humiliated captive, therefore, had a corresponding impact. Frenchmen who had lent themselves to the recruiting project were serving with no love for the English, so long their traditional enemies, but only because they had considered it politic to associate themselves with the stronger side. They began at once instead to fear that they might have chosen the weaker. Upon their counsel and example the

Indians had always been accustomed to rely. As a consequence of this sudden tidal wave of doubt, all five musters were shattered by wholesale desertions long before they had reached any scene of action. Gautier was forced to turn back at Rock River on the Mississippi, Langlade at Milwaukee River, Bennet at St. Joseph's. Bird's and McKee's assembled levies as suddenly melted away. As evidence of the seriousness of the disaffection, among the Indians as well as the French, Half King, the principal Wyandot chief who had since the war's outset been among the most aggressive leaders of frontier attacks, hastily made a formal offer of peace to the Americans and presently visited Pittsburgh to press his overture in person. Informed of the course of events by his western commanders, Governor Haldimand in September was gloomily reporting to the cabinet, "It is much to be apprehended that our Indian allies have it in contemplation to desert us." Much of the damage was repaired in time to regain Indian support in the following campaign season. But, meanwhile, the loss of Kaskaskia and Vincennes to Clark had set back the timetable of the English war effort in the west by a full year. As ensuing events were to prove, that year of delay was vital.

A second effect of Clark's initiative, even more significant than the confusion spread among French and Indians, was the encouragement given the inhabitants of the frontier. In the midst of all the extremities that they were enduring they remained a people ever eager to detect the first sign that the general danger might be sufficiently abating to countenance a renewed reach for the land in the west they so yearned to possess. News of Vincennes, supported by the spectacle of the captive Hamilton's progress eastward over the mountains, was accepted by many as such a sign. In the late summer of 1779, through the winter and well into the spring of 1780, thousands streamed westward to lend the support of their numbers to the harassed stations of Kentucky and to establish totally new settlements in Tennessee. Soon they were to be subjected to new dangers, even more oppressive than before, but their coming had brought by the narrowest of margins enough added strength to withstand them. Few victories, surely, have had decisive effects more immediate or more enduring than Clark's at Vincennes.

XIII

༇

Washington

AFTER THE INITIAL EFFORT in 1775 to promote Indian neutrality, Congress had for the next three years been unable to contribute national assistance to the defense of the western frontier. Supremely critical campaigns in the east had strained every national resource. With the fate of Boston, New York, and Philadelphia at issue Congress had little concern to spare for the fate of Pittsburgh, much less Harrodsburg. Aside from the exertions of the frontier people themselves, the only significant military efforts made in behalf of the frontier during the next three years had been the invasion of the Cherokee country, Holston's reinforcement of Kentucky, and the muster of Clark's Illinois expedition. With none had the central government any connection. The first had been conducted by regional militia, and the other two had been Virginia enterprises.* It was only after the relief of tension following Burgoyne's surrender that Congress was able again to take thought to the frontier problem. Affected by the sufferings of the border inhabitants and spurred in

* Clark eventually became a brigadier general in the Virginia militia, and in 1793 received a French major general's commission, but at no stage in his career did he serve in either the Continental Army or the United States Army.

particular by the apparent extent of Tory disaffection advertised by Hamilton's proclamation, Congress on November 20, 1777, appointed a special committee to investigate and report conditions on the upper Ohio.

The committee's reports of March 31 and April 27, 1778, stressed: (1) the frontier's desperate situation which threatened to oblige its abandonment; (2) the total inadequacy of continued passive defense; (3) the many fallibilities of the militia system; (4) the disruption of public order by the Pennsylvania-Virginia and Tory-Patriot rivalries; and (5) the imperative need for regular troops to spearhead a counteroffensive. Congress responded May 2nd by voting two regiments of continentals for transmountain duty. Hand, partly in deference to his own request, but also because confidence in his judgment had been diminished by the Squaw Campaign and McKee's escape, was replaced by Brigadier General Lachlan McIntosh. McIntosh was a citizen soldier whose military qualities were respected by Washington and who had had Indian fighting experience on the Georgia frontier, but whose chief claim so far to public notice had been that he had in a recent duel killed Button Gwinnett, a Signer. On June 11th, Congress after further deliberation ordered an attack on Detroit as the one decisive counter that might end Indian depredations in the west.

But after Wyoming's demonstration of so much nearer dangers, the Detroit project was hastily countermanded and much of the support formerly intended for McIntosh delayed or withheld. Nevertheless, he assumed command at Pittsburgh August 6th with many loud announcements of his determination to subjugate all Indians, including, first, the long suffering and long friendly Delaware. Hampered by lack of men and supplies, he undertook a floundering advance into the fringe of the Indian country to establish Fort McIntosh on the Beaver and Fort Laurens on the Tuscawara. The Indians were less impressed by what had been intended as a demonstration of American strength than by what struck them as new evidence of American weakness. Fort Laurens, far from serving as a check on Indian belligerence, became a target for Indian attack. During the few months of its precarious existence, its besieged and starving garrison was saved from surrender only by the relaxation of the Indian effort after Vincennes, and the post was abandoned in July 1779 by order of McIntosh's successor, Colonel Daniel Brodhead.

Meanwhile, Brant's devastation of the Mohawk, culminating in the final horror at Cherry Valley, had fired congressional fury and centered congressional attention upon the New York frontier. The massive association of swarms of vengeful and embittered Tory partisans with marauding packs of Iroquois warriors had made it a political as well as a military and a humanitarian necessity to strike back. On February 27, 1779, Congress authorized Washington to organize an expeditionary force of sufficient strength to extirpate the Tory-Iroquois menace. Congress could vote ends, but upon Washington fell the responsibility for assembling the means. As custodian of the hard core of regulars in the Continental Army it was for him, this year as in every other year of the Revolution, to determine, among a bewildering range of demands, the most vital need upon which to spend this limited central force.

In the past and again in the time soon to come, Washington's interest in and sympathy with the frontier provided historically significant contributions to the westward movement. Unlike most of his prominent contemporaries, his confidence in the west's future importance was informed and complete. It was a confidence based on a lifelong, comprehensive, and judicious firsthand knowledge of the frontier. No other man has ever had personal frontier experience of comparable range and variety. At 16 he was surveying for the Fairfax estate in the wilderness beyond the Blue Ridge. By the time he was 21 he was so accomplished a woodsman that he was able to take in stride the desperate winter journey over the mountains to challenge the French commander at Le Boeuf. He commanded the first army to attempt to force the mountain barrier. He was the senior American officer with Braddock and the commander of one of Forbes' two divisions. It was his flying column which made the final dash to occupy the Forks of the Ohio. He had, meanwhile, personally supervised the construction of the more difficult sections of both great military roads over the mountains. As commander in chief of Virginia's military forces, he had during the three years intervening between Braddock's and Forbes' campaigns been personally responsible for the defense of Virginia's borders against the perpetual Indian inroads of that disastrous period. During those critical two decades preceding the Revolution which had been climaxed by the American settlers' first crossing of the mountain barrier, his western experience had been far more than merely military. He had been long and intimately associated with such extraordinary frontier figures as George Croghan, Andrew Lewis, Christopher Gist, Henry Bouquet, and Thomas Cresap. He and his brothers, Lawrence and Augustine, had been among the original members of the Ohio Company. His marriage in 1759 and subsequent devotion to the management of his Mount Vernon plantation had not diminished his interest in frontier affairs. He had continued to accumulate claims to western lands in addition to his land-company interests by buying the land warrants of his fellow veterans of the French War and through the operations of William Crawford, his Pittsburgh land agent. In 1770 he had made a personal exploration of the upper Ohio region during which he penetrated to what was then the extreme distance of the mouth of the Kanawha. In 1773 and 1774 the first official Kentucky surveyors had taken care to allot specific tracts to him. By the outbreak of the Revolution his claims west of the mountains had totaled more than 30,000 acres, including more than 50 miles of Ohio River frontage.

Yet, in spite of these western interests, sympathies, hopes, and investments, he did not throughout the Revolution permit these predilections to sway by a hairsbreadth his estimate of his responsibilities as commander in chief. No matter how desperate became the situation in the west, he not once could be prevailed upon to approve the dispatch of a regular force of any consequence beyond the mountains. His attention was constantly fixed on the primary principle that the first of all needs was to win the war. In his judgment there was little value in saving the west if meanwhile the war were lost, and he never wavered in his conviction that it could only be decisively won or lost on the eastern seaboard. Therefore, with that patient resolution which was his and his country's greatest strength, he husbanded his scant military resources and waited for the eventual moment of that decision.

However, in the spring of 1779, two strategic considerations induced him to feel that a portion of his central force could be safely devoted to an invasion of the so much nearer Iroquois country. The first was that the Mohawk granary was of such importance to his army that a strong effort to save it seemed definitely justified. The other was that there was no indication of the French fleet's return from the West Indies, and except in association with it he could in any event undertake no offensive operations against the English army in New York. It, therefore, appeared that a feasible opportunity had arisen for the temporary detachment of regular troops, who would otherwise have lain idle, to a task force strong enough to strike a powerful blow at the Tory-Iroquois collaboration.

Horatio Gates declined the command, as Washington had hoped, and it went to Major General John Sullivan, whom he much preferred. Sullivan was an energetic, politically alert, young New Hampshire lawyer who had gained rank and considerable military proficiency through continuous hard service from the opening moments of the Revolution. Since becoming a major general, he had taken a prominent part in the siege of Boston, the retreat from Canada, and the battles of Long Island, Princeton, Trenton, Brandywine, Germantown, and Newport. The new demand now to be made upon him was more challenging than any that he had met before. Gates, in declining the command, had testified to an appreciation of the dangers in prospect, based on his having been with Braddock. Washington, better than any other man, understood the unparalleled hazards of wilderness campaigning and, having once decided to approve the enterprise, did not stint his support of it. He made available 16 regiments of continentals, an augmented regiment of artillery, a troop of cavalry, and a battalion of Morgan's Rifles. It was the most formidable American regular army ever to invade the Indian country.

The over-all campaign plan was bold and comprehensive. Instead of concentrating his army on either the New York or the Pennsylvania border, which would have given his opponents, John Butler and Brant, an opportunity meanwhile to attack the area left unprotected, Sullivan mobilized his army in two divisions, to march from bases in either state to a junction at Tioga on the Susquehanna near the New York-Pennsylvania line. Though not under Sullivan's direct command, Brodhead was at the same time to march north from Pittsburgh to assail the Mingo and Seneca towns on the upper Allegheny. The central fastnesses of the Tory-Iroquois alliance in western New York were thus to be subjected to concentric, simultaneous attacks by organized and disciplined forces of very great strength. Sullivan with his First Division of three brigades, commanded by brigadier generals Edward Hand, Enoch Poor, and William Maxwell, was to advance north from Easton through Wyoming, while the Second Division, consisting of the fourth brigade with some additional troops, commanded by Brigadier General James Clinton, struck south from the Mohawk down the long-haunted concentration corridor for Tories and Indians between Unadilla and Oghwaga to the appointed meeting at Tioga.

As a preliminary to the major campaign, Clinton early in the spring dispatched Colonel Goose Van Shaick with an expedition of 580 continentals and militia levies to attack the Onondaga Castle. Making a swift surprise march from Fort Stanwix, the expedition on April 20th burned three Onondaga towns, captured 38 women and children, and killed 12 of their fleeing warriors. As a military operation the achievement was of doubtful value. The Onondaga had never taken a whole-hearted interest in the war and had been increasingly disposed to make peace, but were now recommitted to belligerence. By late June Clinton had assembled his brigade, 1600 strong, on the shores of Otsego Lake where he lay in camp for weeks while awaiting orders from Sullivan to start for the perilous rendezvous with the main army deep in the Indian country.

It was not until June 18th that Sullivan was able to march from Easton after having already suffered a delay of six weeks due to roadbuilding and supply difficulties. In getting his army over the mountains to Wyoming and up the forbidding gorges of the Susquehanna to Tioga, he was confronted by the same historic labors, trials, and perils that had plagued Braddock, Forbes, and Bouquet when leading their regular armies into the wilderness. Washington had been well enough pleased with some of the earlier delay. He had not quite given up hope of the return of the French fleet and was keeping in mind the possibility, if Sullivan had not meanwhile penetrated beyond reach into the interior, of recalling his continentals for seaboard operations of more strategic importance. But the French admiral, Comte D'Estaing, did not reappear in American waters until September, and then sailed no farther north than Savannah while Sullivan's delays continued to run on from weeks into months.

Most were entirely beyond his control. Pennsylvania proved as tardy with promised support and supplies as in the years of Bouquet's disappointments. The pacifist Quaker party was openly opposed to the expedition, considering its objective an unwarranted imposition upon inoffensive Indians. Various influential Pennsylvania land interests would secretly have preferred to see Indian attacks on Wyoming continue until the Connecticut intruders had been dispossessed. Of a promised corps of 750 Pennsylvania borderers, much needed by Sullivan for his screen, only a few dozen appeared. Some of his long unpaid New Jersey troops mutinied, and he was aggravated by desertions from other units. By these and similar frustrations he was held at Wyoming for another five weeks. It was only by the extraordinary personal exertions of himself and his officers that, eventually, sufficient boats, wagons, horses, beef cattle, and flour were accumulated to permit him to get his army with its heavy supply and artillery trains moving northward again.

Butler and Brant had been aware since early spring of the dimensions of the menace that was gathering. Butler's host of Tory agents, infesting not only every frontier community but even the ranks of Sullivan's veteran regiments, kept him fully informed. To these reports was added fresher information gained in a series of early spring raids that probed the border from Stone Arabia and the Schoharie in the north to Kittanning and Turtle Creek in the west. The Iroquois were shocked by news of Clark's capture of Hamilton but, having been accustomed to look to Butler, Brant, Johnson, and Haldimand himself as their English contacts, were not so impressed as had been the western Indians by the lieutenant governor's ruin.

Van Shaick's Onondaga attack, moreover, had provided convincing testimony that the Americans would accept peace under no circumstances but at the price of total Indian submission. For this the Iroquois, though increasingly disturbed by reports of the strength of Sullivan's gathering army, were as yet far from ready.

In May John Butler, with 350 Rangers, his son, Walter, second in command, and 14 regulars, commanded by Lieutenant John McDonnell, advanced from Niagara to Canadasaga on Seneca Lake. Thereafter his progress toward Tioga was as slow as that of the invaders. His supply problem was even more excruciating than Sullivan's. Every Iroquois town was well stocked with food, but in the wilderness there existed no transportation facilities or distribution system to permit the accumulation of stores to maintain an army in the field for the duration of a campaign which, as events were to prove, was to be prolonged over a period of six months. The Indians were slower to assemble than had been expected and then in only a third of the number that had been hoped, but in late June Brant, whose services the cabinet had recently rewarded by the bestowal of a full colonel's commission, led an advance guard of 300 to Oghwaga where he could keep a closer watch on the movements of Sullivan and Clinton.

When Sullivan's ponderous advance continued, attempts to distract him by flank attacks were undertaken in late July. McDonnell, after a sudden night march, surprised Fort Freeland on the West Branch, laid waste a number of settlements in the district, and routed a relief force, the several engagements costing an American loss of 16 killed and 30 prisoners and spreading terror along a wide section of the border. To the east, Brant descended again on Minisink, taking captives and cattle and crushing a militia column venturing out from Goshen with a loss variously estimated by the survivors at 40 to 100.

But Sullivan turned a deaf ear to cries for help from either east or west, grimly reminding the supplicants that the one sure way to guard the border was to carry the war to the Indians, and kept on northward through the Susquehanna gorges until he reached Tioga, August 10th. The long expected word having reached the waiting

Clinton, the Second Division had started south from Otsego Lake the day before. His progress was swifter and more dramatic than had been Sullivan's. A dam built to hold back the waters of the lake was broken, and Clinton's 220 supply boats swept southward on a crest of flood water.* Sullivan had feared an attack by Butler on the weaker of the two segments of his army before they could be united, and dispatched a column of 1000 picked men under Hand and Poor to meet Clinton. The precaution was unnecessary, for Butler, his so much inferior force further weakened by sickness and hunger, was unable to undertake any offensive move. The two divisions were united at Tioga on August 22nd.

Four days later Sullivan marched westward to execute Washington's directive instructing him to devastate the Iroquois homeland so thoroughly that their attacks on the frontier would be forever discouraged. After leaving his invalids and a garrison at his fortified base camp at Tioga, he still had in his command nearly 4000 veteran continentals. Aside from its numerical strength it was an army better fitted for the peculiarly trying task of invading Indian country than was any other to be until Anthony Wayne's 14 long years later. Against the greatest of all dangers, surprise attack, which had occasioned the wilderness downfall of so many other regular armies, he was expertly guarded. In his forward and flanking screens were Morgan's Rifles (commanded in this campaign by Major James Parr), a number of special companies of volunteer rangers and borderers, and a contingent of Oneida scouts. Among his officers and advisors were men of the most varied frontier experience, including John Harper, Moses Van Campen, James Deane, John Jenkins, Marinus Willett, William Butler, Peter Gansevoort, Edward Hand, and the Reverend Samuel Kirkland.

Butler, his army of 350 starving Rangers and 400 skeptical Indians outnumbered five to one, had been obliged to watch his opponent's increase in strength while himself remaining unable to interfere. His one chance appeared to him to be the selection of a defensive

---

* To build up the storage of water in the lake a number of beaver dams in the surrounding area were breached. It was soon discovered necessary to keep nightlong guard posts at each site since otherwise the beaver rebuilt their dams each night.

position offering an opportunity for that tactical surprise which alone might offset the imbalance between the two forces. On a wooded ridge in front of the Indian village of Newtown, five miles east of the present Elmira, New York, a ridge Sullivan must cross in continuing his westward advance, Butler established a defense line of breastworks, trenches, and foxholes. Most of his Indians were stationed on a wooded height extending in an arc to his left from which they could descend upon Sullivan's flank at the moment of his frontal attack assault upon the main defense line. These were identical dispositions to those with which at Wyoming and Niagara Butler had achieved overwhelming success. They did not, however, suffice this third time. The essential element of surprise was missing.

At 11 o'clock on the morning of August 29th, Sullivan's forward patrols informed him of the fortified hill confronting his advance. Instead of being encouraged by his own so much superior strength to plunge ahead into Butler's trap, Sullivan held up for three hours until his reconnaissance patrols had made him fully aware of Butler's precise posture. Thereafter it was he, not Butler, who was in control of the situation. He continued to withhold a frontal assault while extending Poor's brigade by his right flank, first to drive the Indians from the height on Butler's left, and then to undertake an enveloping movement. Meanwhile, his artillery opened fire on Butler's whole line. Five-and-a-half-inch howitzer shells, bursting in a forest, splintering trees, and starting fires, create a far greater commotion than on a more open battlefield. Veteran troops accustomed to ordinary cannon fire have often proved unable to endure it for long. Most of the Indians had never before so much as heard a cannonade and even those on a part of the field where the bursts were occurring far behind them were disturbed by an immediate fear that they had been surrounded. Brant, limping from a buckshot wound in his foot incurred in a recent raid, was able still to rally them to resist for a time. He led one counterattack before which one of Poor's regiments momentarily recoiled. But he could soon perceive that Poor's continued advance, pressed relentlessly by disciplined formations clearing each successive thicket by bayonet, threatened a fatal encirclement and so advised Butler. Realizing all opportunity for surprise had evaporated, Butler ordered a general retreat. So immediate was the American pursuit that he himself narrowly escaped capture. His retreat necessarily continued all the way to the Genesee, inasmuch as most of his Indians scattered to their towns to save their families and such of their possessions as they could carry. Resistance to Sullivan's invasion had ended.

Newtown was primarily a matching of tactical maneuvers, more of a chess game than a battle. There had been only two or three flurries of close, hard contact during Poor's enveloping movement. Butler reported 5 Rangers and 12 Indians killed. Sullivan reported 5 killed and 36 wounded. However bloodless, as a tactical victory it could hardly have been more decisive. The Tory-Iroquois alliance which for a twelvemonth had dominated the New York-Pennsylvania frontier had been utterly and completely defeated. The Iroquois heartland, from which for generations loping columns of the continent's fiercest warriors had emerged to despoil the lands of victims far and near, now lay open and defenseless.

Proceeding with the same methodical attention to detail that so far had characterized his campaign, Sullivan embarked on a program of calculated destruction so thorough that it could be expected to eliminate every Iroquois capacity to make war. He left behind his heavier baggage and most of his artillery, and marched steadily northwestward, entering town after town unopposed. The demoralized and despairing inhabitants fled before him so precipitately that he was unable to take prisoners in compliance with Washington's direction that hostages be seized to help insure future Iroquois behavior. The expedition's punitive exertions were limited, therefore, to the destruction of property. This Sullivan's soldiers undertook with great zest and on an awesome scale. Centuries of victory and prosperity had raised the Iroquois standard of living far above the wigwam level. Most of their houses were substantial edifices of log or squared timbers, some were frame, and a few were even painted. Their towns were surrounded by cornfields, gardens, and orchards. They owned herds of cattle and horses, droves of hogs, flocks of poultry. Their storehouses and barns were filled with grain, hay, produce, and smoked fish and meat. As the invaders passed, they left of all this nothing but smoking ruins.

On August 11th Brodhead had, meanwhile, set out from Pittsburgh with a force of 605 regulars and volunteers to attack the Seneca and Mingo towns on the upper Allegheny. Aside from a brush with one Seneca war party en route south to raid the frontier, he encountered no opposition. The Iroquois had been too dispirited by their inability to cope with Sullivan to resist this added threat.

These simultaneous and apparently irresistible invasions, Butler's headlong retreat, and the total demoralization of the Iroquois stirred growing alarm in Niagara, which was still, as in the years of French dominion, the key to the northwest by virtue of its control of the indispensable portage between the St. Lawrence and the western Lakes. But neither Sullivan nor Brodhead estimated his situation with enough assurance to attempt a junction with the other or to undertake a further advance upon Niagara. After burning 11 undefended Allegheny towns, Brodhead returned to Pittsburgh, September 14th, having suffered not a single casualty. Sullivan kept on to the Genesee where he capped his devastations, September 15th, with the destruction of the Great Seneca Castle, the inner citadel of Iroquois militarism, before he, too, turned back.

His approach to the Seneca Castle was marked by the fearful death of Lieutenant Thomas Boyd, an episode that attracted more attention than any other event of the campaign. Boyd, an officer of Morgan's Rifles, had been sent out on a night reconnaissance patrol. His detachment of 25 men, too large for concealment and too small for defense, was detected, surrounded, and overwhelmed by superior numbers. Only eight escaped. Next day the advancing army came upon the bodies, all unspeakably mutilated. The tragic incident had, however, served one purpose. Butler had at last determined to attempt another stand, and had his reassembled and reinforced army of 800 in a concealed position awaiting Sullivan's approach. The commotion attending the encirclement of Boyd had revealed his position and he resumed his retreat.

Upon completing his desolation of the Seneca capital on the Genesee, Sullivan that same day began his withdrawal to the American frontier, separating his army into several columns in order to devastate a number of districts that had been missed during the advance. He regained Tioga September 30th and Easton October 15th, having covered in a month the distance that had required three months on his outward march. His victorious army was greeted by general public rejoicing. It was universally imagined that he had ended the peril to the New York-Pennsylvania frontier. Washington had devoted a large proportion of his so carefully husbanded Continental Army to the task, but to all appearances the enormous risk had been justified. Sullivan had driven the formerly feared Tory-Iroquois horde into dispirited flight, had destroyed 41 Iroquois towns, had forced upon the English the burden of maintaining the thousands of homeless Indians, must surely have permanently impressed the Iroquois with the invincibility of American arms, and all this he had achieved at a cost of only 41 dead, of whom 4 had succumbed to sickness and 2 to accident.

Yet of all these infinitely desirable effects, not one proved to outlast by long the dying echoes of his withdrawing army's drums. It was true enough that the English supply system was taxed by the need to support the Iroquois through the winter, but it was equally true that their total dependence made the Iroquois even more amenable to English wishes. They had been taught to fear a fully organized American regular army, but remained as scornful as before of settlers and settlers' militia. Before the snow was off, they were raiding again and, embittered by the ravage of their homeland, were more bent than ever on ravaging that of their enemy. During that harsh winter following a summer marked by so many American victories, all Indians, east and west, finally faced up to the comfortless fact that for them there was no longer a choice between peace and war. The English army post represented the sole source for the implements, guns, gunpowder, and gun repair upon which the survival of their hunting society depended, and the price insistently exacted was active support' of the English war effort. The Americans, meanwhile, had no better counteroffer than submission and dispossession. The American border offensive of 1779, with all its remarkable successes ranging from Vincennes to Newtown, had served no more than as a delaying action. For the next three years the frontier suffered even more painfully than during the earlier years of the Revolution. The military lesson was pounded relentlessly home. As long as the English held Niagara and Detroit, so long must the American frontier remain in jeopardy. That was to prove a very long time, indeed. Neither was occupied by the United States for another 17 years.

XIV

ॐ

The Frontier People

THE MAJOR BATTLES and sieges of the Revolution's border war
—Vincennes, Oriskany, Newtown, Wyoming, Boonesborough,
Donnally, Wheeling—had had effects impinging only upon the outer
circumference of decision. The actual and totally decisive issue remained the capacity of the inhabitants to endure trials and dangers
which each year of the conflict had become more severe. The dooryard of the average settler was the decisive battlefield, and the fortitude of his ragged and hungry family was the determining factor.

The frontier people who bore up under this ordeal were by 1779
beginning much more strikingly to manifest those traits of self-
reliance, intransigence, and adaptability which have set them apart
from all other peoples and contributed so notably to the total American character. This was a phenomenon even more extraordinary
than it then appeared. Ordinarily, characteristics so sharply divergent
develop in a human strain only through generations of transition. In
them they had developed in one. The frontier people of the Revolution were as distinct from their fathers' generation as they were
from Chinese or Hottentots. The Indian onslaughts of 1755 and
1763 had driven them into terrified flight or helpless submission, yet

in 1769 and 1775 they had become a people so different that they were crossing the mountain barrier in the face of the same Indian danger and were now defying a far greater one. For a period so brief this represented a tremendous change. In the interval there had occurred, if not the birth of a nation, certainly the birth of a people.

The spontaneity of the transition was made the more remarkable in that it had developed in a population that had appeared so little prepared for it. The settlement of the old frontier east of the mountains during the first half of the eighteenth century had represented the last outward lap of the era's tide of trans-Atlantic immigration. The new inhabitants had sought land in the edges of the wilderness because only there could it be had cheaply enough for them to hope to possess. A very large proportion of them were of varying tongues and nationalities, Germans, Scotch-Irish, Huguenots, and of the English stock most were ex-redemptioners or colonies of imported indigents introduced by great landowners. The confused newcomers had been unacquainted with any of the demands of a primitive background. Among their many diversities their one conformity was extreme poverty. The problem of clearing enough land in time to raise enough to eat was their great concern. They had occupied their new homes at a time when border peace had long prevailed. They were no more familiar with the realities of Indian war than they had been before leaving their former European homes. Even after the crisis was upon them, they had had little impulse to band together for mutual defense. Bred in tight little old-world communities, they continued to regard their unfamiliar neighbors as strangers and therefore suspect. Accustomed to order and governmental authority, they thought only of awaiting an army's hastening to their rescue. They were slow to perceive how much they had in common in their common danger.

The shocks of 1755 and 1763 could, therefore, have been expected to break the spirit of a people who seemed to have so little instinct for self-preservation. But instead of a breaking point these led to a turning point. Possibly they had been partially prepared to meet the challenge by the variety of lesser demands that had already been made upon them, the uprooting from their ancestral background, the miseries of the ocean crossing, the outlandish novelties of the new world, the grinding rigors of their attempt to maintain a family in a forest clearing. At any rate, the turning came as extemporaneously and as impulsively as an accidental explosion. One year the terrorized settlers were too demoralized to attempt to defend themselves, the next they had themselves become the aggressors, and the year after they were crossing the mountains into the Indian country. Prolonged suffering had miraculously served not to crush but to arouse them. The vitalization was fostered by the sudden rise among them of a scattering of natural leaders. These had been produced by the stresses of the times as erratically as sports appear among plants under abnormal conditions. The more noteworthy were the long hunters who first ventured into the transmountain wilderness and the militia colonels of the Valley of Virginia and the Holston who had forged the frontier's first military effort, but there were others of the most widely varying types. The frontier people had as suddenly become ready to respond to leadership. They had been made so by dangers which were proving extinction the sole alternative. So desperate was their need that the initiative of one aggressive member of a community had become enough immediately to rally his formerly bewildered and discouraged neighbors about him. The process was illustrated by the career of James Smith of Pennsylvania.

He was captured at eighteen while serving as packer with Braddock, and spent his next five years in Indian captivity.* After his escape and return to his frontier home, he roused his neighbors to a more belligerent resistance, even persuading them to paint themselves red and black and, instead of awaiting attack, to sally from their stockades to meet approaching Indian war parties in the woods. In 1764 he was one of the few Pennsylvania borderers who served with distinction in Bouquet's Muskingum expedition. In 1765 he demonstrated the frontier's new aggressiveness by leading his Black Boys in attacks on government packtrains carrying conference presents intended to appease the Ohio Indians. In 1766, having through

---

* He wrote a book entitled *An Account of the Remarkable Occurrences in the Life and Travels of Colonel James Smith,* describing in fascinating detail life in a contemporary Indian town, which was published in Lexington, Kentucky, in 1799.

his Indian contacts gained an inkling that a great Iroquois land sale was in the wind, he determined to make a personal inspection of western lands so that he might be in a position to pre-empt the best. In so short a time his imagination had proved able to bridge the stupendous gap between the trials of Indian captivity and the prospects of seizing upon acreage 800 miles deep in the Indian country. With five companions he passed through Cumberland Gap, explored, among other regions, the enchanting middle reaches of the Cumberland, and descended the Tennessee to its mouth. Here his companions went on to the comparatively tranquil Illinois, but Smith, alone, except for a mulatto boy, Jamie, returned overland through the Kentucky hunting grounds of the fiercely contentious Shawnee to the Holston, where he was arrested as a suspicious character because his account of his movements was considered incredible. It was obviously a little too early to undertake to settle the distant Cumberland, but he soon took a part in the establishment of the first settlements west of the mountains on the Monongahela and served as colonel of militia during the Revolution. The range of his personal experiences had thus enabled him to play every most significant frontier role, Indian captive, beleaguered settler, long hunter, land seeker, pioneer, border commander, but most of all to serve as a personal example capable of stirring an emulative resolution among his fellow settlers.

In attempting to account for the extraordinary resilience of the frontier people, one singular trait stands out among the impulses by which they were moved. This was the prevalence among them of an inextinguishable optimism. From occasional seizures of the deepest depression they immediately recovered. The more bitterly dissatisfied they were with their present condition, the more certain they were that it was bound to improve. The less attractive the land they possessed, the more alluring appeared the land awaiting them somewhere farther to the west. With their homes in ashes and their neighbors dead or fleeing, they remained persuaded that these, though grievous, were but passing afflictions. And no matter how desperate their own situation, they were always confident that elsewhere all must be going better. Bad news they were eager to reject or judge much exaggerated. In more favorable rumors, however wild, they placed immediate credence. For them the war was forever on the verge of ending, the Indians always preparing to submit, victory was perpetually in sight, and prosperity in the most distant west about to come within the reach of all.

Their actions confirmed this optimism. It represented a state of mind so persistent that it extended beyond confidence in their own fate to an equal confidence in the fate of their country. Captain John Bowyer, reporting on his innumerable difficulties with the muster, transport, and supply of his local militia company, interjected a reference to his frontier community's impression of Washington's recent Brandywine and Germantown defeats and the consequent fall of Philadelphia: "I sepose you have learned before this time That General Washington has give How a Compleat Drubing near Schoolkill." George Morgan, reporting in the spring of 1778 on the general progress of the war for the benefit of David Zeisberger at his remote Delaware mission, assured him: "I think our affairs below are in a good way and hope this Summer will put an end to the Contest." Colonel John Campbell, in his famous express to Clark at the Falls in June of 1778 informing him of the French alliance, further informed him that "General How is said to be on the Wing from Philadelphia and I hope to have the pleasure of informing you soon that there is not a British Soldier except Prisoners on any part of the Continent of America." This all-pervading and unquenchable optimism is more revealing, however, when evidenced in connection with any frontier inhabitant's daily affairs. Gabriel Madison, a settler among whose cousins were a President of William and Mary College, a Bishop of Virginia, a future Governor of Kentucky, and a future President of the United States, wrote in a family letter announcing his intention of setting off down the Ohio to Kentucky, "I shall leave this place in a day or two for the falls," then mentioned in passing, "there is Certain Accounts Brought to Pitt that the Indians are very thick on the river," and returned to the subject only in a postscript: "I shall rite to you by the first opy (opportunity) from the falls if I get there."

Given this optimistic determination of a whole people to believe only good news, the reports of the 1779 victories of Clark, Sullivan, Brodhead, and Shelby produced an immediate and profound effect. The spectacle of Hamilton's progress as a prisoner through one frontier district after another was seized upon as unmistakably supporting evidence that the war in the west must already have been won.* People who had been listening for years to stories of the fabulous excellence of Kentucky land and who in any event invariably assumed any distant land to be in every respect superior to any they had so far known became convinced that unless they made haste they would be too late to obtain their share. That fall hundreds of families toiled over the Wilderness Road to Kentucky. With the next spring's high water hundreds of boats carried an even greater rush down the Ohio. The Indians had by then recovered from the shocks of Vincennes and Newtown, but there were so many craft at once on the river that most passed unscathed through Indian attacks which, though persistent, cut off only the more unfortunate.

Contemporary estimates placed the six months' increase in Kentucky's population at nearly 20,000. The inhabitants' formerly precarious position was momentarily so bolstered that for the first time in Kentucky's history people felt able to emerge from their stockades to build their own cabins on their own land. Not only was Kentucky materially reinforced, but a new and separate western colony was established that winter on the southern bend of the Cumberland at the site of the present Nashville, Tennessee.

This sudden, unpremeditated, almost convulsive, westward surge was as extraordinary as it was significant. It was the supreme demonstration of the frontier people's unique and absolute genius for reaching directly for what they wanted without regard for danger or difficulty. The first two great pulses in the westward movement, those of 1769 and 1775, had come during periods of border peace. But this third and greater surge of 1779–80 came in the midst of a desperate war which had been waged the most violently of all along the frontier and which was still many long painful years from being

---

* John Stuart had died March 26th while Hamilton was an eastbound prisoner of war. England had thus been suddenly deprived at the outset of the 1779 campaign season of her chief Indian administrators, in the south as well as in the west.

won. The people making it were, for all their outward assurance, far from oblivious to the new hazards they were courting. They were inhabitants of the Holston and the upper Ohio who had been fighting for years to hold the homes they already occupied, who had been confined to their stockades for many months of each of those years, and who were bitterly familiar with all the recurring horrors and dreary vicissitudes of border war. Yet they were on the spur of the moment pushing on hundreds of miles westward to new homes on the Kentucky and the Cumberland where, as no one knew better than they, they must find every peril intensified.

One final deterrent, an astounding natural prodigy, accompanied their westward lunge like an ominous and infinitely dismal orchestration. The winter of 1779–80 was by far the coldest of which there is any record or memory. In the east, Long Island Sound, New York harbor, the Delaware, the Chesapeake, and the Potomac were solidly frozen over and snow became everywhere so deep that all travel and most business was suspended. In the midcontinental west, the season from early December to late February was even more frigid. All lesser streams froze to the bottom. Ice formed many feet thick on rivers as far south as the Cumberland and the Tennessee. Prevented from feeding by the depth of the snow, vast herds of buffalo, deer, and elk perished. Most of the settlers' cattle and hogs died from the cold. Birds fell, stiffened, from the trees. Much of the cane was killed. Trees, their heartwood frozen, split with reports like gunshots. Many emigrants, snowbound among the ridges and gorges of the Wilderness Road, lost their stock and starved until they were staggering skeletons by the time they finally reached Kentucky. Yet as soon as spring floods released the flow of rivers, the westward rush was resumed by raft or boat by other hundreds of families. These were a people who had decided to move west.

The difficulties were to persist and to multiply. The Indian war, far from having been won, blazed up more furiously than ever, and was to continue for many more bitter years. Spain was soon to deny them their one hope of a market by closing the Mississippi. Their own country was for long to ignore their interests. They were unable even to maintain possession of the land they had come to obtain. But by none of these enormous disappointments were they in the least discouraged.

Of all their disappointments, the land problem provided the most acute. On January 22, 1779, Virginia had at last enacted a definitive land-tenure statute, and in September had sent out a commission headed by Colonel William Fleming, the heroic veteran of Point Pleasant, to attempt to disentangle the infinite confusion of competing and overlapping Kentucky land claims. The act had paid lip service to regard for the rights of actual settlers, but was so entangled with legalistic obscurities that hundreds of thousands of acres passed into the hands of eastern speculators and few of those families who struggled westward that winter and spring ever succeeded in gaining final titles.

Another of Virginia's efforts in behalf of the frontier that year was more effective, if only temporarily so. Governor Henry directed the organization of a punitive expedition to put an end to Dragging Canoe's Chickamauga raids on the Holston, the Wilderness Road, and Kentucky. In April of 1779, Colonel Evan Shelby assembled an army of 600 volunteers at Long Island on the Holston, including a North Carolina contingent under Major Charles Robertson and Colonel John Montgomery's Virginia battalion which had been raised to reinforce Clark. Instead of attempting to advance through the mountains upon the Chickamauga towns, situated near the junction of the present state lines of Tennessee, Alabama, and Georgia, Shelby elected to make his enterprise a naval expedition. He built boats and canoes and swept southward on the spring high water of the Holston and the Tennessee. This totally unexpected method of approach, so swift and silent, took the Chickamauga completely by surprise. They resisted only long enough to permit their women and children to escape. Shelby burned all eleven of their towns. A considerable booty of horses, furs, trade goods, and war supplies from the English base at Pensacola was taken. Montgomery kept on down the Tennessee to join Clark in the Illinois. The remainder of the army rode back up river on the captured horses. The military effect of the expedition was negligible. Dragging Canoe's followers had suffered a loss of only six warriors. They had soon

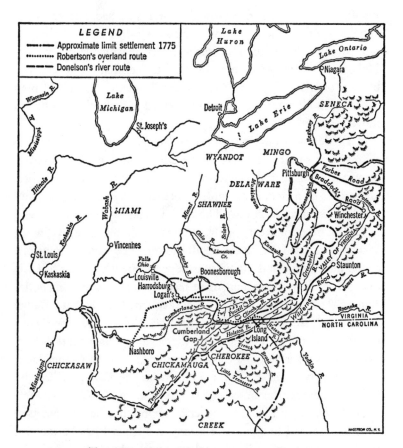

THE WAY WEST DURING THE REVOLUTION

The two major routes followed by the westward movement were governed by the breaches in the mountain barrier provided by the two military roads in the north and by the pre-Revolutionary extension of settlement along the Holston toward Cumberland Gap in the south. In the north settlers crossed the mountains by either Forbes' or Braddock's road, then traveled by boat down the Ohio to Limestone Creek where they followed the Great Buffalo Trace to the Kentucky settlements. In the south they pushed directly westward over the 200 miles of mountain trail which became the segment of the route to which the term Wilderness Road was primarily attached.

rebuilt their towns, had replanted their crops, had received fresh supplies from Pensacola, and were resuming their raids. An important psychological effect, however, was that meanwhile many more Holston residents had been encouraged to feel that the routes west by way of the Wilderness Road or the Tennessee River had been made much safer and had therefore decided to make their westward move forthwith.

In all this westward surge of 1779-80, there was no segment so dramatic or so representative of the effort and danger involved as the founding of central Tennessee. Like most such migratory undertakings of the period, it was much more carefully planned than outward appearances indicated. The country about the southern bend of the Cumberland, commonly referred to at the time as French Lick, or Big Salt Lick, or the Bend, had long been known to be one of the most fertile and inviting in the west. French traders had frequented it for 70 years, and more recently many long hunters, including James Smith, Casper Mansker, Michael Stoner, Daniel Boone, and Anthony and Isaac Bledsoe, had enthusiastically reported upon the attractiveness of the region. Three years before, Clark had filed a Virginia claim to 3000 acres on the Cumberland. In 1778 thirty fugitive Tory families from the Carolinas had, by Indian indulgence, taken temporary refuge there.

Therefore, when Richard Henderson approached James Robertson with his proposal to establish a colony at French Lick, he found a ready and sympathetic listener who was already familiar with the subject. Henderson's original settlement of Kentucky had passed from his control when Virginia had claimed that region as a county, but he was confident that the southern portion of his 1775 Cherokee purchase, along the middle Cumberland, would prove to be in North Carolina when the Virginia-North Carolina boundary line, then being run westward over the mountains, was completely surveyed. He proposed, therefore, to establish a second new colony and, just as he had selected Daniel Boone to found Boonesborough, he had elected now to recruit Robertson.

Henderson could have hit upon no better man for his purpose. James Robertson had been among the first settlers on the Watauga, had commanded a company at Point Pleasant, and had been a frontier tower of strength in every emergency since. He embarked upon the enterprise with vigor and a most practical attention to detail. In the winter of 1778–79, he led a small party to the Cumberland to see the country for himself and to arrange for the planting of a first corn crop. He then went on to the Illinois to make sure that no loose ends were left dangling with respect to Clark's interests. His bargain with Clark was simple. If the boundary survey when completed placed the land in Virginia, he would deal with Clark, otherwise with Henderson. Returning overland to the Holston, he seized the opportunity to bring with him a string of the Spanish-bred horses much in demand in Virginia.

Upon his return he undertook the organization of his colonization project. With him was now an associate of comparable vigor and initiative, John Donelson. According to their carefully prepared plan, which was successfully carried out in every detail, Robertson with a part of the men and the livestock would circle overland through Kentucky; Donelson, with the rest of the men, the women, and children, and all the heavier stores, would go by boat down the Tennessee to the Ohio and then back up the Cumberland to their common destination. Robertson's overland party was much oppressed by the terrible winter, lost some of their stock, but kept on, crossed the Cumberland on the ice, and began building cabins, having even persuaded en route a number of Kentucky-bound families to join them.

The same unnatural winter stranded Donelson almost before he had started. He had built a flotilla of shallow draft barges to transport some 35 family groups, their furniture, farm equipment, and supplies. Nearly half were carried aboard his flagship, christened *Adventure,* a huge heavily timbered scow of proportions to make it a direct prototype of the later Ohio River flatboats. In the party were Robertson's wife and five children and Donelson's daughter, Rachel, later the wife of Andrew Jackson.

Resuming the voyage with the return of warmer weather late in February, Donelson on March 7th approached the Chickamauga country, devastated by Shelby the spring before. In addition to the Indian danger, this was the leg of the journey presenting the most threatening navigational perils. Here the mountains became more precipitous and the river narrowed to boil through rock-studded gorges. One whirlpool, commonly called The Suck, had been recognized as a particular hazard since a first mention in De Soto's journals. The first day, as the fleet approached the gorges, the Indians appeared to hesitate to attack so large and strong a party, but the second day they pounced on a weakness in its defenses. The Watauga contingent, commanded by Thomas Stuart, had been stricken by an outbreak of smallpox and by agreement their boats were following at some little distance in order to avoid contaminating the others. The Indians overwhelmed this trailing and weaker division of the flotilla, killing and capturing all. Of the 28 men, women, and children there was but one known survivor, the six-year-old Thomas Stuart, Jr., later ransomed.*

The main party could hear the screams of the victims behind them, but were prevented by the swiftness of the current from attempting assistance and were by then themselves intensely preoccupied with the difficulties of passing The Suck, now immediately before them. The Indian sniping from the wooded slopes overhanging the gorge was increasing and one man had already been killed. John Cotton's canoe overturned in the rapids and the Indian fire was concentrated on the rescuers. Four persons were hit in the boat of Abel Gower, Robertson's brother-in-law. Gower's young daughter, Nancy, seized the tiller and had steered the boat through the rapids before the blood soaking outward through her clothing revealed to her companions the fact that she, too, had been wounded.

All the other boats got past The Suck except the small one of John Jennings, containing his wife, a friend of the family, Mrs. Ephraim Peyton, whose husband had gone overland with Robert-

* The Cherokee were already suffering from a smallpox epidemic during which 2500 died.

son, her baby to which she had given birth the night before, Jennings' teenage son, another young white man, a young Negro, and a Negro woman. Jennings' boat lodged on a rock. The Indians, perceiving his predicament, closed in along the adjacent shore. Jennings, a noted marksman, stood them off while ordering the three young men to throw overboard the cargo to lighten the boat. All three, however, terrified by the tumult, dove into the river and attempted to swim to the farther shore. The Negro drowned and the two white youths were captured.* The three women, though the clothing of each had repeatedly been frayed by the Indians' almost pointblank fire, assumed the task of casting out the cargo, then jumped into the water to rock the boat, and finally succeeded in shoving it free. Two days later Jennings overtook the fleet in his waterlogged and bullet-riddled craft. Of the five who had stayed with their battle-scarred ship, only the day-old baby was lost, whether by gunshot or drowning was not recorded. In his journal Donelson remarked that even after the variety of trials to which she had in the three days been subjected, Mrs. Peyton's "health appears to be good at this time."

Sporadic attacks by Indians following along the shore continued to afflict the expedition for the next week. There were repeated alarms; five more men were wounded, but there were no more killed. As they drew farther from the Chickamauga country, the attacks dwindled and finally ceased. On March 20th the Ohio was reached. Here a number of families, including that of Donelson's own son-in-law, decided to head for Natchez or the Illinois instead of struggling back up the Cumberland to a location where they would again be within reach of the Chickamauga. Donelson and thirty families persisted, however, and labored up river. Their food supply had been exhausted by the unforeseen duration of their winter-delayed journey and they subsisted on buffalo, excessively lean after the hard winter, and greens collected along the banks. On March 31st they were cheered by a fortuitous encounter in the midst of this remote wilderness with the indefatigable Henderson, engaged in the boundary survey. He further encouraged them with the assur-

---

* The one was burned at the stake, but young Jennings was ransomed by the trader, John Rogers, an ancestor of Will Rogers.

ance that there was no longer doubt that the new Cumberland settlement was situated south of the Virginia border.*

The fleet reached its destination April 24th, four months and two days after the boats had been boarded at Long Island. Donelson noted in his journal: "This day we arrived at our journey's end at the Big Salt Lick, where we have the pleasure of finding Capt. Robertson and his company. It is a source of satisfaction to us to be enabled to restore to him and others their families and friends, who were entrusted to our care, and who, some time since, perhaps, despaired of ever meeting again." But there was also, as was always the case with movers who had struggled desperately westward toward their new homes in the wilderness, the inevitable letdown as the newcomers for the first time candidly surveyed their new situation. Donelson testified to this in the next sentence of his journal: "Though our prospects at present are dreary, we have found a few log cabins which have been built on a cedar bluff above the Lick by Capt. Robertson and company."

The new settlement got at once to the first business of every new settlement. An ordinance for self-government was drafted and signed or marked by the 256 resident adult males. The central station was named Nashborough (later Nashville),† after Francis Nash, a North Carolina officer who had fallen at Germantown. The new community had need for all the coherence it could muster. Its capacity to endure was almost at once tested by a series of Indian attacks more persistent than had marked the first year of any other new settlement. Not only the Chickamauga, but the Creek and even the Chickasaw, considered the new settlers trespassers who must at any cost be expelled. The first assault struck the outlying Renfro's Station. The death list ran to 20 and only one woman escaped. Among those killed in succeeding attacks were some of the

---

* The Virginia surveying party had, in addition, veered 12 miles north of the true line which accounts for the curious jog in Tennessee's northern boundary still observable on maps today.

† Earlier settlements of the Revolutionary period were customarily given English names, e.g., Harrodsburg, Boonesborough, Leestown, but after the French alliance there was a tendency to favor more Gallicized forms such as Louisville, Nashville, Maysville.

colony's most notable figures, including John Jennings, Abel Gower and his son, Abel, William Neely, a long hunter who had accompanied Robertson on his first visit to the Cumberland, and Robertson's oldest son, James. The scanty reserves of food and ammunition were failing and the ability to continue resistance appeared more and more doubtful. Few frontier leaders were more experienced than Donelson. He had for many years taken a prominent part in the Holston frontier's wars and disputes with the Cherokee, had served as a militia captain in the 1777 defense of Boonesborough, and had abundantly proved his resolution on the recent river journey. Basing his judgment on this long experience, he decided defense of the settlement was no longer feasible and removed with his family to Kentucky.*

Robertson, however, was resolved to stand fast and persuaded the majority of the settlers to stand with him. Continuing hostilities interfered so drastically with planting and harvesting that hunger remained a constant concern. Ammunition ran short. That winter Robertson made a hasty trip to Kentucky to hunt for supplies and to make a vain attempt to recruit additional settlers. The day of his return was enlivened by the birth of his son, Felix, and another attack on his station in which Major Robert Lucas, local militia commander, was killed. But Robertson's determination to stay was unshaken. Depredations along the Cumberland, the most exposed of all frontiers, continued almost without interruption until 1794. The inhabitants remained stubbornly immovable.

Any attempt to appraise the unique qualities of the frontier people must give particular attention to the section of the frontier extending through the Valley of Virginia to the Holston. It was among these narrow valleys and steep ridges that their peculiar genius reached its fullest expression. That memorable region had provided the dynamic center from which had radiated the chief impulses achieving settlement of the Monongahela, the Kentucky, and the Cumberland, and continued during the Revolution to constitute the

* Four years later he was killed by Indians while en route from the Kentucky to the Georgia frontier. His widow and family returned from Kentucky to reside on his Cumberland lands.

central citadel of frontier strength. Its inhabitants had been the first to cross the mountain barrier to the banks of streams flowing west. They had furnished the first long hunters and, in 1766, the first rude intruders to press on toward the upper Ohio in defiance not only of Indian displeasure but of the English army's. They had in 1773 furnished the first surveyors of Kentucky, and in 1774 by their own unaided initiative they had defeated the Shawnee in the decisive frontier war, so absurdly miscalled Dunmore's War, which had finally cleared their way to Kentucky. In the Cherokee War of 1776, they had held their border and then forced Cherokee acquiescence in the further advance of their settlement down the Holston. In 1777 they alone had dispatched defenders to the support of the beleaguered stations of Kentucky. In 1779 they had occupied the Cumberland and had added thousands of their boldest to the occupation of Kentucky. Now, in the spring of 1780, they were confronted by the most exigent of all the many demands that had so far been made upon them. This new danger sprang not from the wilderness they so long had faced, but from the seaboard behind them.

On May 12, 1780, Charleston had fallen. Cornwallis was moving northward, intent on restoring English dominion from Florida to Maryland. His advance was accompanied by the ruthless devastations of his two lieutenants, Lieutenant Colonel Banastre Tarleton and Major Robert Ferguson, devoted to the punishment of Patriot inhabitants and the mobilization of their Tory rivals. Everywhere across the south detachments of Tories and Patriots were marching and countermarching, making night dashes and dawn attacks, lying in wait and achieving surprises, burning and pillaging, paying off old scores and running up new ones. These local campaigns were being savagely waged, with quarter seldom given and little concern for the fate of noncombatants. Many guerrilla bands, without serious political leanings, saw in the general disorder their opportunity to murder and rob indiscriminately. As a final confusion, Creek and Cherokee war parties, persuaded by their English advisors that the time at last had come to move in support of an English army in the field, were contributing their special talents to the universal tumult.

The northward surge of this tide of destruction drove hundreds of refugees to the sanctuary of the Holston. Despite the near certainty that the success of the English offensive would precipitate a new Cherokee invasion of their own region, the inhabitants decided to dispatch aid to their hard-pressed compatriots east of the mountains. While Colonel John Sevier remained behind to hold the border against the expected Cherokee attack, Colonel Isaac Shelby in July crossed the mountains with 400 mounted riflemen. This unique corps of frontier cavalry, able to move with extraordinary rapidity and to strike with an aimed fire power of shocking force, was a reinforcement of such importance that retreating detachments of North Carolina militia were able to reassemble and briefly to mount a counteroffensive. In a whirlwind two-week campaign the Tory garrison of Thicketty Fort was forced to surrender, one of Ferguson's columns was defeated at Cedar Spring with a loss of 30 casualties and 50 prisoners, and Colonel Alexander Innes was routed at Musgrove's Mill with a loss of 63 killed, 90 wounded, and 70 captured. The effect of these local successes was dissipated, however, by the crushing defeat of Gates' main army at Camden, August 16th, and the succeeding collapse of formal American resistance in the Carolinas. Shelby returned to the Holston to rejoin Sevier and to reorganize for the imminent greater emergency.

Cornwallis, delayed by sickness among his troops, the midsummer heat, the need to refit, and the gadfly attacks of roving bands of still defiant Patriot partisans, was unable to resume his northward advance until late September. Ferguson, in command of his left flanking force, marched along the eastern slopes of the mountains, ravaging each district as he passed, and as he approached the Catawba dispatched an insolent threat to the Holston that he "would march his army over the mountains; hang their leaders, and lay their country waste."

Ferguson's taunt was not needed to arouse the Holston. From the moment of Shelby's return the westerners had remained as determined as before to support their fellow countrymen in the east. Sevier and Shelby, the colonels, respectively, of North Carolina's two Holston counties of Washington and Sullivan, had agreed upon a rule of thumb by which roughly half their men able to bear arms

would be retained at home to guard against the still expected Cherokee attack and the other half devoted to the expedition. An appeal
for backing of the enterprise was sent to William Campbell, colonel
of Virginia's Holston county, also named Washington. Campbell
was briefly delayed by his preoccupation with suppressing an insurrection of New River Tories whose hopes had been reinvigorated by
news of Camden, but he arrived at the appointed time. The rendezvous was held September 25th at Sycamore Shoals, a site already
made historic by the Cherokee Purchase which had led to the
settlement of Boonesborough. Sevier brought 240 men, Shelby
another 240, and Campbell 200 to which, before the expedition
marched, were added another 200 Virginians enlisted by his cousin,
Arthur Campbell.* The westerners were accompanied by 160 refugee
militiamen from eastern North Carolina under Colonel Charles
McDowell.

The long column of buckskin-clad riflemen crossed the mountains
among peaks already covered with snow and dropped down on the
headwaters of the Catawba. Here they were joined by remnants of
local militia, raising the army's total to 1500. The Holston force had
been raised without waiting for any sort of governmental authoriza-
tion and, since they were now embarked upon a campaign in conjunction with more formally raised troops, a tactful appeal was sent
to Gates to assign them a commander. In the meantime, William
Campbell, commanding the largest Holston regiment, was selected
to serve, and they continued to move too fast ever to receive Gates'
reply. Ferguson, informed of the sudden change in his situation by
two American deserters, relieved his feelings by a proclamation denouncing his new antagonists as "Back Water men," "barbarians,"
and "a set of mongrels," but he was too experienced a soldier not to
appreciate the menace that loomed before him. He began at once a
curiously indecisive retreat toward the South Carolina border during
which he marched 60 miles the first two days and then idled the

---

* Sevier's recently wedded young wife, Catherine, who had leaped into his arms
at the siege of Fort Caswell and had now undertaken the responsibilities of a household that already contained ten children, devoted these days of her honeymoon to the
campaign outfitting of her bridegroom and the three of the sons who were over
sixteen.

next two days. Campbell pressed his pursuit with a picked detachment of the 900 men of his command who possessed the best horses.

On October 6, 1780, Ferguson, for reasons never made clear, announced with a petulant display of defiance his decision to hold up his flight toward the protection of Cornwallis' main army and instead to stand and give battle. He may have been overimpressed by the natural defensive strength of his camp site on King's Mountain. This was a low, though steep, brush-covered, rock-studded, flat-topped hill surrounded on all sides by forest. His army of 1100 was composed, aside from several staff officers from the English regular establishment, of professionally drilled and equipped Tory regiments, most of them from the Carolinas, but including elements from New York and New Jersey. Most of them had been as long organized and as well trained as the most seasoned of Washington's continentals.

The pursuing Americans, their number increased to 1200 by a last-minute junction with several South Carolina militia units, approached King's Mountain toward noon on the 7th, dismounted, encircled the hill, and prepared immediately to attack. James Collins, a 16-year-old participant, for the rest of his life vividly recalled the temper of these frontier volunteers, led by commanders they had elected among their neighbors: "Each leader made a short speech in his own way to his men, desiring every coward to be off immediately."

It had been a cloudy morning with a thin rain but in the afternoon, just before the American assault, the sun came out. Ferguson was astounded by the precipitancy of the attack and the vigor with which it was pressed but, riding back and forth among his defense formations, organized an obstinate resistance. The Americans, holding their fire, attempted straight off to rush the crest, engaging the array of English bayonets with rifle butts, hunting knives, and tomahawks. Captain Abraham De Peyster, Ferguson's second in command, remarked uneasily that they were "the same yelling devils that were at Musgrove's Mill."

The immediately developing battle lasted less than an hour, but was fought with desperate ferocity. The Americans were repeatedly repulsed from the edge of the hilltop by the local bayonet charges of Ferguson's disciplined Provincials. They met the challenge by resort to the traditional Indian tactic in coping with regulars under forest conditions. They gave way readily before the bayonet charges but at the same time undertook enveloping and encircling movements, forcing the advance as hastily to withdraw, then resumed the assault. In the earlier stages the field was dominated by the deadly accuracy of the American rifle fire. It was the defenders, not the attackers, who were suffering the far heavier casualties. This advantage was presently lessened as the continuous firing produced clouds of smoke which limited visibility to a few yards. The decisive surge to victory was generated by the readiness of the attackers to close in and to persist in driving ahead until they had driven their assault home. These undisciplined volunteers had risen to a sustained offensive pitch of which only veteran regulars are ordinarily considered capable.

Sevier's division was first to reach the crest but was soon met there by Shelby, driving up from the other side of the hill, who greeted him with the quizzical observation: "They've singed off your hair." Ferguson, still endeavoring to rally his forces, was killed. The American pressure converging from all sides was becoming irresistible. Many of the defenders were beginning to wave white flags, but so great was the confusion that it was some time before the firing could be halted. De Peyster at last managed to complete a formal surrender. Except for a few fugitives who crawled away through the underbrush, Ferguson's entire army had been killed or taken prisoner. There was a strong disposition to deny quarter to many who were identified as having been partisan leaders guilty of past atrocities, but Sevier and Shelby succeeded in saving the remainder of the prisoners after nine had been hanged. Due to the heterogeneous character of the hastily assembled American army, estimates of its casualties remained incomplete. It was generally considered at the time that the loss in killed approximated 75. Brigadier General William Davidson, who was on his way to assume command but who arrived after the battle, reported Ferguson's loss included 150 killed and 810 prisoners.

The victory at King's Mountain had far-reaching consequences not only as a turning point in the war in the south but in its effect on the course of the Revolution as a whole. It forced Cornwallis to give up hope of establishing effective Tory control of the Carolinas and delayed his projected advance into Virginia by a full year. This was a fatal delay, as was to be evidenced by Yorktown. Far from least among its consequences was its moral effect west of the mountains. It was a final and unmistakable signal that the frontier had come of age. The frontier people had long since proved their capacity to defend their homes. Now they had demonstrated their readiness also to defend their country. Many westerners were not yet fully convinced that they had a country, but the men who had fought at King's Mountain were thereafter sure that they had one and that they were a part of it.

XV

ၦ

1780

THE EXCEPTIONAL RIGORS of the hard winter were accompanied by one compensation. For months the frozen wilderness lay silent and without movement. Each frontier community was obliged to feel concern only for its own inner struggle with starvation. But along with the merciful absence of threat from without there was also a disturbing absence of news from anywhere, whether of friend or enemy. Even rumor had been stilled. What might be brewing at English bases and in Indian towns could only be conjectured. In their enforced seclusion people brooded over the possibilities to be revealed by spring. There was much reason for hope that the successes of 1779 might have very considerably improved their situation. Then came the sudden thaw, the raising of the curtain, and the suspense was ended. What was revealed were greater confusions, starker threats, and more deadly dangers than any they so far had experienced. Though with the spring came a rush of new settlers, most of them were less able to contribute help than were in need of help, and along with them came a whirlwind of Indian raids, striking earlier and more viciously than ever.

What had happened during the winter was that the English high command had determined to renew in 1780 with more vigor than before the effort to implement its basic strategic plan for winning the war. As it had been since the outset, this was, brutally and simply, to suppress the Revolution by driving the frontier in upon the seaboard centers of population. The 1780 opening move in this campaign was the promotion of more general and more thoroughly organized Indian raids. The Indians lent themselves to this renewed effort with more ardor than they had formerly evidenced. A winter's reflection on the American victories of 1779 had served to remind them the more forcibly that their English friends were their sole source of supplies and that the settlers, on the other hand, were their mortal enemies. The second phase in the over-all design for 1780 was coincidentally to revitalize the Tory movement in as many frontier districts as possible. The measurable success of this program was partly due to the continuing tendency of eastern Tories to move to the frontier, and partly to the increasing number of former Patriots who had come to the conclusion the Revolution could never be won. The third, and most ominous, development in the design was the launching of strong invasion columns from Montreal, Oswego, Niagara, Detroit, and Mackinac to exert concentric pressures on the frontier in conjunction with the major and more orthodox military effort of Clinton and Cornwallis to repossess the southern states. From the headwaters of the Connecticut to the tidal plains of Georgia, the frontier was beset by attackers, ranging from raiding parties of a dozen warriors to invasions by armies of a thousand, supported by white battalions equipped with artillery.

In the north, the New York frontier had confidently expected that Sullivan's triumphant devastation of the Iroquois country the year before had blunted, if not ended, the Iroquois menace. The reverse proved true. In failing to move on the English base at Niagara, Sullivan had left the Iroquois capacity to make war little impaired. The new year had scarcely begun before they were back, vengefully determined to visit upon white communities as much as or more than theirs had suffered. As early as February they were making unprecedented raids on snowshoes. In April, Brant, his personal morale undoubtedly enhanced by his marriage at Niagara the winter before to Catherine Croghan, assembled stronger forces for a more formidable onslaught. Operating from his base camp at Oghwaga, he demonstrated once more the military proficiency which enabled him to keep a 150-mile stretch of the frontier in constant turmoil for weeks on end. Advancing and withdrawing, reappearing at unforeseeable points and intervals, he burned Harpersfield, raided Ulster, revisited Cherry Valley, and did not even neglect his favorite victim, Minisink, far down the Delaware.

In the continuing feud between the Butler and Johnson factions, Butler had lost face with both Indian chiefs and English authorities as a result of his inability to cope with Sullivan. Guy Johnson had moved his headquarters as Indian Superintendent to Niagara, and in 1780 Sir John Johnson at last took the field as commander of the year's principal and more formally organized Tory-Indian effort. With a column of 500 regulars, Rangers, Greens, and Indians he made a surprise march through the wilderness from Crown Point to burst in the middle of the night upon Johnstown, May 21st. Setting up his headquarters in his old home, Johnson Hall, he embarked upon an unhurried and largely unopposed pillaging of the lower Mohawk while gathering in 167 Tory recruits. By contemporary report he was able also to dig up two barrels of silver which he had buried before his flight from his estates in 1776. By the time New York's Governor Clinton had assembled a strong enough force of militia to intervene, Johnson with his loot and prisoners was safely back in Crown Point.

Brant had meanwhile extended his raids from in sight of the Hudson in Ulster to the edge of the wilderness at German Flats. He next turned on the Oneida towns to punish that nation for its assistance to the Americans. His force now strengthened to a total of 600 Indians and 200 Tories, he pursued the fleeing Oneida to a sanctuary under the walls of Fort Schuyler (Stanwix). The fort was as usual desperately short of supplies, there was fear for the garrison's ability to withstand a siege, and a relief column was hastily organized by New York commanders. Having centered American attention on the fort's apparent peril, Brant made one of his extraordinary, circuitous forced marches through the wilderness and next emerged far down the Mohawk where on August 2nd he set upon Canajo-harie. The principal Mohawk town and the seat of his forefathers, it had, during the decade before the war, been encircled by the west-ward advance of the frontier, had been evacuated by the Mohawk at the outbreak of the war, and during the war had been occupied by white settlers. Here he had long made his home, had resided during his first two marriages, had conducted his missionary activi-ties, and had held those warming reunions with the white friends of his Lebanon school days. He destroyed the place with even more than his customary ruthlessness. Fourteen who ventured to resist were killed. He burned more than a hundred houses and barns, the church in which he had once led services, a mill and two forts, and carried off 60 prisoners. His Mohawk had been driven into exile, but he was leaving their dispossessors equally homeless.

With this continuing devastation of the New York frontier the militia had proved quite unable to deal, each detachment being primarily concerned with the maintenance of its local fort as refuge for the local inhabitants. Washington, who had the year before been able to spare 16 regiments of continentals to mount Sullivan's offen-sive, was this year unable to extend the slightest support. His dwindling resources were already strained to meet demands he considered more vital. Preoccupied with the problem of feeding his starving army, with the suppression of mutiny in some of his most trusted brigades, with the need to send aid to the imperiled south, with the obligation to co-operate with the arrival at Newport in July of the first French expeditionary force, and finally with the nerve-shattering crisis of Arnold's treason, he made no move to inter-fere even though the enemy was depriving his army of its principal supply source. In one sense his restraint was a successful counter to the English hope to require him to detach American forces from sea-board operations to frontier defense, but this at the time was small comfort to the border's despairing inhabitants.

The second stage of the organized invasion of the New York frontier from the north for a time threatened more immediately de-cisive consequences. In October Major Guy Carleton * with 600

* Nephew of the former governor.

soldiers and 200 Indians advanced down Lake Champlain to strike toward Schenectady and Albany, while Sir John Johnson with 600 regulars, Rangers, and Greens marched from Oswego past Oneida Lake, was joined by Brant with 600 Indians at Unadilla, and on October 16th burst upon the frontier from the headwaters of the Schoharie. These operations had been planned to coincide with Benedict Arnold's expected delivery of West Point which would have permitted Lieutenant General Sir Henry Clinton, who after Saratoga had become English commander in chief in America, to have dispatched a third and stronger force up the Hudson from New York. They represented a repetition, on a smaller but what may have seemed to Haldimand and Clinton a more practical scale, of Burgoyne's 1777 attempt to cut the colonies in two.

Due to the fortuitous apprehension of the unfortunate Major John André, West Point was saved and its fortified blockade of the Hudson preserved. Denied support from New York, the northern invasions fell short of their objectives. Carleton captured Fort Anne October 10th and Fort George October 11th, but turned back after reaching Ballston in Saratoga County. Johnson and Brant laid waste the Schoharie, threatened Fort Hunter, but then turned away from Albany and the projected junction with Carleton and instead moved westward up the Mohawk. Though now committed to withdrawal, they were destroying whatever had escaped destruction in former inroads. No forts were taken, but several detachments of militia were crushed with a loss in killed variously estimated at 60 to 100. Extricating with some difficulty his by now exhausted army from the threatening but sluggish pursuit of Brigadier General Robert Van Rensselaer with 1500 hastily assembled militia from the Hudson valley counties, Johnson got safely back into the Indian country and then to Oswego. The primary English intention had been thwarted, but the year ended with the entire New York frontier west of Schenectady a smoking and desolate desert, its surviving inhabitants homeless, hungry, and desperate.

In the south where the 1780 English effort to promote a general Indian invasion had been made to seem most likely to succeed by the English regular army's successes on the adjoining seaboard, it proved on the other hand a comparative failure. Stuart's successor as Indian Superintendent, Alexander Cameron, was experienced and diligent but he lacked Stuart's flair for inspiring Indian confidence in the disinterestedness of his judgments. The Creek and Choctaw were disturbed by Spain's entry into the war and the quick Spanish capture of Natchez and Mobile. The Chickasaw made sharp attacks upon Spanish river traffic and upon the Americans at Fort Jefferson and on the Cumberland, but were only concerned with their own territorial interests. The Cherokee, from whom most had been expected, were in the grip of a smallpox epidemic. As a result of these and other deterrent factors, there was much painful raiding of the southern frontier but no massive Indian invasion. The Chickamauga took the most assiduous interest in these piecemeal attacks, but among their parent Cherokee the senior chiefs, with judicious regard for the proven striking power of their settler enemy on the Holston, strove to keep their warriors under restraint. These pacific intentions served no purpose. Tired of awaiting the so long expected Indian invasion, Arthur Campbell and John Sevier with 700 Holston horsemen descended upon the unresisting Overhill Cherokee and, in Christmas week of 1780, burned all their principal towns on the Little Tennessee and the Hiawasee. The punitive expedition withdrew, however, without pushing on into the country of the belligerent Chickamauga beyond, and the Cherokee were left with the impression that it was as safe to fight the whites as to seek peace with them.

In the west, the punctuality and violence of 1780's spring raids gave immediate warning that this was to be another such year as 1777. The extraordinary migration to Kentucky represented a weakening of the upper Ohio defenses repeatedly and bitterly lamented by Brodhead.* The remnants of his two regiments of regulars stationed at Fort Pitt were meanwhile daily becoming further enfeebled by hunger and desertion. The magnificent func-

---

* Among Indian attacks on immigrant boats in transit down the river, one attracted special attention on account of the personalities involved. Two boats were intercepted off Capitiana Creek, 21 miles below Wheeling, and 20 persons taken. One was 14-year-old Catherine Malott who while in captivity became Simon Girty's wife.

tioning of the frontier militia system on the Holston had no counterpart on this border. The local jealousies aroused by the Pennsylvania-Virginia dispute, the dislocation of population produced by the migrations to Kentucky and from the east, and the prevalence, particularly among the newcomers, of loyalist or defeatist sentiments, combined to frustrate the efforts of Brodhead and the county lieutenants to organize either defensive or offensive operations. Due to the spiraling inflation, no governmental authority was longer able to provide more than a dribble of pay or supply for either soldiers or militia. As a last resort, Pennsylvania attempted to stimulate frontier defense efforts by the offer of a bounty of $1000 (paper) for each Indian scalp, a device which proved a serious threat only to the still friendly Delaware.

The weakening of the Pennsylvania frontier resulting from the migration to Kentucky was not attended, however, by an equivalent strengthening of Kentucky. This was clearly indicated in a March 10th petition to Clark from the inhabitants of Boonesborough, which stated in part: "The few among us who have long experienced the intollerable hardships of maintaining our Post against the Barbarous savages, Derive very little consolation from the vast addition of Numbers now scattered through the various Parts of this Country. The almost incredible number of Distressed and defenceless Families settled through our woods for the sake of sustinance instead of adding to our strength are in fact so many allurements, and must become a daily sacrifice to the savage brutality of our inhuman enemies; who from their unavoidable success will be encouraged to reitterate their attempts."

The principal English effort in the west in 1780 was concentrated on a powerful three-pronged drive, originating in the main English bases at Detroit and Mackinac, and aimed initially at the Illinois and Kentucky. This was in essence a repetition of Hamilton's grandiose design of the year before which had been strangled in its dismal infancy by Clark at Vincennes, but this time so much more care had been lavished on preparation, supply, and recruitment that hopes for it were higher even than had been his. English expectations were literally unlimited. What was foreseen was that, in conjunction with concurrent English operations from Pensacola, control of the entire Mississippi might be wrested from the Spanish while, at the same time, American resistance was being extinguished throughout the Ohio basin. To achieve this momentous result veritable armies of Indians were assembled and their ranks stiffened by cadres of French militia, Tory partisans, and even a few English regulars.

All got under way on schedule in early May. Captain Emanuel Hesse, a prominent trader who had had professional military experience with Bouquet's Royal Americans, set out from Mackinac, descended the Wisconsin, regrouped at Prairie du Chien, and swept down the Mississippi. By then his force of English and French partisans, Chippewa, Ottawa, Sauk, Outgami, Winnebago, and Sioux had increased to 950. His ultimate objective was New Orleans, but his necessary first strikes were at the Spanish defenders of St. Louis on one bank of the river and the Americans and French defenders of Cahokia on the other. Meanwhile, Charles Langlade, with a smaller force, was coming down the Illinois in a companion advance intended to confuse and distract any defense dispositions that might have been set up to oppose Hesse.

The third and main English invading force, based on Detroit, was commanded by Henry Bird, who by now had had four grim years of experience with wilderness campaigning. Every well-considered detail of his planning, preparation, and organization seemed to have added another element of strength to his enterprise. Most of his thousand Indians were Shawnee, Wyandot, and Mingo, nations which during the Revolution had been among the most belligerent and aggressive of all western Indians. To insure control of so large a body of such normally intractable followers, he had enlisted the services of Alexander McKee, Matthew Elliott, and Simon, James, and George Girty, men of lifelong Indian experience who commanded the confidence of their innumerable Indian friends. Instead of relying on French militia for his white contingent, he had a small detachment of regulars and two companies of veteran Rangers from Niagara. Far exceeding in importance any of these factors, he had also with him two cannon of a caliber able to breach a palisade and thus to require any Kentucky stockade to surrender on demand. So truly formidable a blow had never been aimed at the frontier. That Kentucky received just in time some warning of its imminence was due to a series of unrelated events, each sufficiently dramatic in itself, which had appeared to portend not the frontier's salvation but its overthrow.

In June of 1778, Colonel David Rogers had set out with 30 men from Fort Pitt under Viriginia's instructions to obtain a shipment of military supplies from the Spanish at New Orleans. Of all the many notable wilderness river journeys—Fraser's, Croghan's, Willing's, Linn's—his had been the most laborious, adventurous, and protracted. When at length he reached Arkansas Post, he was informed by the Spanish commandant there that the supplies he sought had already been shipped to St. Louis under arrangements made by Oliver Pollock, Virginia's agent at New Orleans, but that before obtaining them he himself must appear in person at New Orleans. This mortifying requirement committed him to many more months of delay, hardship, and peril, but he accepted the burden with patience and fortitude. With six of his followers he ran the English blockade on the lower Mississippi and reached New Orleans. Spain was still officially neutral, but after some sparring with suspicious English agents he was surreptitiously given his permits. In order to get around the English river posts, he was obliged to make a several-hundred-mile detour through swamps and canebrakes and did not gain St. Louis with his reunited party until a year and two months after his original embarkation at Pittsburgh. Here he at last achieved possession of the shipment of military stores, the most significant portion of which was a very large supply of gunpowder, and got on with it to the Falls. Fully appreciating the immense value of the convoy and the circumstance that the most dangerous leg of the journey was still ahead along the reaches of the upper Ohio, Clark reinforced his escort with 23 men under Lieutenant Abraham Chapline. Also joining Rogers here was Colonel John Campbell with a shipment of flour destined for Fort Pitt. At the Falls the convoy had, as a result, been augmented to a fleet of five boats manned by 65 men. In persevering with so much determination through so many months of extraordinary labor and hardship during which he had

THE GREAT ENGLISH OFFENSIVE OF 1780

Clark rushed from Fort Jefferson to assist in the defense of Cahokia, then back to Fort Jefferson, then overland in disguise to Harrodsburg in time to organize the counterattack which resulted in the destruction of the Shawnee towns, Chillicothe and Piqua.

traveled over 4000 miles, Rogers had surely deserved a kinder fate than was in store for him. But, made overconfident by the strength of his recent reinforcement, he permitted himself to be lured into an ambush at the mouth of the Licking on October 4, 1779, by a war party of 130, led by Simon Girty. Rogers and more than 40 were killed. Only 13 escaped. Among the captured were Campbell and Chapline. The loss of the provisions was a stunning blow to the starving garrison of Fort Pitt, and the loss of the powder as great a blow to the entire frontier. In its military effects the disaster, therefore, represented the opening engagement of the soon to develop 1780 campaign.

Among these effects, however, was one neither the victors nor the vanquished had foreseen. In taking young Chapline, the Indians were soon to be reminded that they had again taken a tiger by the tail. At 24 Chapline had already had wilderness experience as extensive and intensive as any man could have had. He had come to the frontier at 15. He had been with Harrod at the establishment of Harrodsburg and served with Harrod's company at Point Pleasant. He had returned to Kentucky and been captured with Boone at the salt camp. He had soon escaped, his captors having been thrown off guard by his apparent willingness to accept betrothal to an Indian maiden. He had got back to Kentucky in time to serve with Clark at Kaskaskia and Vincennes. Now that he was again a captive, the Indians remembered their former difficulty with him but were, nevertheless, so impressed by his capacity to endure torment that again they offered him adoption into an Indian family. Again he escaped, this time at a most critical moment. He reached the Falls May 19th with word of Bird's coming invasion, brought in time to give Kentuckians at least some opportunity to gather to resist.

Upon Clark, Viriginia's commander in the west and throughout the Revolution the western frontier's defender in chief, fell responsibility for contriving emergency measures to parry the monstrous three-headed blow that was descending. He had few weapons toward which he might reach. The great depreciation had made it so difficult to maintain pay and supply that even his Illinois regiment had been reduced to a skeleton force.* In the first flush of his Kaskaskia and Vincennes successes, Clark had been able to maintain his forces by requisitions for supplies drawn on the French in the Illinois and, through Pollock, on the Spanish in New Orleans. But Virginia questioned his accounts and proved at first reluctant and then unable to honor his bills, poisoning his relations with the Illinois French, bankrupting Pollock, and shattering his supply system. Literally the only additional men available to Clark in the 1780 crisis were the local militia of each community, necessarily concerned primarily with their local defense, and the floating population of land seekers and land speculators' agents, whose first impulse was to flee the country. Clark, nevertheless, rose to the occasion with a display of personal initiative and energy seldom matched by any commander.

Since early April he had been occupied with the construction of Fort Jefferson on the Mississippi at Iron Banks, five miles below the mouth of the Ohio, a new post intended chiefly as an offset to the pretensions of the country's new but grasping ally, Spain. First word of the summer's enormous threats to reach him was an appeal for help from de Leyba at St. Louis and Montgomery at Cahokia. Clark rushed north to the Illinois with the few men that could be spared at Fort Jefferson, arriving May 25th, the day before Hesse launched his attacks on the two towns. Both assaults were repulsed. The more considerable action developed at St. Louis where Spanish soldiers and French inhabitants dug entrenchments and set up an unexpectedly spirited resistance. According to the Spanish official report the defenders lost 22 killed, 7 wounded, and 70 prisoners. Lieutenant Governor Patrick Sinclair at Mackinac reported to Governor Haldimand that the attackers had brought back 43 scalps and 18 prisoners.

Hesse's Indians had been led to anticipate easy victory and rich plunder, and were so disconcerted by the brusqueness of their reception that he was obliged at once to back away. He had already been distracted by the difficulty that invariably and inevitably dogged every

---

* As one example of the deterioration in the national, as well as the state, military establishment, in every letter of the period written by Brodhead to Clark he begged Clark to attempt to apprehend deserters making their way down river from the Fort Pitt garrison.

commander who had ventured to conduct a large military force into the wilderness. Lack of transport made it literally impossible to maintain adequate stores. This difficulty was magnified many times when Indians were concerned. They were constitutionally opposed to every regulation necessary to maintain order in an army's most routine marching and camping. Even veteran warriors who had proved their valor and endurance on innumerable raids remained the poorest of soldiers. The longer the campaign the greater always became Indian impatience with discipline. They particularly rejected, because it was so foreign to their lifelong habit, the need to ration food. They wolfed or wasted whatever was issued, and as soon as they were hungry were seized with the impulse to return home or to scatter to hunt. The surprising resistance of St. Louis and Cahokia aggravated the discontent of Hesse's Indians, and he was soon committed to a retreat as rapid as had been his advance. Most observers at the time reported that the Indians' discouragement became complete when they learned that Clark himself had arrived to take command of their adversaries. In any event, Clark swiftly organized a volunteer French-Spanish-American force under Montgomery to pursue the fleeing invaders. Langlade was chased until he had re-embarked upon Lake Michigan. The retreat of Hesse's main column was hustled as far as Rock River where Montgomery burned several Indian towns before returning.

Clark had been denied the congenial privilege of leading this pursuit. He had learned from Detroit informants of the assembly of Bird's army, realized there was greater need for him in Kentucky, and hastened back to Fort Jefferson. The partially built post had meanwhile been invested by the Chickasaw, incensed by its unsanctioned erection on their territory. Clark had another of his narrower escapes in breaking through their lines and getting into the fort. It was still necessary to get on to Kentucky. He and two companions disguised themselves as Indians, eluded the watching Chickasaw and, a little later, an Indian party that had been dispatched particularly to intercept him, crossed the Tennessee and the Cumberland on driftwood rafts, successfully passed through the nearly 300 miles of intervening wilderness, and reached Harrodsburg in time to organize Kentucky's mobilization to meet the great emergency. Despite the known imminence of invasion, crowds of claimants were still milling about the land office. Clark's first move was to close it for the duration of the campaign.

Bird had ascended the Maumee and then had come down the Miami with most of his force and stores in boats and canoes. He had intended to strike first at Louisville, but so great was the excitement of his Indians over the prospect of blasting entrance to settlers' stockades with the cannon that after some discussion it was determined instead to make directly for the populous central section of Kentucky. Ruddle's Station on the Licking, a new but larger than average settlement with 300 inhabitants, was the first to be assailed on June 20, 1780. The cannon proved fully as efficacious as had been foreseen. After two shots the defenders were forced to realize resistance was hopeless, and the station became the first stockade in Kentucky's violent history to be surrendered. Isaac Ruddle was given Bird's personal guarantee that the lives of the inhabitants would be spared, but no sooner had the gate been opened than the Indians ignored their commander and rushed upon the cowering people within. The value of live prisoners in Detroit was forgotten as completely as had been Bird's pledge. Their sadistic excitement mounted to a frenzy in which each warrior strove to exceed each former excess of his companions. If one dispatched a man, the next struck down a woman and the third a child, with the bestial competition presently developing into every variation of dismemberment and mutilation. Before the day had ended a majority of the helpless prisoners had been butchered.* The invaders marched on to Martin's Station, unlimbered their cannon, and the smaller station was compelled also to surrender, delivering up another 50 prisoners. The way into the heart of Kentucky appeared open, with each previously invulnerable stockade doomed to yield on demand to the summons of the cannon.

---

* No reliable estimates of the number who died in the massacre remain. Official English reports state that 100 of Bird's prisoners eventually reached Detroit. Of the 350 prisoners that he took in Kentucky a few of the missing may be assumed to have escaped or been adopted by their Indian captors, but it must be presumed that most of those unaccounted for perished.

But for all its fierce energies, the invasion contained within it the seeds of its own disintegration. Like Hesse, Bird was losing all control over his savage command. The Indians had been infuriated by the angry vigor of his attempts to save the lives of prisoners. Conscious of having already won remarkable victories, accustomed to the hit-and-run tactics of raiding, they were tired of the prospects of a more prolonged campaign. The supply problem, moreover, had become critical. At Ruddle's enough cattle had been captured to have supplied the army for many days if kept alive and on the hoof, but in spite of Bird's protests the Indians had cut down the cattle with as much zest as they had the prisoners. In the heat of summer the beef was rapidly spoiling. The final impulse toward the army's demoralization was administered by two well-meaning Tory deserters from Harrodsburg who brought the news that Clark, who had been thought to be hundreds of miles away in the Illinois, was in Kentucky and taking personal charge of marshaling Kentucky's defenses. The Indians, already dissatisfied with Bird, with the duration of the campaign, and with the lack of enough to eat, were in no mood to face so redoubtable an opponent. Bird had no other recourse than to get out of Kentucky as fast as he could, dismiss his Indians to their respective towns, bury his cannon on the upper Miami, and return to Detroit, probably as disillusioned and disgruntled a commander as has ever been obliged to accept a substitute for victory.

The shock of Bird's invasion had stirred in Kentucky a universal determination to retaliate, and Clark had no difficulty raising a force of volunteers comparable in experience and spirit to those the Holston had for so long been accustomed to muster. Every station contributed the majority of its ablest defenders. At the August 1st rendezvous at the mouth of the Licking 998 Kentuckians appeared. Among their leaders were most of Kentucky's most noted pioneers, Benjamin Logan, Daniel Boone, James Harrod, Levi Todd, William Linn, Hugh McGary. Clark had even been able to bring with him from Louisville a six-pounder cannon, captured in the Illinois, with which presently the tables were to be turned on the Indian ravagers of Ruddle's and Martin's.

The primary objective of the expedition was punishment of the

Shawnee, the most hated of Kentucky's many Indian enemies. Marching up the Miami with his heavier stores in boats and canoes, Clark struck the Shawnee before any of their allies could be summoned to their support. Astounded by the unexpectedness and rapidity of his advance, the Shawnee hastily evacuated their nearer town, Chilicothe. Clark burned it, destroyed some hundreds of acres of ripening corn, and marched on their next town, Piqua. Here the Shawnee, though outnumbered three to one, made a desperate stand. The engagement that developed was brief but furious. Clark's little cannon proved its value by splintering the principal Shawnee blockhouse. The Shawnee left their fortified log houses and took to the woods, then fiercely counterattacked the advancing Americans. They were opposed, however, by white men who by now were as adept at bushfighting as they. The outnumbered Shawnee were driven from the field. Most who survived the action made good their escape when Logan's encircling column, delayed by an intervening swamp, was unable to get into position in time to cut them off.

It had been a battle while it lasted. The Americans had lost 20 killed and 40 wounded, of whom a number died. They had brought off 73 scalps. There had been no quarter given or asked on either side. Two of the fallen were especially mourned. One was Samuel Moore who had been one of the first settlers of Harrodsburg in 1774 and one of Clark's two Kaskaskia spies. The other was Clark's cousin, Joseph Rogers. He had been a Shawnee captive since 1776 when he had been taken in the attempt to retrieve the gunpowder cache when Gabriel Jones had been killed. At the height of the battle he had made a desperate dash toward the oncoming American line, but had been pierced by many bullets from both sides and died in Clark's arms.

The Kentuckians looted and burned Piqua and destroyed more acres of Shawnee corn. But the familiar wilderness supply problem had become so acute that, instead of being able to develop their advantage, they were compelled to make an immediate, hungry, and headlong withdrawal across the Ohio. They, nevertheless, could feel assured that they had struck the Shawnee a blow which, if not decisive, had still impressed not only them but all Indians with new respect for Kentucky's ability to strike back.

Considering the enormity of the threats that had loomed in the spring, the frontier had come through the infinitely dangerous summer of 1780 with colors flying high indeed. The personal achievements of Clark, commander extraordinary, had reached new heights. Not only had he successfully repulsed invasions over a thousand-mile front but he had routed, pursued, and humiliated the invaders. Most of all, frontier defense had gained one more precious year.

XVI

༒

The Road to Detroit

THE SUCCESSFUL REPULSE of the 1780 English offensive in the west
had been a kind of military miracle, and yet all that had been
gained by frontier defense had been one more year of survival. In
the year that followed the menace was as constant, the danger more
desperate. It had been made clear to the slowest understanding that
as long as the English base at Detroit existed Indian attacks were
bound to continue. But it required no keener perception to grasp
the companion fact that an attempt upon Detroit was confronted by
stupendous hazards. It was separated from the American frontier
by 400 miles of wilderness, the way to it was flanked and guarded
by the fortified towns of eight of the most war-minded of all Indian
nations, and it could be readily reinforced and supplied by means of
English control of Lakes navigation. Still the challenge remained.
Only by meeting it could the frontier ever achieve relief.

Recognition of this imperative necessity was accompanied by the
realization that in 1781 the project had become immensely more
difficult than when it had been tentatively and momentarily authorized by Congress in 1776 and 1778. Wartime depreciation had
bankrupted the frontier, the states, and the nation. Any accumula-

tion of military supplies had been made all but impossible by the lack of any other medium of exchange than simple barter. Musters even of local militia required that men be fed and furnished ammunition, and this was becoming with each passing month a more nearly insoluble problem. Despite this near paralysis of organized military effort, Clark persisted in his insistence upon an expedition against Detroit. In this determination to achieve the seeming impossible he was as firmly supported by Thomas Jefferson, Virginia's second Revolutionary governor, as he had been in 1776 and 1777 by Governor Patrick Henry.

Jefferson was later able more dramatically to demonstrate his interest in the west by a series of forever famous public acts culminating in the Louisiana Purchase and dispatch of the Lewis and Clark expedition, but never was his interest more clearly evidenced than in this crisis. It came the more naturally to him in that it had been bred in him from childhood. His father, Peter Jefferson, was a member of the Loyal Land Company and he inherited much of his parent's disposition to accumulate acreage. He was born in the shadow of the Blue Ridge on a recently established plantation on what was then Virginia's frontier, three miles from the farm where, eight years later, Clark was born. Another neighbor was Thomas Walker. That most experienced and best informed of all authorities on the early frontier became the guardian and mentor of the 13-year-old Jefferson upon his father's death. Dr. Walker was not only a veteran woodsman and explorer but an educated man with a scientific interest in every phase of wilderness phenomena. From this association the exceptionally intelligent and impressionable youth had drawn his belief in the west's limitless potentialities and the so nearly unlimited range of his own scientific curiosity. He was later writing Clark, for example, relative to the deposits of prehistoric bones in Kentucky, "a specimen of each of the several species of bones now to be found is to me the most desirable object in Natural history and there is no expense of package or of safe transportation which I will not gladly reimburse to procure them safely." In outlining in 1803 the objectives of the Lewis and Clark expedition, he emphasized above all else his direction that all members of the party keep daily journals reporting everything, however minor, that they observed, with the data to be gathered concerning the far Indian nations ranging from "what quarter of the earth did they emigrate as related to them by their ancestors" to "what are their musical instruments" and "what time do they generally consume in sleep." From his boyhood on his interest in everything about the west had been as insatiable.

This lifelong fascination with the land beyond the mountains had thus prepared him to strain Virginia's last remaining resources to support and even to elaborate upon Clark's project. Jefferson's plan envisaged a muster of 2000 militia from Virginia's Holston, Valley, Kentucky, and Ohio frontier counties. Clark was commissioned brigadier general to raise him to a rank commensurate with command over so substantial an army. Jefferson appealed to Washington for the necessary artillery and certain extra stores and boats. It was contemplated that Clark would assemble his main force at Pittsburgh, descend the Ohio to the Falls, there pick up the Kentucky contingent, and on March 15th strike northward through the center of the Indian country, crushing Indian resistance on his way to the reduction of Detroit.

Washington gave the undertaking his hearty approval. He had since the outbreak of the war understood the full urgency of the need for eliminating the Detroit spawning ground for Indian attacks and had each year since hoped in vain that some intermission in other demands might enable him to assign continental troops to the task. He was gratified that Virginia had undertaken the responsibility. On December 29, 1780, he wrote Brodhead directing him to furnish Clark every assistance. He not only directed the supply of the artillery, stores, and boats Jefferson had requested but further instructed Brodhead to transfer to Clark as strong a regular detachment as could possibly be spared from the Pittsburgh garrison.

Clark reached eastern Virginia in December of 1780 to confer with Jefferson on plans for the expedition. But plans and hopes were alike disrupted by a sudden invasion of Virginia, not from the wilderness but from the sea. On January 4th Benedict Arnold, now an English brigadier general, landed at Westover with 1600 regulars and the next day seized undefended Richmond. Clark dropped his preparations long enough to lead a detachment of local militia in a guerilla action in which 17 of the invaders were killed, but was soon driven off by superior numbers. Jefferson remained convinced that, in spite of the enormity of this new peril in Virginia's tide-water, there was greater need for Clark on Virginia's frontier and got him off for Pittsburgh, as formerly scheduled, on January 22nd. After his departure the threat to eastern Virginia increased at an accelerating pace. Cornwallis, at last completing his northward advance, joined Arnold at Petersburg. The insufficient American forces under Baron de Steuben and the Marquis de Lafayette were compelled to avoid battle while most of seaboard Virginia was occupied or ravaged, including Jefferson's home, Monticello, and the state government forced to flee over the Blue Ridge to a temporary capital at Staunton. The Valley which for 30 years had been obliged constantly to expect attack from the west was now obliged as well to guard against attack from the east. Persuaded that Virginia's plight demanded leadership with more military experience, Jefferson resigned as governor on June 3rd and was succeeded by General Thomas Nelson.

Arriving at Pittsburgh, Clark found conditions nearly as chaotic as those he had left behind. The frontier was in a fever of dread of a reported invasion from Niagara, supposedly being hatched by John Connolly, who had escaped his American imprisonment and resumed advocacy of his 1775 design. But among the many fears besetting the frontier, this was one that was for the moment needless. For English policy had taken another turn and in an opposite direction. There were not this year to be attempts in the west to mount large, cumbersome and, as experience had proven, unmanageable Indian invasions. Instead the Indians were being encouraged to undertake many more and much harder raids. Throughout the spring and early summer these became more numerous and more violent. This was a tactic with which the long frontier had from the war's outset found it far more difficult to deal than the more ponderous organized invasions.

Adding to the general dismay, a new danger loomed. The nearest and only still neutral nation joined the ranks of the frontier's Indian enemies. The Delaware, except for a few Moravian converts under the immediate influence of Heckewelder and Zeisberger, had this spring embraced the English cause. After years of ineffectual struggle to establish friendly relations with the Americans, they had at last decided that their own safety required co-operation with their fellow Indians and adherence to what was seeming increasingly to be the stronger side.

While threats multiplied, the frontier's capacity to resist had been progressively reduced. The worthlessness of paper money and consequent failure of supply had crippled every effort to maintain an organized defense. Clark's conquests were being necessarily relinquished. The American garrison had been withdrawn from Kaskaskia and before the year was over would be from Vincennes. On June 8th the recently established Fort Jefferson was abandoned. Fort Randolph and Fort Laurens had long since been given up. Everywhere the inhabitants depended for survival chiefly upon their own exertions. The frontier was very nearly as defenseless, in any organized sense, as at the outbreak of the war while the Indians were united, better armed and supplied, and being continually exhorted by English officers and their own chiefs to redouble their attacks.

The desperate plight of each frontier community was precisely revealed in a letter of April 16, 1781, from John Floyd to Jefferson, describing conditions in Kentucky's Jefferson County: "We are all obliged to live in Forts in this County, and notwithstanding all the Caution that we use, forty seven of the Inhabitants have been killed & taken by the Savages, Besides a number wounded since Jany. last— Amongst the last is Major William Lyn [Linn]. Whole families are destroyed, without regard for Age or Sex—Infants are torn from their mothers Arms & their Brains dashed out against Trees, as they are necessarily removing from one Fort to another for safety or Convenience—Not a week passes & some weeks scarcely a day without some of our distressed inhabitants feeling the fatal effects of the infernal rage and fury of those Execrable Hell hounds. . . Of those who have Escaped, many have lost their stocks, and have not any Land of their own, nor where withal to purchase—Our

dependence to support our familys is upon getting wild meat & this is procured with great difficulty & danger; and should it fall to the Lott of some in this County who are thus situated to serve as Regular Soldiers according to Law, their familys must inevitably starve." *
Floyd was detailing the situation in his county. Similar conditions could have been reported from any of the 20 other counties on the western frontier.

Clark's already extreme recruiting difficulties were further handicapped by Brodhead's reluctance to co-operate. Despite Washington's direct orders, which had been tempered only by a distant commander's customary deference to the judgment of the responsible officer present on the scene, Brodhead withheld support in order to get on with his own designs. He was meanwhile also having his own troubles. His small regular garrison was hungry, unclothed, unpaid, discontented, and being constantly reduced by desertions. As he had written Washington in a letter January 23, 1781, his entire force very little exceeded 300 men of whom many were "unfit for such active service as is necessary here." He had added, "My soldiers will be naked by the first of March & yet I can obtain no clothing for them." Investigators for the Board of War had reported to Congress on March 15, 1781, that supply of the Pittsburgh garrison had been so deficient for the last year that there was present danger of the post being of necessity abandoned. In order to keep his garrison alive, Brodhead was driven to sending out parties to hunt buffalo and even into appealing to the Christian Delaware for food. Many of his somewhat self-willed measures to cope with his situation had failed to gain public approval. In April a petition signed by 419 of the leading inhabitants of the upper Ohio frontier was sent to

---

* In another letter of April 16th, to Clark, Floyd added a personal note: "I have been more infortunate in my little hunt last Winter than the rest. I hired seven or eight men, went to Lees Cabbins with Horses loaded with Salt, gave 1000 pounds for the Building Canoes, killed and saved 54 Buffaloe 4 Elk & 2 large wild Hogs & brought it down safe to between Goose Creek & Beargrass where my vessels were overset by a Gale of Wind & sunk my whole Cargo to the bottom. Besides the Meat Tallow &c I lost five Guns, my saddle bags Surveying affairs Warrants Field Books & all my Memorandums about Land for seven years past. (and as people say in their Advertisements) & many other articles too tedious to mention—This is my second defeat at Sea; but I am yet alive & hearty." See note p. 310.

Washington, denouncing Brodhead's general conduct as well as his exercise of command and urging his removal.

Castigating his accusers with equal vehemence, Brodhead hastily launched his own project, an attempt to punish the newly belligerent Delaware. With a column of 150 soldiers from his garrison and 134 militiamen, he surprised and burned Coshocton, one of the nearer Delaware towns. The feat was tarnished by the militia's deliberate killing of 15 Delaware warriors after they had surrendered. The campaign served no purpose other than to harden Delaware hostility. Their immediate response was to burn nine Kentucky prisoners, one on each of nine successive days. After Coshocton they were to rival the Shawnee in the persistence and violence of their animosity.

Upon his return from the expedition, Brodhead went east to face a congressional investigation, leaving Colonel John Gibson in command. Gibson was more sympathetic to Clark's design but felt bound by Brodhead's order that no regular support be furnished Clark other than Captain Isaac Craig's artillery company which had been formed in the east for his particular needs. Clark appealed to Washington, but Washington's final decision was to accept Brodhead's judgment that no additional continentals could be spared from Fort Pitt. Washington summed up the entire American military situation in his report to the Board of War of June 8, 1781: "You must be convinced from your very intimate knowledge of our Military affairs that it is out of my power to send any reinforcements to the Westward. If the States would fill their Continental Battalions we should be able to oppose a regular and permanent force to the Enemy in every quarter. If they will not, they must certainly take measures to defend themselves by their Militia, however expensive and ruinous the system."

In estimating his recruiting expectations Clark had primarily relied on a strong response from the Valley counties which had in former years so often risen to meet any demand. But their first concern now was necessarily the English invasion of Virginia. On June 21st the Valley frontier's hesitation was made official by the assembly's voting to abandon the expedition. Clark was left depending on recruits from the Ohio counties and those he might hope to find awaiting him in Kentucky. It was already so late in the season that any prospect that anything could be achieved against Detroit was fast fading. Still Clark persisted. Most inhabitants of the upper Ohio frantically favored an attack on Detroit as the one possible means of ending the perpetual Indian threat, and with much public collaboration he had been able to establish so adequate a magazine of supplies that he was even able to loan some to the Pittsburgh garrison. But recruits were harder to come by. The tremendous distances contemplated for the expedition, 860 miles to the Falls and then another 400 to Detroit (600 if Clark elected to take the Wabash route), suggested that men who joined it would be kept away from home for six months to a year. Ill will between Pennsylvanians and Virginians contributed to others' hesitation. Pennsylvania's territorial claims had finally been acknowledged by Virginia as extending to Pennsylvania's present boundaries, but there remained much local rivalry and innumerable disputes over individual land titles. Many Pennsylvanians were encouraged by their county officers to consider Clark's project as primarily a Virginia land-grabbing expedition. Privately, Clark betrayed his exasperation with people of both states who seemed so unready to rise to his own pitch of urgency. On June 12th he was writing William Fleming, "The inhabitants cry out for an Expedition, but too few I doubt will turn out, affraid I believe that they will be led on to something too desperate for their Delicate stomacks." Men who followed Clark had some reason to expect that they might be led on to something desperate. On June 23rd there came one bit of encouragement when Pennsylvania's Westmoreland, influenced by a singularly stouthearted county lieutenant, Colonel Archibald Lochry, voted to furnish a contingent of its militia.

By ceaseless exertions, incredible patience, and occasional outbursts of rage, Clark at last assembled 400 volunteers at Wheeling, centered about Colonel Joseph Crockett's Virginia regiment and Craig's artillery. He was unable to wait for Lochry who was on his way to join him with his 107 devoted Westmoreland volunteers. Small as was Clark's force, it was being daily reduced by desertions as men

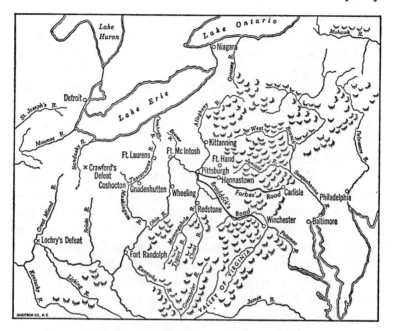

FRONTIER DEFENSE ON THE UPPER OHIO

became more fully aware of how forlorn had become the hope with which they were associated. On August 8th, Clark started down river in order to deter further desertions by placing a greater distance between his army and the settlements, leaving instructions for Lochry to make haste to overtake him. Waiting for him down the Ohio was Brant and the one encounter during the Revolution between these two foremost champions of their respective races.

That spring of 1781 the New York frontier had known its darkest hour. Raids had begun as early as January and continued into the summer. So feeble and inert had become the stockade-bound defense that the raiders' chief difficulty had been to find something to destroy that had not previously been destroyed. The inhabitants were confined to their 24 stockades from which they dared to emerge to plant their fields only when accompanied by a military guard. Brant had concentrated his personal attention on a blockade of Fort Schuyler (Stanwix). In May, after a flood and a barracks fire, the

long struggle to maintain American control of this key to the Oswego portage was abandoned and the historic post was evacuated.
Fort Herkimer had become the frontier's westernmost defense bastion. Raiding parties continued to roam the New York frontier
almost at will, one penetrating as far as Sussex County, New Jersey,
and another to the outskirts of Kingston. Once prisoners were taken
east of the Hudson. Schenectady expected attack and many residents
of Albany had packed in readiness for flight.

Colonel Marinus Willett, the indomitable young veteran of Ticonderoga, Quebec, Oriskany, and Newtown, belatedly assigned to
take command of the frontier's defense, brought by his personal
example new energy and spirit to inhabitants whose last hopes were
expiring. He kept his small and hardy mobile force of some 150
continentals and volunteers centrally located at Canajoharie from
which he dashed out to set upon raiding parties. One which had
recently burned Currietown he pursued and dispersed with a loss
of 40 Indians killed. He was fully aware, however, of the proportions of his task. In his report of July 6, 1781, to Washington he
described in detail the burden he had assumed. Years of war had
left the border little strength with which to continue to resist. New
York's frontier Tryon County had had at the outbreak of the war
2500 enrolled in its militia. There now remained less than 800 able
to bear arms, demonstrating how heavy had been the loss in population. In accounting for the reduction, Willett ascribed one third to
the number killed or captured, one third to those who had gone over
to the enemy, and the other third to those who had fled eastward.
According to Willett's estimate the New York frontier had thus
lost half its manpower by direct enemy action.

Washington could provide little assistance beyond the tiny regular
corps with which Willett had been furnished. His Continental Army
had been shaken by the spring's new and more general mutinies in
the Pennsylvania and New Jersey line, made the more terrifying
by the afterglare of Arnold's treason. If the heroic Arnold could
betray his fellow countrymen, there seemed during those desperate
early months of 1781 no one upon whose constancy there fell no
shadow of doubt. Washington was, in spite of the mutinies, obliged

to detach troops from his ragged and hungry little army to support Greene's campaign in the Carolinas and Lafayette's in Virginia. He had, moreover, been assured of the return this year of the French fleet and his attention was already fixed on the opportunity to make the memorable march to Yorktown. All in all, this year more than in any former year, he was compelled, sad as he regarded the necessity, to let the calamity-ridden frontier continue to shift for itself.

With so little left to complete the ruin of the New York frontier, it was decided in early summer that Brant might prove of greater service in the west where his presence could be expected to add new spirit to the western Indians' war effort. He conferred in July with Lieutenant Governor Arent De Peyster at Detroit and joined at Sandusky the Indian levies being assembled by McKee, Elliott, and the Girtys to support Captain Andrew Thompson's Rangers in preparation to resist Clark's expected invasion. When word at last came that, instead of striking directly toward Detroit from Pittsburgh, Clark was moving down the Ohio, there developed a race to intercept him somewhere along the lower river.

Clark was proceeding with less rapidity than was his custom in order to give Lochry a better chance to overtake him. In his August 9th message to Lochry, the last dispatch Lochry was ever to receive, he said: "I am heartily sorry that after waiting so long for you I should set out but a day before your arrival ... the militia with us continue to desert, and consiquently I cannot remain long in one place ... I shall move on slowly ... I have suffered much lately but you again encourage me." Brant reached the mouth of the Miami in time to sight Clark's boats on the river, making this the nearest to a personal clash between the two that was ever to occur. But the more lethargic main English-Indian force under McKee and Thompson was still far behind. Brant had with him an advance party of only 30 Indians, and he was forced to watch from concealment while his great opportunity passed.

He was able, however, to capture Lochry's dispatch boat bearing a message urging Clark to wait, and thus became aware of the approach of the following smaller force. Sixty more Indians had meanwhile joined him. Using one of Lochry's captured couriers as a decoy, he lured Lochry ashore August 24th and set upon him in a sudden surprise attack of bewildering violence. Lochry's volunteers were seasoned frontiersmen, long inured to wilderness emergencies. They included Captain Nehemiah Stokely's company of rangers, each a veteran scout, woodsman, and bushfighter. Yet so fierce and unexpected was Brant's onslaught that the whole command was taken at as great a disadvantage as might have been the most untried home guard. Thirty six, including Lochry, were killed and 64 captured. Not one man of the Westmoreland regiment escaped.

Kentuckians had looked forward anxiously to the return of Clark, their great defender, as their one real hope. But he reached Louisville under a cloud of frustration and failure in somber contrast to the train of triumphs which so far had marked his brilliant career. On September 5th, 6th, and 7th he conducted a series of councils attended by Kentucky's county lieutenants, Benjamin Logan, John Floyd, and John Todd, by Colonel John Montgomery of the Illinois Regiment, Colonel Joseph Crockett of the Virginia Regiment, Major George Slaughter, commanding the Louisville garrison, and by numerous other officers. The purpose of the councils was to decide whether to persist in the attempt on Detroit, to undertake instead a limited offensive against the Shawnee in conjunction with a possible thrust westward by Gibson from Pittsburgh, or to continue to stand on the defensive. Clark put the issue bluntly to the county lieutenants: "I wait as a Spectator to see what a Country is determined to do for itself when reduced to a State of Desperation; I am ready to lead you on to any Action that has the most distant prospect of Advantage, however daring it may appear to be." The Illinois officers, with unshaken faith in Clark's star, continued to advocate an attempt on Detroit, but the majority at the council held the available force of at most 700 men too small and the season too late. Clark agreed that an alternative attack upon the Shawnee at a time when they would have been able to complete their corn harvest was not worth the effort. The final decision was, therefore, to remain on the defensive. Clark was for the first time seized by one of those fits of discouragement to which lesser men are subject. On October 1st

THE ROAD TO DETROIT [263]

he was writing Governor Nelson: "I have lost the object that was one of the principal inducements to my fatigues & transactions for several years past—my chain appears to have run out. I find myself enclosed with few troops, in a trifling fort, and shortly expect to bear the insults of those who have for several years past been in continual dread of me."

For his great rival, Brant, those same September days were bringing similar frustrations and disappointments. After the extinction of Lochry, he proposed to move at once upon Clark at Louisville before the defenders had recovered from the shock of that disaster. Prisoners and captured correspondence had informed him how weak was Clark's force and how stirred with dismay was Kentucky. But most of his Indians, as usual made as eager to go home by a victory as they ever were by a defeat, were increasingly reluctant. When Brant was within nine miles of Louisville, captured prisoners revealed the councils' decision to abandon any attempt to stage an American offensive. Relieved of any prospective threat to their own towns, the Indians seized upon this information as a further excuse to evade the risk of braving the lion in his lair. Thompson's Rangers, starving and many of them sickened by subsisting on unripe corn, were as intent upon turning back. Deprived of most of their force, Brant and McKee, still grimly determined to achieve something more, turned away from Louisville southward into central Kentucky with the 200 still resolute Indians who had remained with them. What had been envisaged as a formidable offensive had now degenerated to the level of an oversize raid, devoted to spreading terror, stealing horses, destroying property, and pouncing upon whoever could be found outside a stockade. Among the victims were Daniel Boone's brother, Squire, at the moment engaged in making a most untimely move with a party of settlers from Boonesborough to a new location on the Beargrass. Among the killed were a number of women and children. Floyd, sallying to the rescue with only 27 men, was, in the words of his report to Clark, "cut to pieces" with a loss of all but seven of his small force. With his remaining Indians by now totally satisfied with their loot and their successes and without cannon to reduce even one stockade, Brant was forced to withdraw across the Ohio after a few days. In his first and only western campaign he had won startling local victories but nothing more nearly decisive than to have provided his fellow Indians with some temporary elation. Kentucky, distraught yet defiant, still stood. Brant was so disgruntled by his failure to achieve more that, according to contemporary report, he so far forgot his usual dignity as to become involved in a private quarrel in which he laid open Simon Girty's head with his sword.

While Brant, McKee, and Thompson were endeavoring to intercept Clark, Matthew Elliott with 250 Indians, most of them Wyandot, drawn from the same originally defensive mobilization at Sandusky, undertook a strike at the upper Ohio frontier with Wheeling as a primary objective. From his mission station on the Tuscarawas, Zeisberger, as he had so often before, managed to get off a warning to Fort Pitt. As a result, any opportunity to take Fort Henry by surprise was denied, and most of the inhabitants of the region were able to gain their stockades in time. The expedition became, like Brant's in Kentucky, only an oversize raid, forced to be content with the destruction of outlying property and the killing or capture of upwards of twenty stragglers who had been slow to take refuge. Unfortunately, two of the captives mentioned the missionary's warning. Confirmed in their long-held suspicions that the Moravians had been partial to the frontier, the incensed Wyandot on their way home pillaged the mission, forced the colony of Christian Delaware to remove to Sandusky, and delivered Heckewelder and Zeisberger to Detroit for interrogation by De Peyster. In the long record of tribulations which had continued to afflict the Moravians since the opening months of the French War, this exile was the next to the catastrophic last chapter.

For the frontier the dreary year had proved the most discouraging yet, with the perpetual deferment of hope approaching more narrowly than ever the final extinguishment of hope. But before it ended there came to the New York border one stark glare of action which produced at least some measure of grim consolation. The denuding of the Hudson defense line by Washington's sudden march to Yorktown had not escaped the attention of English commanders. Brigadier General William Heath had been left with only 2000 men to hold the Hudson highlands, while in Clinton's New York City garrison idled upwards of 16,000 English regulars and Hessians. Haldimand saw in this situation an opportunity to revive for a third time the three-pronged Hudson offensive on the original Burgoyne pattern. This time it was, if possible, more ineptly managed than the first two. Clinton, with an inertia astounding even in a commander of his incomparable sloth, made no move to threaten Heath. St. Leger, dispatched southward by Lake Champlain from Canada, paused at Ticonderoga, bemused by obscure negotiations with Ethan Allen's Vermont faction which regarded Vermont's territorial dispute with New York as a more important quarrel than the war with England. Only the third and least of the three projected offensives got under way.

Major John Ross, with a fast-moving force of 161 regulars, 150 Rangers, 120 Greens, and 52 miscellaneous Tory partisans, with Walter Butler his second in command, set out from Oswego October 10th. To his and Haldimand's furious disappointment only 130 Iroquois of the 600 expected had joined him. Brant's absence in the west had proved how essential was his personal leadership of the Iroquois. Making a wilderness circuit by way of Oneida Lake and the Unadilla, Ross on October 25th burst upon the frontier on the lower Schoharie at Warrensbush. Aware by now that he could expect no support from either Clinton or St. Leger, he was compelled to turn back after penetrating to within 12 miles of Schenectady. He crossed to Johnstown to seize cattle to feed his starving force and began his retreat up the Mohawk. The vigilant Willett, having made an all-night march from Canajoharie, was at his heels with his few continentals supported by some hundreds of hastily assembled militia. The movements of both armies were much impeded by continuing heavy rains which had turned roads to quagmires and flooded all streams. Willett was repulsed in a sharp engagement at nightfall, and Ross resumed his retreat, taking to the forest north of the valley.

Still not content that Ross should escape without punishment, Willett reassembled his force, gathered provisions, and on the 28th resumed the pursuit. The rain had turned to sleet and snow. Ross had meanwhile lost most of the intervening three days through the duplicity of his Indians who had endeavored to guide him along wilderness trails leading west in the direction of Niagara instead of north toward the St. Lawrence. Shortly after daylight on the 30th Willett's advance patrols overtook Ross' rear guard at the crossing of West Canada Creek. Walter Butler, conducting a delaying action at the ford, was one of the four Rangers killed in the skirmish. Willett broke off his pursuit and Ross made good his escape, but to the New York frontier the fall of Walter Butler represented an outstanding victory. From the time of his court-martial at German Flats, and increasingly after his jail break at Albany and his reappearance at Cherry Valley, frontier abhorrence of the Tory-Indian enemy had been centered in his person. He had been invested in border estimation with every imaginable manifestation of the most monstrous cruelty. There was more rejoicing in Tryon County over his death than over the coincidental news from Yorktown.

Upon learning that for the second time an entire English army had been forced to surrender, Congress was moved by Washington's dispatch from Yorktown to proceed in a body to the Dutch Lutheran Church to "return thanks to Almighty God for crowning the allied arms of the United States and France with success." Everywhere on the seaboard bells were rung, bonfires lighted, salutes fired. People were beginning to sense that the war for independence had at last been won. But the war on the western frontier had not yet been won. There Yorktown was to have no perceptible effect. There people faced the winter with no new hope. Their situation was more tellingly described than it could possibly be by any later comment in Floyd's October 6, 1781, report to Governor Nelson on conditions in Kentucky's Fayette county: "On account of the unsettled and dispersed situation of the Inhabitants it is out of my power to send you an exact Return of the Number of Militia in this County, but by the last returns made me by the Captains we had 327 including Officers, and I believe at this time we have about 300, and near one third of these are preparing to go into the Interior parts of the State and many others would follow the Example but are unable to remove by Land having lost most of their Horses already by the Savages & the Ohio runs the wrong way. The Frontier of this County along the Ohio River is 277 miles by computation, and the Inhabitants greatly dispersed & cooped up in small Forts without any ammunition. Eighty four of the Inhabitants of this County have been killed & Captured since last spring & many more wounded. We are now so weakened in the most exposed parts of the County, by having so many Men killed & others removing to Lincoln for safety, that when any murder is done we can not pursue the Enemy without leaving the little Garrisons quite defenceless. The most distressed Widows & Orphans perhaps in the world make up a great part of our Inhabitants."

XVII

༄

France and Spain

THE DECISIVE EVENT of the Revolution was the French alliance. Without massive French support independence could not have been won by any military action that appeared conceivable then or since. After 1778 Washington's every strategic judgment was keyed to his necessary adaptation to the movements of the French fleet and the French expeditionary force. The general war effort was as dependent upon French financial aid. In the latter years of the war, the major source of supply or money available to Congress was the continued advance of French grants. American persistence in the war was underwritten by France and sustained by powerful French military assistance. Of the nearly 40,000 men in the ground and naval forces investing Cornwallis at Yorktown, only 9000 were American and of these 3500 were militiamen of slight value to the besiegers.

On the western frontier, the support of our other Revolutionary ally, Spain, was very nearly as decisive in the early years of the war. The emergency supply of gunpowder made available by the Spanish in New Orleans provided the thread upon which hung the frontier's survival in 1777. Clark's conquests of 1778 and 1779 were made possible by a supply system which relied on the beneficence of hypocritically neutral Spain. Due to the geographical pattern of mountains and rivers, the western frontier was in closer transportation contact with New Orleans than with Philadelphia and more dependent upon the Mississippi than upon the Hudson, the Delaware, or the Potomac.

As decisive as was French and Spanish aid, an enormous forfeit was exacted for it. The price was American recognition of Spain's claim to the entire Mississippi Valley. In the French and Spanish view, the crest of the Appalachians could properly be considered the natural and preordained western boundary of the new American republic. From 1778 on both world powers exerted constant pressure upon their infant protégé—a pressure made the more difficult to resist by the desperate American need for their support—to require acceptance of this western limitation.

To deprive England of her immensely valuable English-speaking American colonies had been the great French incentive in entering the war. It was a motive intensified by memories of France's worldwide territorial losses in the recent great war for empire, known in Europe as the Seven Years' War and in America as the French and Indian War. But this wish to reduce England's power was accompanied by no wish to raise in America a new power which might in the future by reason of a common language and natural commercial relations combine with England to maintain a perpetual control of the Atlantic. This French impulse to limit the future importance of the United States was demonstrated from the first year of the war. France looked with no favor on the American invasion of Canada in 1775. No French effort was made to raise the overwhelmingly predominant French population in support of the invaders. The bishop of Canada threatened to excommunicate French residents who aided the rebels. The French inhabitants of Quebec, nine tenths of the population of Canada, remained, with the French government's approval, docilely neutral under their new English rulers throughout the war, even during the later years of the conflict when France was dispatching fleets and armies to campaign with Washington. The French purpose in supporting the Revolution was definitely and precisely restricted. What was sought was a United States independent of England but still so weak that it must remain dependent on France.

Spanish policy at the outbreak of the Revolution was a fainter duplicate of the French attitude. The great value to Spain of the 1763 acquisition of Louisiana was its service as a new buffer of vast distances between any aggressor on the continent and her central treasure house in Mexico. The nearest foreign threat was the presence of England in West Florida. Spain, despite a traditional horror of democracy, therefore at first welcomed the Revolution insofar as it promised a weakening of this English threat. From his secret service fund, Bernardo de Gálvez, the brilliant young governor of Louisiana, advanced Pollock $74,087 to be used for gunpowder and other supplies furnished Linn, Rogers, and Clark and approved of Pollock's dedicated efforts to keep supplies moving in support of the Revolution on the western frontier.* This benevolent neutrality was based on the theory that whatever was bad for England in North America could not escape being good for Spain.

Spanish eyes were opened, however, by James Willing's incursion. Willing was a former Natchez merchant who was able to persuade Congress to sanction an expedition against the recently established English settlers there, the majority of whom, he maintained, were Tories. His presumed objective was to open the Mississippi to American navigation and by the confiscation of Tory property to furnish Pollock with additional funds to procure supplies for frontier defense. He was commissioned captain in the nascent American navy and in January of 1778 set out from Pittsburgh with 27 "marines" in a river barge cheerfully christened *Rattletrap*. Whatever may have been the former sentiments of the Natchez settlers, Willing's descent soon converted them into rabid loyalists. To his little force of continentals had been added 70 frontier volunteers, hunters, trappers, traders, adventurers, fugitives, picked up en route. They fell upon the at first unresisting Natchez planters with all the

---

* Pollock additionally obligated himself personally to a total of $136,466. When Virginia declined to honor his drafts, he was bankrupted. Ten years passed before he was reimbursed by Virginia and the United States.

gusto of a horde of buccaneers, seizing anything of value that was movable. The items of property carried off the sale in New Orleans ranged from jewelry and household effects to 100 slaves. Aside from antagonizing the residents to a pitch of fury that turned them into fervent English partisans, the immediate military result of the exploit was to stir the English Pensacola command to the hasty establishment of garrisoned and fortified posts on the lower Mississippi, thus closing the river to American navigation much more effectively than before. Willing soon became involved in altercations with Pollock and the Spanish authorities, resigned his commission, and while attempting to get back to Philadelphia by sea was captured by the English. Some 40 men of his expeditionary force laboriously made their way back northward under Lieutenant Robert George to join Clark the following spring in the Illinois.

What chiefly impressed the Spanish about the Willing episode was its sudden revelation of the startling energy and aggressiveness of American frontiersmen. This unwelcome impression was confirmed by Clark's totally unexpected successes in the Illinois. The initial Spanish impulse to support the American war effort in the west swiftly cooled. It had become apparent that the thin ripple of American settlers crossing the mountains to seek land in the central valley represented a far more dangerous threat to future Spanish interests than did the English presence at Natchez, Mobile, and Pensacola. The rapid hardening of this attitude was soon evidenced by the positions taken in Philadelphia by Conrad Gerard, first French minister to Congress, and Juan de Miralles, first Spanish agent in the United States. On February 15, 1779, while Clark was struggling through the Wabash floods toward Vincennes, Gerard was lecturing Congress on the international facts of life. He pointed out that Franco-American success in their common war against England depended on France's gaining control of the sea which in view of English naval superiority could only be achieved by a combination of the French and Spanish fleets. But Spain, he said, could be persuaded to enter the war against England only if assured possession of the Floridas and control of the Mississippi. Congress readily agreed to Spain's Florida claim while, after some soul searching, continuing to maintain its own claim to the Mississippi as the future western boundary of the United States. In the process, however, Congress had been made unpleasantly conscious of the diplomatic shape of things to come. Gerard had coldly warned that France "would not prolong the war by a single day to secure the United States the possessions which they coveted."

Spain almost surreptitiously declared war on England May 8, 1779, but, unlike France, expressed no sympathy with the American struggle for independence. Her sole interest was Spanish territorial advantage, with her major objective, after the recovery of Gibraltar, the strengthening of her already solid grasp on the Mississippi Valley. This aspiration was speedily given substance by the most forceful action. With a remarkable exhibition of energy and initiative, Governor Gálvez overwhelmed every English post on the lower Mississippi after an initial attack before the defenders had learned of the state of war between the two nations. He took Fort Manchac September 6th, Baton Rouge and Natchez September 21st, and in a series of naval engagements seized control of Lake Pontchartrain. In this first campaign he captured 8 English ships, 550 English regulars, and 600 English militia and seamen. With Gálvez' capture of Mobile March 14, 1780, Spain had established complete domination over the lower Mississippi and its sea approaches to add to her former possession of the entire west bank. There now remained no English military positions nearer the Mississippi Valley than Detroit and Mackinac.

Lacking available English adversaries to attack, Spain filled the vacuum by certain formal gestures intended to forestall American pretensions in the central valley. On November 22, 1780, Captain Baltazar de Villiers, commander at Arkansas Post, crossed the river, raised the Spanish flag, and proclaimed possession of the formerly English east bank in the name of the King of Spain. On February 12, 1781, Captain Eugene Pourre, after a midwinter march from St. Louis with 65 militiamen and 60 Spanish Indians, seized the ungarrisoned English trading post at St. Joseph's in what is now southern Michigan, raised the Spanish flag, carried away the English flag, and before marching home again formally claimed the region for

Spain. Finally, after two former attempts had been dispersed by hurricanes, Gálvez on May 10, 1781, reduced Pensacola, the major English base in the south, and thus completed Spanish possession of West Florida.*

To these Spanish military successes and territorial assertions in the West, Congress could make no significant response. Cesar Luzerne, Gerard's successor as French minister to the United States, had arrived in September, 1779, with the instructions of his government to support Spain's western claims by registering the most emphatic French insistence upon Congress that they be recognized. Congress dispatched John Jay as United States minister to Spain, but he was kept fuming in anterooms by the Spanish cabinet and after nearly two years in Madrid failed to gain as a token of Spanish friendliness even a Spanish recognition of American independence.

Virginia, with her wide western land interests, made the only American moves to resist Spanish aggressiveness. The American settlements in Kentucky and Clark's Illinois conquest were declared to be Virginia counties. With Jefferson's hearty approval, Clark built Fort Jefferson in the spring of 1780 as another counter to Spanish designs upon the east bank of the Mississippi. But Virginia's grip on the Illinois could not be maintained, and supply difficulties and Chickasaw attacks forced Fort Jefferson's abandonment in 1781. Thereafter, the nearest American garrison to the Mississippi was Fort Nelson at Louisville, 480 miles up the Ohio.†

Meanwhile, the variety of pressures and maneuvers confusing the various claims to the west, ranging from those of individual settlers to those of world powers, had been curiously exemplified by the expedition of the French adventurer, Mottin de la Balme, in 1780. La Balme was a French cavalry officer who had come to America under Lafayette's auspices and been commissioned by Congress

---

* Among the terms of the surrender was a condition binding the garrison not to serve again during the war against Spain or her allies. Since the United States was not a formally recognized ally of Spain, the English troops were shipped to New York where they were available for service against American forces.

† The Chickasaw were equally jealous of Spanish encroachments on their territory and from 1781 through 1783 fiercely harassed Spanish traffic on the Mississippi, in one instance capturing and holding as hostages the wife and two sons of Francesco Cruzat, St. Louis commander.

Inspector General of Cavalry. He soon resigned, engaged in various mercantile and land speculation enterprises, and in June of 1780 came to Pittsburgh on a secret mission, approved by Luzerne, which apparently had as well the support of certain land-company interests and the sympathy of some anti-Virginia elements in Congress. His ostensible purpose was to rally the French inhabitants of the Illinois, restore the former French influence over the western Indians, and lead the two against Detroit. Setting off down the Ohio accompanied by the Grenadier Squaw to assist him in his first contacts with Indians, he reached Kaskaskia where he was enthusiastically welcomed by the French inhabitants. He began at once to persuade them of the advantages of repudiating Virginia's rule and in looking to him instead of Clark for leadership. Clark's preoccupation that summer with his Piqua counterattack after Henry Bird's invasion of Kentucky gave La Balme his opportunity. In October, with 90 French volunteers and a few French Indians, he made his tentative move toward Detroit. All depended on his ability to win the intervening Indian nations, presumably disillusioned by their recent defeats, away from their English alliance. But he failed with the first nation he approached, the Miami. After he had enjoyed some initial success in pillaging English trading posts on the upper Wabash, the neighboring Miami, far from responding to his appeal or wavering in their English allegiance, fell upon him with fatal violence. He and 30 of his credulous followers were killed and his expedition totally dispersed. In the most unlikely event that by some more fortunate Indian intrigue he had succeeded in gaining possession of Detroit, there is no certain evidence whether he then would have proposed to raise there the American flag, the Spanish flag, or the French flag.*

In Philadelphia, other maneuvers bearing upon possession of the west were in progress on a more worldly, calculated, and dangerous level, though in an equally conspiratorial atmosphere. Luzerne, bland, ingratiating, friendly, had worked his way into the confidence of Congress. As the accredited representative of an indispensable

---

* His close friend, Lafayette, throughout the Revolution advocated the promotion of an insurrection of the Quebec French.

ally, he was necessarily admitted to every most secret war council. He was better acquainted with current factional disputes within Congress than were most of the American participants. The war hero, General Sullivan, recent commander of the invasion of the Iroquois country, now representing New Hampshire in Congress, had become his intimate consultant and ardent supporter. All of these official and personal advantages he devoted to increasing the pressures exerted by France to persuade Congress to yield to Spain's claim to the west.

Congress squirmed away from the apparently inevitable. American pride was stung by the thought that the new republic was to inherit at birth so severe a territorial limitation. But there was some difficulty finding solidly legalistic counters to the French and Spanish argument that under no recognized theory of international law could the west be considered territory over which any of the American states could claim sovereignty. Before the French War the west had been French. At the end of that war it had been formally ceded in part to England, in part to Spain. By the 1763 proclamation of the King of England title to all English territory west of the mountains had been specifically reserved to England and denied to any province. Any claim to the west by the United States could therefore now only be established by conquest achieved during the present war. But this was a war being fought in co-operation with France and Spain and to any such distortion of mutual war aims both powers were wholly opposed. That some thousands of American settlers had already pushed as far west as Kentucky was not yet considered a telling argument by anybody.

As the great debate continued, only the southern states with land claims in the west stood firm. The northern states without western land interests began increasingly to doubt the wisdom of risking alienation of France over an issue that did not seem to them of sufficient importance to justify a prolongation of the war. Virginia and North Carolina delayed the surrender for a time by an intra-congressional alliance with New England by which support of New England's fisheries claims was exchanged for support of the south's western land claims. Then there came a diplomatic thunderclap in

Europe which made further debate academic. With the connivance of France, the governments of Russia and Austria, neither of which had as yet recognized the United States, offered on May 20, 1781, to act as mediators in the war between England, France, and Spain and proposed that during the negotiations a truce be instituted with each party to the war holding its present military positions. This meant that in America hostilities would cease with English forces still in possession of New York City and most of the southern seaboard. It also meant that such a truce could be declared whenever France chose, for by now it was overwhelmingly evident that Washington could keep his army in the field only so long as France continued to support the effort.

King George refused the mediation, but Congress had meanwhile yielded. On June 15, 1781, new instructions were voted to guide the American peace commissioners, the governing clause in which read: "You are to make the most candid and confidential communications upon all subjects to the ministers of our generous ally, the king of France; and to undertake nothing in the negotiations for peace or truce without their knowledge and concurrence; and ultimately to govern yourselves by their advice and opinion." Luzerne with every reason confidently informed his government that the Americans had by now so clearly recognized the realities of their situation that they were prepared to accept the Ohio or even the Alleghenies as the future boundary between the United States and the territory of Spain.

The American commissioners selected to stand ready to conduct peace negotiations when and if such discussions were initiated were John Adams, Benjamin Franklin, John Jay, Henry Laurens, and Thomas Jefferson.* But upon Franklin, because of his enormous prestige on both sides of the Atlantic, fell the main responsibility. Only he was of stature capable of influencing European public opinion or confronting foreign ministers on equal terms and, therefore, only he could accept the burden of making difficult and final

---

* Jay was in Madrid until June 1782, Laurens had been a prisoner in the Tower of London since his capture at sea in October of 1780, and Jefferson remained in the United States.

decisions. His fame rested primarily then, as it has since, on his representing so striking an example of the universal man. He was regarded as much in his own time as he is still in ours as a great scientist, statesman, philosopher, diplomat, legislator, politician, inventor, editor, author, sage, wit, businessman and ladies' man. Everything interested him and whatever excited his interest he strove to understand. In this diplomatic crisis the fate of the west and of the new republic's future room to grow was largely dependent upon his judgment. As with the earlier supremely critical frontier decisions of Patrick Henry, Washington, and Jefferson, the western interests of the United States had again fallen providentially into the custody of a public servant able fully to comprehend the immensity of the values and forfeits involved. Franklin was as prepared as had been they to meet the challenge. Far from least among the myriad concerns of his long life had been an interest in and an understanding of the frontier, based on years of personal experience with wilderness affairs.

When he had come to Philadelphia as a boy of 15 in 1723, the city itself was little more than a frontier station. The border was less than a day's ride away. Lancaster had been settled only five years and Easton was not to be for another 29. The Indian trade was a major Philadelphia enterprise. Border peace for a generation encouraged the province's rapid progress and continued to present the Indians as easily hoodwinked simpletons, but Franklin was quick to recognize the gravity of the threat inherent in the French seizure of the Forks of the Ohio. At the Albany Congress he came to grips with the problems of Indian diplomacy and frontier defense and became so aware of the danger that upon his return he undertook personal responsibility for the procurement of the wagon transport required by Braddock. When Braddock's defeat exposed Pennsylvania's borders to Indian devastation, Franklin was placed in command of the province's northwest frontier with power to issue commissions, raise troops, and erect blockhouses. In 1763 he was again involved in frontier defense problems when he returned from five years' service as the province's agent in England in time to command Philadelphia's resistance to the march upon the city of frontiersmen, enraged by inadequate governmental support during the attacks of Pontiac's Indians. As the most influential member of the Pennsylvania assembly during these repeated frontier defense crises, his anxiety to guard the border was balanced by his inclination to use the emergency as a means to extract political concessions from the proprietors. This balanced view did not, however, spring from any doubt of the west's importance. No American after Washington was more fully wedded to the conception of westward expansion. He did not approve of promiscuous settlement because of the certainty of precipitating new Indian wars, but from 1756 on he was constantly, diligently, and intimately associated with the more orderly expansion envisaged by land-company designs. Serving in London for 17 of the next 18 years as agent for Pennsylvania, and later for Massachusetts, New Jersey, and Georgia as well, he took constant advantage of his official position to promote land-company interests. He was instrumental in winning Shelburne's consent to the Fort Stanwix purchase and in the overthrow of Hillsborough which countered that obstinate minister's opposition to expansion west of the mountains. In 1775 Franklin returned to America on May 5th to learn as he disembarked of Concord and Lexington. The next day Pennsylvania's assembly elected him to the Continental Congress in whose deliberations he was to take a leading part until after the Declaration of Independence when he entered upon his greatest service to the Revolutionary cause by becoming the new nation's representative-in-chief in Europe.

Under the tremendous and complex pressures of international power politics he now had need of all his seasoned vision and judgment. No one more clearly appreciated the consequences were France and Spain to succeed in enforcing acceptance of their territorial demands. Earlier in the war he had compared being asked to give up the west to being asked to give up the street door to his house. But in the desperate summer of 1781 he felt obliged to take a more realistic attitude. In reply to Adams' and Jay's indignant protests over the surrender embodied in the congressional instructions, he counseled patience and reminded them, in effect, that beggars cannot be choosers. That the war could not be won unless

French aid was continued was an inescapable fact that in his estimation was too potent to be ignored. French confidence and friendship must therefore be painstakingly nourished by deference to major French wishes. He had been compelled to make the same hard decision as had Washington in a similar dilemma. Washington had sacrificed frontier defense to the need to maintain freedom of military action on the seaboard. Franklin sacrificed American hopes to claim the west in order to insure France's continued interest in the war. It was grimly clear to him that first things must come first. First the war must be won. First independence must come. Only then, if then, might the west be considered.

On the desolated western frontier, the inhabitants faced another starving winter and another haunted spring. Generals, diplomats, ministers, and world powers might pronounce, and negotiate, and maneuver, as they dealt with the ultimate disposition of the west. One other fact still remained, one more potent than any other. The settlers were there. After seven years of war, they were still there. It was upon their capacity to continue to endure their increasingly fearful trials that depended the real issue of their future and the nation's future.

XVIII

༜

The Year of Sorrow

THE NEWS of Yorktown had been the last straw to convince the people of England that further opposition to American independence was self-defeating. On March 4, 1782, the House of Commons resolved "that the house will consider as enemies to the King and country all who shall advise, or by any means attempt, the further prosecution of offensive war, for the purpose of reducing the revolting colonies by force." The American commissioners in Europe were on the qui vive to detect and interpret the first English peace overtures. In America every indication from abroad made it the more clear to Washington and Congress that they had won. Before the year 1782 was out, the victory had been made fully manifest as a new English government recognized the United States with an offer of peace on astonishingly favorable terms, and English troops evacuated Savannah and Charleston. But this extraordinary success for most American aspirations had been accompanied by no such sunrise of hope for the inhabitants of the western frontier. They were to recall 1782 as The Year of Sorrow.

To the frontier people, the Revolution had seemed but a prolongation of the unending border war which had begun so disastrously in

1755. Since that frightful year there had been occasional years of relative calm, interspersed among the years of catastrophic Indian invasion following Braddock's defeat, and during Pontiac's uprising and the explosive hostilities of the Cherokee War in 1760 and the Shawnee War in 1774, but there had been no year without murders and outrages and threats, no spring which a man might face with any real assurance that his planting might proceed and his family remain secure. A whole generation had grown up under this perpetual shadow. The shadow had become a pall with the outbreak of the Revolution. Since the summer of 1776 there had been no single moment's relief. In the forever deepening gloom gibbered the specters of every kind and degree of fear.

The basic insecurity oppressing the individual settler was the frantically difficult task under the best of circumstances of supporting his family in a wilderness clearing. The next most pervasive was loneliness, the sense that he had been cut off from the protection human society normally affords its members. The number of his other anxieties was measured only by the number of his desperate needs, for none of which did there appear any hope of satisfaction. Over all these distressing forms of insecurity hung the most oppressive of all, the appalling imminence of death, captivity, mutilation, torment. This ultimate apprehension, however, was a continuing menace so dire that people after a time tended to become almost inured to it, their sensibilities anesthetized by the very duration of their familiarity with it, so that the average settler often appeared more exacerbated by more practical concerns. He was particularly exercised, for example, by his apprehension that even were he to prove able to save his wife and children from the Indians, while meantime proving also able to save them from starvation, there was far less likelihood of his proving able in the end to save from the devices of eastern speculators and legislators the land which he had endured so much to gain. This multiple burden of mortal danger, incredible hardship, incessant anxiety, and continuous frustration the frontier people had borne for 27 years. It had been a strain that had tempered and toughened, but also brutalized, until, like the wounded wild animal, their first and chief impulse was to gnash at whoever or whatever came near.

In 1782 the strain had become yet more agonizing. The previous winter had been so mild that raids had scarcely ceased before they had begun again in February. On the New York frontier that spring, the remaining inhabitants were desperately building additional blockhouses, the English were strengthening Oswego, and Brant was gathering a striking force of 600 warriors to resume his devastations of the Mohawk Valley. At the other end of the frontier in Georgia, the Creek were more aggressive than they had been so far during the war, pushing war parties as deep among the settlements as the outskirts of Savannah. On the Holston, outlying settlements found themselves in the same peril as in every former year, though the previous March John Sevier had again punished the Cherokee, this time by making a daring crossing of the Alleghenies from the west to destroy 15 of their Middle towns.* On the Valley frontier, Governor Benjamin Harrison was reporting to the assembly that "many families have been either killed or carried off, the earliness of the attack gives them reason to apprehend it is only a prelude to what they have to expect." On the Cumberland, Robertson was fending off Creek and Chickamauga raids, though gathering some hope of proving able to negotiate a peace with the Chickasaw's renowned chief, Piomingo. In Kentucky, the early spring raids were so severe that April 15th John Todd was writing Clark of his fears that the more exposed settlements must be evacuated.

But it was on the Pennsylvania frontier that the strain was most nearly approaching the breaking point. The destruction of Lochry's force, with the loss of 100 of Westmoreland's ablest fighting men, had been a terrible blow. The storm of early spring raids pounded salt into that still open wound.† This was the one frontier west of

---

* The military effects of these repeated punitive operations against the Cherokee were mixed. One result was to drive many more embittered young warriors into Dragging Canoe's packs of inveterate raiders. Others made the long journey north to offer their services to their former enemy, the Shawnee.

† Among these raids was the ambush of a woodcutting party at Fort McIntosh in which five soldiers were killed or taken, indicating the freedom with which war parties penetrated even to the immediate vicinity of the military posts established to guard the frontier.

the mountains that had ever been advanced the support of continental troops, but the weakness and wretchedness of the regular garrison at Pittsburgh had by now served only to intensify resentment of the central government's neglect. The tattered little force, the remnants of the 8th Pennsylvania and the 7th Virginia, had been unpaid for two years, never been supplied with clothing or fuel, been barely fed, and been so depleted by desertion and disease that the remaining 300 were too few to defend Fort Pitt and Fort McIntosh against any serious attack, much less undertake any offensive operation.

Washington had the autumn before sent out a new western commander, Brigadier General William Irvine, a warmhearted Irishman who had been an English naval surgeon, a settler at Carlisle as early as Pontiac's War, had served with distinction in the Continental Army, and was much the ablest officer to assume this thankless post since Hand. He arrived glowing with the news of Yorktown and in his first order of the day designated a parole of "General" and a countersign of "Joy." But he had been disillusioned by his first look at the grotesque condition of the fort and its garrison. On December 2nd he had written Washington: "I never saw troops cut so truly a deplorable, and at the same time dispicable, a figure. Indeed, when I arrived, no man would believe from their appearance that they were soldiers; nay, it would be difficult to determine whether they were *white men*." A total want of funds or resources made it impossible for Irvine greatly to improve either their appearance or their morale, though, for all his natural kindliness, he was a stern enough soldier to improve their discipline somewhat by frequent applications of a hundred lashes and an occasional hanging.

Irvine was away from Pittsburgh from January to March 25th on winter leave at his home in Carlisle, having had no reason to suspect that Indian attacks might be resumed so early. Infuriated beyond endurance by the raids and the renewed demonstration of the regular establishment's incapacity to make any move in their defense, the inhabitants of Washington County determined to take matters into their own hands. It had been established the previous October by a probing column of the county's militia that the Delaware had moved from their former homes on the Muskingum to new towns on the

Sandusky and that the mission Delaware had also been moved there under duress. But the abandoned mission towns of Gnadenhutten, Schonbrunn, and Salem still stood, and it was assumed that they were being used as intermediate bases by belligerent Indians attacking the frontier. It was even hoped some of these transients might be surprised there were a sudden descent made, and in any event it was considered a necessity that these way stations for raiders be demolished. At a muster on the eastern shore of Mingo Bottom, 160 mounted settlers volunteered to go on the expedition and again elected David Williamson, colonel of one of the county's militia battalions, their commander. Sixty were unable to swim their horses through the icy waters of the flooded Ohio, but the other hundred got across and rode up the forest trail leading to the mission towns 50 miles to the west. The fury of their hatred of all Indians was further fired by the discovery en route of the mutilated bodies of a white woman and child left impaled on stakes beside the path by recent raiders.

At the mission towns ahead unforeseen prey awaited their vengeance. The long succession of tragic misfortunes which had beset the Moravian mission since its inception was about to produce a culminating horror. During the French War the converts' resolve to remain peacefully detached from all hostilities had brought upon their mission the punitive attacks of belligerent Indians and equally outraged white settlers. In Pontiac's War they had been driven in helpless submission from one refuge to another while losing a third of their number to disease and violence. In 1772 they had conceived that they had at last found sanctuary in the remote depths of the wilderness on the Tuscarawas, only to discover with the outbreak of the Revolution that their new homes were in a no man's land and that their pious hopes to remain neutral were distrusted by both parties to the conflict. Since being carried off to the Sandusky the previous fall, they had been deprived of the comfort and guidance of their white ministers, but even their stern Wyandot wardens had at length taken pity on their hunger. In the late winter permission had been granted some 150 of them to return temporarily to their former homes to gather their unharvested corn. It was this delayed gleaning of their frostbitten fields that was interrupted by the descent of the borderers.

On the night of March 6th Williamson's men hid in the forest a mile from Gnadenhutten. Daylight revealed the unexpected number of Indians working in the fields around the town. There was no mistaking their identity since, as a feature of their religious training, the converts had abjured Indian paint and ornamentation and dressed and wore their hair according to white fashion. Nevertheless, the attackers made their approach to the town with as much military stealth and energy as if it were being defended by Shawnee or Wyandot warriors. Care was taken to surround the place so that there might be no escape. Six Indians, including one woman, who chanced at intervals to be encountered in the woods outside the town were killed.

When the assailants suddenly closed in, the Moravians made no effort to resist or escape and were at first not even frightened. They readily accepted the preliminary white assertion that all that was intended was to remove them to Pittsburgh where they would be fed and kept safe until the war was over. Most professed to prefer this prospect to a return to their harsh Sandusky exile. The Moravian contingent at Schonbrunn had meanwhile fled into the forest, having been warned in time by one of their number who had stumbled upon the body of one of the six Indians killed in the intervening woods during the white approach to Gnadenhutten. But those at the third town, Salem, having had no such timely warning, unhesitatingly accepted a white delegation's assurances of friendliness and joined their companions in Gnadenhutten.

A total of 90 Moravian men, women, and children had been assembled, disarmed, and confined in their chapel where they awaited, still trustingly, the indicated move to Pittsburgh. There had been ten years of intercourse between the mission and the frontier, frequent social and commercial contacts, most of the Indians knew many of their captors by sight, some even by name, and there was even yet no suspicion of white intentions. But what was now going on outside the chapel was the holding of a kind of kangaroo court as the undisciplined intruders debated with increasing heat what disposition actually to make of their prisoners. A minority, afterwards said to have numbered at most 18, favored taking them unharmed to Pittsburgh as had been promised. They argued that the Moravian Indians were Christians whose conduct had always been inoffensive and recalled how often their pastors, Heckewelder and Zeisberger, had furnished the frontier with information and warnings. But the much more vehement majority continued to insist that the prisoners still were Indians. Search of the three towns had disclosed many articles of white manufacture, branded horses, and similar indications which could be construed as evidence that some at least of the residents had been engaged in attacks upon the frontier. Later assertions were made that blood-stained clothing and even scalps had been found. Whatever view might be taken of these inferences, there could be little doubt that hostile war parties in their excursions to and from the frontier had habitually demanded and necessarily been granted shelter by the pacifist mission communities. The majority verdict, therefore, was death. The minority advocating clemency turned their backs and made no further protest.

When informed of their fate the Moravians begged for time to prepare themselves. They spent the night praying, singing hymns, and exchanging farewells. At dawn they were dragged with ropes, two or three at a time, to one or the other of two houses, thereafter referred to by the white participants as the "slaughter houses." Most were dispatched with a cooper's mallet, a tool belonging to one of the mission artisans. When one executioner's arm tired, the hammer was passed to another eager to take his turn. Of the 90 killed, 29 were men, 27 women, and 34 children. All were scalped and the trophies taken home by frontiersmen who by now had become accustomed to set as high a value on these tokens of personal prowess as did any warrior.

After the loot was collected, including nearly a hundred horses, the three mission towns were burned to deny their future use as bases for raiders, and the expedition returned, feeling its action fully justified. News of the event aroused universal condemnation in the east. The Pennsylvania assembly termed the episode "an act disgraceful to humanity." But no effort was ever made by the authorities of either the United States, Pennsylvania, or Virginia so much as to investigate the occurrence. On the frontier the feat was almost as universally approved. The frontiersman's creed, forged in the flames of so many years of border war, had been reduced to a simple axiom: The only good Indian was a dead Indian. The intensity of this feeling was further emphasized, to Irvine's great mortification, by an attack the morning before his return by frontier militia on a small island off Fort Pitt where were encamped a dozen or so friendly Delaware who had for years served the garrison as guides and hunters, including two who had been given American captains' commissions. The detachment of regulars assigned to guard them was disarmed and dispersed and all of the Indians killed except two who escaped by swimming.

The achievement at Gnadenhutten coupled with the continued ineffectuality of the regular establishment had stirred the frontier to embark upon another independent undertaking. This was to be a deeper and more powerful strike at the central nest of Indian hostility on the Sandusky. This one, unlike Williamson's earlier unauthorized effort, had Irvine's official blessing. He was unable to offer the material support of regular troops, but he did assign to the expedition a surgeon's mate, John Knight, and his own personal aid, Lieutenant "John Rose," a young Russian nobleman who had fled incognito to the new world after killing an antagonist in a duel.

The 488 militiamen who assembled at Mingo Bottom were faced with the usual preliminary necessity of electing a commander. There was such violent difference of opinion that for a time there seemed little likelihood there would be an expedition. Williamson was strongly supported on account of his part in the Moravian affair and failed by only five votes to match the count for a far more distinguished rival. The command went to Colonel William Crawford, one of the most esteemed figures on the frontier. He had been an officer in the French War, Pontiac's War, and the Shawnee War, had been in 1766 one of the first settlers west of the mountains, had long served Washington as his western land agent, had participated with the rank of colonel in many campaigns of the Revolution in

both the east and west, and had, since he had served under him at
the capture of Fort Duquesne in 1758, been one of Washington's
closest friends.

The expedition set out May 25th by the same Moravian trail
Williamson had taken. All were in high spirits, elated by their
numbers, and confident that success was certain. Most were mounted,
for in the western frontier campaigns of the Revolution the horse
played as essential a role as in the later Indian wars on the Plains.
But for all their enthusiasm they were four days covering the first
50 miles to the Tuscarawas and another six days the next 100
miles to the Sandusky. The totally undiciplined militiamen were
slow to break camp of a morning, wasted their provisions, strayed to
hunt, and were forever pausing to debate what to do next. Crawford
was a veteran officer who had had 25 years of experience in commanding both militia and regulars and who enjoyed the affectionate
respect of his followers, but he still found it utterly impossible to
keep them under any sort of command control.

This slow progress proved a fatal delay which destroyed the
chance of surprise upon which the campaign depended. Indians had
observed the advance from its second day, and Indian runners had
spread the alarm far and wide. Caldwell had had time to bring up
a column of Rangers and Lake Indians to reinforce the Wyandot,
Delaware, and Mingo residing in the threatened area and to interpose the combined force between Crawford and the nearest Sandusky towns. The two armies collided late in the afternoon of June
4th among the scattered islands of woodland dotting the Sandusky
plains and a brisk engagement continued from about four until dusk.
The Americans collected their 4 killed and 13 wounded and took
up a position for the night in one of the woods. The next day there
was desultory long-range firing but they were primarily absorbed in
their own differences of opinion over what move next to make.
Caldwell was well content with the delay since he was being constantly reinforced. The arrival of McKee with 150 Shawnee enabled
him to develop an encirclement.

The Americans became increasingly aware of their disadvantage
and in another anxious council of their many commanders deter-

mined to attempt a withdrawal during the night, a decision with which Crawford agreed. An unexpected outburst of Indian firing precipitated a panic, however, and the attempted withdrawal became so hurried that some of the wounded were left behind. The Indian line was passed and in that sense the breakout was a success, but in the confusion and darkness the column disintegrated into a wild flight in which every man thereafter shifted for himself. With daylight packs of Indians hunted down as many fugitives as they could catch, some continuing the pursuit as far as the Ohio. Among those captured were Crawford himself, a son, a son-in-law and a nephew, as well as the doctor, Knight, and John Slover, the expedition's chief guide.

There have been wide variations in the estimates of the American losses. Lieutenant John Turney, who had assumed command of the Rangers after Caldwell was wounded, reported to De Peyster that he had counted 100 American bodies on the field. McKee and Elliott asserted that 200 to 250 Americans had been killed in the battle and during the pursuit. On the other hand, Major William Croghan, writing July 6th from Fort Pitt to Virginia's Secretary of War, stated that after the last straggler from the expedition had got back across the Ohio not more than 50 were still missing, while Rose reported to Irvine that the loss had not exceeded 30. In any event, it had unmistakably been a rout, only the more humiliating if the casualties had been this light.

Terrible as had been the expedition's defeat, in public estimation the fate of its commander seemed yet more terrible. Greatest among Crawford's many misfortunes during the hapless campaign was that the pursuing warriors who had pulled him down were Delaware. Delaware hatred of Americans, stemming from the excesses of the Squaw Campaign and the assassination of White Eyes and fostered by years of frontier refusal to accept their appeals for peace, had been raised to an insane pitch by the recent massacre of their Moravian kinsmen. They were immediately determined to make a spectacle of the retribution to be inflicted upon this most notable of all frontier leaders ever to fall into Indian hands. Among those present were Matthew Elliott and Simon Girty, each of whom later maintained that he had endeavored to persuade the Indians to desist.

Of all the atrocities of which Indians were capable none preyed so fearfully upon frontier imagination as did the Indian practice of burning prisoners. It was a prospect that haunted every captive and every inhabitant who realized that he might any day become a captive. People speculated endlessly on the grisly subject. Some maintained that it was only on the rarest occasions that the Indians burned a prisoner, others that they invariably did, some that they never burned women, others that the squaws, the foremost participants in most forms of torment, took particular relish in burning white women and children. There was a more morbid interest in how Indians did it even than in when or why they did and on this point most testimony was hearsay, rumor, and totally uninformed opinion. For all the dreadful reality of their fear of it, the calamity remained on the white side of the frontier a process cloaked in mystery, a horror awaiting in some distant and unknowable world. But with this last and most dramatic repetition of the fabulous barbarity the mystery was stripped away. The procedure was described in complete and precise detail by the surgeon, John Knight, an attentive and scientific eyewitness, making of it a documented and explicit page in the history of that infinitely troubled time. As he described the satanic ritual:

"When we were come to the fire the Colonel was stripped naked, ordered to sit down by the fire, and then they beat him with sticks and their fists. Presently after I was treated in the same manner. They then tied a rope to the foot of a post about fifteen feet high, bound the Colonel's hands behind his back and fastened the rope to the ligature between his wrists. The rope was long enough either for him to sit down or walk around the post once or twice and return the same way. The Colonel then called to Girty and asked if they intended to burn him? Girty answered, yes. The Colonel said he would take it all patiently. Upon this Captain Pipe, a Delaware Chief, made a speech to the Indians, viz., about thirty or forty men, sixty or seventy squaws and boys.

"When the speech was finished they all yelled a hedious and

hearty assent to what had been said. The Indian men then took up their guns and shot powder into the Colonel's body, from his feet as far up as his neck. I think not less than seventy loads were discharged upon his naked body. They then crowded about him, and to the best of my observation, cut off his ears: When the throng had dispersed a little I saw the blood running from both sides of his head in consequence thereof.

"The fire was about six or seven yards from the post to which the Colonel was tied: It was made of small hickory poles, burnt quite through in the middle, each end of the poles remaining about six feet in length.

"Three or four Indians by turns would take up, individually, one of these burning pieces of wood and apply it to his naked body, already burned black with the powder. These tormentors presented themselves on every side of him, so that whichever way he ran around the post they met him with the burning faggots and poles. Some of the squaws took broad boards upon which they would put a quantity of burning coals and hot embers, and throw on him, so that in a short time he had nothing but coals of fire and hot ashes to walk upon.

"In the midst of these extreme tortures he called to Simon Girty and begged of him to shoot him: But Girty making no answer he called to him again. Girty then, by way of derision, told the Colonel he had no gun at the same time turning about to an Indian who was behind him, laughed heartily, and by all his gestures seemed delighted at the horrid scene. Girty then came up to me and bade me prepare for death . . .

"Col. Crawford at this period of his sufferings, besought the Almighty to have mercy on his soul, spoke very low, and bore his torments with the most manly fortitude. He continued in all the extremities of pain for an hour and three quarters or two hours longer, as near as I can judge, when at last being almost spent, he lay down on his belly: They then scalped him and repeatedly threw the scalp in my face, telling me 'that was my great Captain.' An old squaw (whose appearance every way answered the ideas people entertain of the Devil) got a board, took a parcel of coal and ashes and laid them on his back and head after he had been scalped: He then raised himself upon his feet and began to walk around the post: They next put a burning stick to him as usual, but he seemed more insensible of pain than before.

"The Indian fellow who had me in charge now took me away to Capt. Pipe's house, about three quarters of a mile from the place of the Colonel's execution. I was bound all night and thus prevented from seeing the last of the horrid spectacle." *

Knight escaped while being conducted to a Shawnee town for burning and after extraordinary privations made his way through the wilderness to Fort McIntosh with the first news of Crawford's fate after his capture. Far from being dismayed by the crushing defeat of their former effort, the frontier colonels appealed to Irvine to lead them in another and stronger offensive. They undertook to raise 700 militia which when combined with his regulars, they urged, would constitute a force fully capable of reversing the verdict. They argued that defense measures had long since been proven useless and that relief for the frontier could only be gained by attack on the centers of Indian hostility. Irvine wrote the Board of War asking permission to organize such an expedition. After much hesitation this was granted, then restricted, then finally withdrawn. The regular military establishment operating under the control of Congress was, at this stage of the war, exhausted, all but prostrate. The threat of further English action on the seaboard had ended. For the east the war was over. No remaining energies could be summoned to dispatch support to frontier campaigns in the west. Washington, writing Irvine August 6th of that summer when every day was making national victory seem more imminent, was unencouraging and, now that the war's long strain was for him almost over, strangely subdued. Regarding the proposed offensive in the west he wrote: "If attempted, I can only give you my good wishes for its success." He added: "I lament the failure of the former expedition, and am particularly affected with the disastrous fate of Colonel Crawford . . .

---

* First published in pamphlet form from a manuscript furnished by H. H. Brackenridge of Pittsburgh and printed by Francis Bailey in Philadelphia, 1783.

No persons, I think, should, at this time, submit themselves to fall alive into the hands of the Indians."

Whatever his hopes of mounting an offensive against the Sandusky towns, Irvine was reminded of the continuing need to look to the defenses of Pittsburgh by a renewal of the threat of invasion from Niagara. John Connolly was at last undertaking the long-projected strike at the Ohio frontier he had first advocated in 1775. He still expected his appearance to provide the signal for a considerable Tory insurrection. He had hoped to have at his command a force of 300 soldiers and 500 Indians supported by 12 pieces of artillery, but with his superiors' receding interest in the war his following had dwindled by the time he reached Chautauqua Lake to 200 Seneca under their veteran war chief Guyasuta, Bouquet's adversary at Bushy Run. Unable with so limited a force to make his originally intended attempt on Pittsburgh, on July 13th he struck at Hannastown, long the political center for Pennsylvanians in their dispute with Virginia and site of the first justice's court ever instituted west of the mountains. The town was burned, 30 inhabitants killed or carried off, and the whole surrounding area devastated. This incursion deep among the settlements into a district 30 miles east of Pittsburgh and 80 miles east of Wheeling caused new consternation as another demonstration of the relative defenselessness of the frontier in the long prevailing military situation which gave the enemy continuing freedom to select time and point at which to strike.

The news of Yorktown had reached Detroit April 3rd, 1782. Lieutenant Governor De Peyster endeavored to conceal its significance from his Indian allies. Their chiefs had had too much painful experience with the aberrations of international diplomacy, however, to remain long unaware of their danger. They realized the need immediataely to consider their position were England to withdraw from the war, leaving them unsupported to deal with their deadly enemies on the American frontier. In late June a great Indian congress was held at Wapatomica, attended by all the nations of the Ohio, the Wabash, and the nearer Lakes, and even by the distant Cherokee. McKee took a leading part as thereafter he was increasingly to do in every Indian council. He was English agent to the western Indians and a captain (later colonel) in the English army, but his point of view remained that of an inhabitant of the wilderness. His enormous and continuing influence over Indians was based in part on his ability to furnish them supplies from English bases but far more on his personal identification with Indian interests. As a trader and as almost a fellow Indian, he was as opposed to the advance of white settlement as could be any Indian. Wapatomica was one of the few major Indian councils in which there were no serious differences among Indian opinions. Their situation was obvious to all. Since there was risk of English military support being withdrawn, it was imperative while they still enjoyed it to make an immediate and climactic effort to break down the American frontier. They further vowed as evidence of the intensity of their hostility henceforth to hold no prisoners for ransom but instead to burn every one they were able to seize. No application of violence and ferocity was to be spared in order to make certain this year of the settlers' expulsion. In late August, De Peyster, as the Indians had feared, did receive orders from Haldimand, in conformance with the home government's directive, to stand thereafter on the defensive and to endeavor to keep the Indians in check. But the Indian offensive had meantime been launched.

Its major purpose was frustrated by Clark, not this time by anything he did but by the mere impact of his past reputation. McKee and Caldwell, who had recovered from his Sandusky wound, were on the march with 150 Rangers and 1100 Indians to deliver what could have been a crushing blow at the Pennsylvania frontier. They had crossed the Scioto when they were overtaken by runners with word that Clark with 4000 men was invading the Indian country behind them. The report was unlikely on the face of it but the Indians, always ready to believe anything of Clark, were intensely disturbed. The army fell back to defend the Shawnee towns. Blue Jacket, the Shawnee chief, made a personal reconnaissance and returned in six days with the information that Clark, far from undertaking an offensive with 4000, was very much on the defensive in Louisville with a garrison reduced to 300. But the opportunity, like Brant's the year before, had passed. The Indians had by now eaten their reserve provisions and more than half of them, much relieved by this reassurance that nothing was immediately to be feared from Clark and having lost patience, as usual, with prolonged military maneuver, scattered to their homes. Their commanders were forced to abandon the attempt at a major invasion and to resort instead to two lesser, though still very strong, attacks. Caldwell and McKee with 50 Rangers and 300 Indians started for Louisville, and Captain Andrew Bradt with 40 Rangers and 250 Indians for Wheeling.

Bradt's attempt on Fort Henry at Wheeling, the third siege of the place during the Revolution, was marked by much commotion and excitement, but came no nearer its capture than had the other two. The investment began September 11th and continued through three days. Three times during the first night and once during the second assaults were made under cover of darkness, a tactic to which Indians had seldom before ever resorted. All were beaten off without the loss of a single defender. The relative invulnerability of a well-built stockade, when defended by a resolute garrison and not threatened by cannon, had again been demonstrated. The third day Bradt's force divided into smaller parties to ravage adjacent areas and the next day withdrew across the Ohio.

For the thirteen months since Lochry had embarked, the upper Ohio settlements had been kept in a constant state of alarm, rage, and grief. These trials had been more than matched by those afflicting Kentucky. There, too, the early raids had been unprecedentedly severe and the raiders had penetrated boldly into the most populous centers of settlement. One of these attracted wide attention. In March a small Wyandot raiding party attempted to surprise Estill's Station, 80 miles south of the Ohio. The residents managed to get their gate closed in time. The Indians ravaged the vicinity and withdrew. Captain James Estill set off in pursuit at the head of 25 hastily summoned neighbors. So far all had proceeded normally according to a pattern repeated many hundreds of times. But what happened next was startlingly different. Instead of continuing their flight the Wyandot suddenly turned to fight. The forces were equal in strength. The engagement was fought with the same determination and ferocity on either side. Neither flinched while both were losing half their number. At the struggle's climax it was the Indians who charged and the white line that broke. The outcome of this miniature battle between representative frontiersmen and Indians made a profound impression on Kentucky. There was new cause for dismay in the realization that the strain of so many years of war was rendering their Indian enemy not less but more pugnacious.

Kentucky's sole organized defense in 1782, aside from emergency musters of local militia, depended upon Clark's Fort Nelson garrison at Louisville, consisting of militia serving under term enlistments. There was increasingly bitter criticism of his failure to establish forts also at the mouths of the Kentucky, the Licking, and the Limestone to block the main Indian invasion routes. The lack of funds and supplies and the unwillingness of militia to serve at any distance from their communities had, however, made this program impossible. Incensed by Virginia's questioning of his military accounts, Clark had resigned his commission at one stage of his dispute with the state's fiscal authorities, but Governor Harrison had declined to accept it. Clark was now endeavoring to construct a fleet of galleys to patrol the Ohio and serve in lieu of forts to discourage Indian incursions. One only was finally completed. With cordage of pawpaw for lack of hemp, heightened gunwales to deflect rifle fire, armed with three small cannon, manned by a crew of 110 "marines" and militiamen,* and commanded by the able artilleryman, Captain Robert George, the warship took to the waters of the Ohio late in July. The single galley proved unable to interfere materially with Indian crossing of the river, but *Miami's* maiden cruise nevertheless served one great purpose. Sight of the strange and bristling craft precipitated the wild Indian rumor of Clark's imagined invasion which caused McKee and Caldwell to turn back from their march on the Pennsylvania frontier.

They were now, however, turning instead upon Kentucky. Assembling 50 picked Rangers and 300 Indians, they launched their strike in early August, with Caldwell in military command of the

---

* Most of the militiamen soon mutinied or deserted. They particularly objected to the labor of manning a galley's oars.

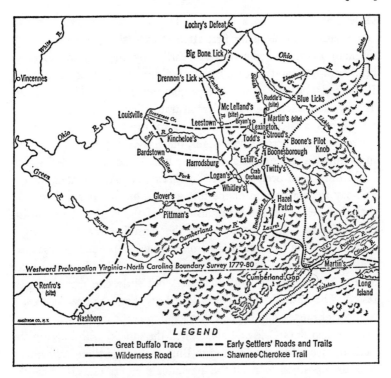

THE KENTUCKY-TENNESSEE FRONTIER IN 1782

expedition and McKee, with help from Elliott and Simon and George
Girty, in charge of the Indians. After crossing the Ohio near the
mouth of the Limestone, they proceeded southwestward along the
great buffalo trace, that pattern of wide tracks trampled many feet
deep into the earth, extending from the grassy prairies north of the
Ohio to the larger salt springs in the limestone country south of it,
which provided a principal avenue of communication in early Kentucky. A third of the force was sent on ahead in small parties to
gather intelligence and to disconcert the inhabitants by widespread
raids. The main body undertook the siege of Bryan's Station, the
most exposed of Kentucky's settlements since the destruction of
Ruddle's and Martin's stations in Bird's 1780 invasion.

Bryan's, a stoutly palisaded stockade, had been built to guard a settlement founded by a family of the original pioneers who had accompanied Boone in his first attempt to settle Kentucky in 1773. William Bryan, killed two years earlier by Indians, was Boone's brother-in-law, and Joseph Bryan, builder of the first cabin here, Boone's son-in-law. These were people prepared to hold a stockade, as they were shortly able to demonstrate. The attack was preceded by various strategems which failed to throw the defenders off guard and then pressed with vigor, but the 44 men within the walls maintained a defense at a cost of 4 killed and 3 wounded which could only have been overcome with cannon. At one stage of the two-day siege a portion of the fort was set on fire, but a change in the wind permitted the extinguishment of the flames. This consistent ability to hold a stockade was the central element of strength upon which the survival of the frontier most depended. It was also, however, always a limited and costly victory. The defenders were able to save their fort and their lives but little else that they possessed. The besiegers of Bryan's killed 300 hogs, 150 cattle, took a number of horses, and burned the ripening crops in the fields.

After two days Caldwell abandoned the attack, withdrew up the buffalo trace across the Licking to Blue Licks, and there deliberately took up a position to await the inevitable pursuit. The alarm caused by the widespread raids of his advance detachments had expedited the muster of Kentucky's militia. Of the first relief party to approach Bryan's, 17 who were mounted had broken through the Indian investment lines under cover of a field of standing corn into the fort to add to the strength of the garrison, but those on foot had been driven off. The day after the siege was lifted a stronger column of 182 men arrived, led by some of the frontier's most famous colonels, John Todd, Daniel Boone, Stephen Triggs, and Robert Patterson. Logan was known to be on his way with another body of militia nearly as numerous, but the first arrivals determined to pursue at once in the hope of overtaking the Indians before they had made good their escape across the Ohio. Early on the morning of August 19th the pursuers pulled in their horses on the bank of the Licking. On a wooded height on the other bank above Blue Licks, site of the capture of Boone and the salt-makers in 1778, a few Indians could be seen moving about. The more thoughtful among the militia commanders advised waiting for Logan, but hot-headed Hugh McGary insisted upon an immediate attack and invited all who were not cowards to follow him. This was a challenge none could ignore and without further consideration the pursuit was resumed.

Fording the river, the militiamen galloped to within a short rifle shot of the presumed Indian position, dismounted, hastily formed their line, and plunged forward. Again, as at Estill's defeat, the forces were approximately equal, and again, though on a much larger scale, the result was an astoundingly unexpected reverse. The one difference was that at Blue Licks the engagement lasted but a matter of minutes. After the first exchange of volleys, the Indians, with a savage readiness to come to close quarters that they had seldom before this year ever exhibited, countercharged. The white line was broken by the fierce impetus of the Indian rush, and the battle became at once a rout. Of the fleeing Kentuckians 77 were killed before they could get back across the river.

Three days later Logan, his force increased to 470, reached the battlefield and buried the dead. He attempted no pursuit, and in any event Caldwell, satisfied with his achievement, had in the meantime completed his leisurely withdrawal across the Ohio. The Indian offensive had not had the total result contemplated by the Wapatomica conference, but the frontier had been more deeply shaken than ever before during the Revolution.

Kentucky was stunned by the shock of Blue Licks. As long as the settlements had existed, Indian raids and invasions had caused untold miseries and deprivations, but there had always been a sustaining hope in the assumption that man for man the individual white man was superior to his Indian antagonist. Now even this comfort had been undermined. The frontier had no more experienced and able defenders than the men who had been overwhelmed at Blue Licks. The hard lesson was driven home two weeks later when another Indian war party of 100 warriors took Kincheloe's Station, the first Kentucky stockade ever to fall except to cannon. Many settlers who for years had stubbornly withstood their former trials lost heart and started back over the mountains. Others would have followed had they been left in possession of one horse to transport enough food to sustain their families on so long a journey. The holding of a one-room cabin and a two-acre corn patch had come at last to seem no longer worth so fearful an effort.

The successive major disasters of Clark's eclipse, Lochry's extinction, Crawford's rout, the burning of Hannastown, and the debacle at Blue Licks had each laid a new and heavier tax upon the frontier's long tried fortitude. Even more oppressive was the incessant raiding to which near neighbors of every surviving inhabitant had fallen victim. There was revealing evidence of the desperate straits of individual communities in the 1782 appeals and petitions for help sent Irvine. As examples:

From Dunkard Bottom: "The enemy are frequently in our settlements murdering, and we are situated in so scattering a manner that we are not able to assist one another in time of need."

From McDonald's Station: "To you we look for aid and assistance, as we are but few in number, not able to repel the enemy."

From Catfish: "The people declare they must immediately abandon their habitations unless a few men are sent to them during harvest."

From Doddridge's Station: "The dangerous situation that our frontiers at present seem to be in obliges us, your humble petitioners, to beg your assistance at such a difficult time as it now is. We are daily open to the rage of a savage and merciless enemy."

From Brush Creek: "The unabated fury of the savages hath been so particularly directed against us, that we are, at last, reduced to such a degree of despondency and distress that we are now ready to sink under the insupportable pressure of this very great calamity."

From Ten Mile Creek: "We, finding our dangers and distresses still increasing upon us through the continual alarms from the encroachments of the savages, are driven to the necessity to apply to you and humbly to implore your assistance."

These prayers of the Pennsylvania frontier for succor from national forces were paralleled by Kentucky's desperate appeals to Virginia. Daniel Boone was writing Governor Harrison:

"I have Encouraged the people here in this County all that I could, but I can no longer Encourage my Neighbors nor my Self to Risque our Lives here at such Extraordinary hazzards. . . The Number of the Enemy that lately penetrated into our County, their Behavour, adding to this our late unhappy Defeat at the Blue Licks, fill us with the deepest concern & Anxiety, the Loss of our worthy Officers & Soulders who fell there the 19th of Augst we Sensibly feel & deem our Situation truly Alarming. We can scarcely Behold a spot of Earth but what reminds us of the fall of some fellow adventurer, Massacred by Savage hands. Our Number of Militia decreases Our Widows & Orphants are numerous Our Officers & worthiest Men fall a Sacrifise. In short, Sir, our Settlements hitherto form'd at the Expence of Treasure & much Blood seems to decline & if something is not speedily done we doubt will wholly be depopulated."

William Christian, most experienced of all border commanders who had led a regiment in the Shawnee War and an army in the Cherokee War, wrote Harrison his dispassionate and considered estimate of Kentucky's military situation:

"Kentuckey it is supposed does not contain above 1000 men at present, the general Part of the young men having come off this summer, as is commonly the case when Danger appears there. The Settlements are so much scattered, that it is difficult, and takes some Days to collect a Force together, particularly to go any Distance from their own Families, when no other man knows what number of the Eenemy have entered the Country, nor where the first Stroke will be made. The last Blow has cast a Gloom over the whole Country, and indeed Sir, their Distress is so great, that I need not attempt to describe it. . . If no succor is sent to Kentuckey . . . it is more than Probable the whole of the Inhabitants will be killed, taken to Detroit or driven away."

To these cries for help from the despairing frontier there could be no response. Irvine's garrison was far too weak to attempt to supply protection to individual communities. Even the last hope of checking the raids by the projected offensive against Sandusky was denied. Washington, assured by Carleton, the new English commander in

New York, that Niagara and Detroit had been ordered to call off the Indians, directed Irvine to abandon the undertaking as a needless provocation. To Kentucky's appeal to Virginia, Harrison could only give the terse and unanswerable reply: "I am sorry to inform you that we have but 4 S. in the Treasury, and no means of getting any more."

While Americans west of the mountains were failing to gain support from their country, events on the other side of the Atlantic were making it seem altogether unlikely that they had a country. The peace commissioners were still attempting to deal, guardedly, in view of the instructions of Congress, with French insistence on the acceptance of Spain's claim to the Mississippi Valley. In August, Jay, who, though a New Yorker without western interests, was the most active of the commissioners in clinging to American counterclaims to the west, proposed as a compromise a line running from the mouth of the Kanawha to the Georgia border which would have saved the Pennsylvania and most of the Holston settlements but left those in Kentucky and Tennessee in Spanish territory. The French foreign office objected to this as "too much" and continued to point to the Proclamation Line as the former English colonies' legally established western border. Behind French and Spanish intentions awaited England's intentions still to be considered. In none of the preliminary conversations of late summer and fall was there any slightest English intimation that any other western boundary for the United States than the Proclamation Line along the crest of the Appalachians would for a moment be considered. The king was declared not at all disposed to grant to rebels territory which 20 years earlier he had barred to his loyal subjects.

It was with the accompaniment of these forbidding developments in the east and in Europe that the long struggle between the settlers' capacity to endure and the Indians' ability to take advantage of the wartime opportunity to expel them reached its final stage, literally its last gasp. In this crisis, as in so many others before, the frontier people found within themselves one more reserve of will and energy to make yet another effort. In September, Sevier with 250 Holston horsemen invaded the Chickamauga country, fought a battle on Lookout Mountain, destroyed the towns which had been reoccupied since Shelby's 1779 campaign, and kept on to burn four Cherokee towns on the Coosa River in Georgia. In November, Clark found his fellow Kentuckians so exercised by the Indian victories of the summer that virtually every man who owned a horse and a rifle volunteered for a surprise invasion of the Shawnee country. His advance with 1050 mounted riflemen was too rapid to allow the Shawnee time to summon assistance from their allies. They, therefore, refused battle and lost only 7 killed and 7 captured, but their principal towns were destroyed, together with an important English supply center on the upper Miami and most of the Shawnee winter food supply. Thus, the Year of Sorrow closed with white successes which, if more modest than the preceding Indian victories, still gave the frontier a kind of last word.

More indicative of the peculiar resiliency of the frontier people than these military activities were the migratory movements of the year. Their restless and gnawing impulse to reach for the new wild land forever awaiting them somewhere to the west was not suppressed even by the terrifying reverses of 1782. For every family toiling eastward toward safety over the Wilderness Road there was another marching westward. Even after taking into account the number of unattached young men who had left, there was in that most perilous year of the war a perceptible increase in Kentucky's total population. On the upper frontier there was an even more astounding westward thrust. Aside from those who embarked upon the river for Kentucky, some scores of families had been stirred by the Delaware withdrawal to Sandusky to cross the Ohio and seize upon new wilderness locations on the Indian side. A few even erected cabins among the fields and ashes of the former Delaware towns on the Muskingum.

These were not the half-crazed ventures of men who had lost their wits. They were moves made by men who were not only fully aware of the risks they were inviting but also aware of the rewards they were seeking. They were considering, planning, and building their future. They were thinking not only of their future as individuals but of their future as citizens. An essential feature of that future in their estimation was a government of, by, and for themselves. On the Holston they were already actively debating the establishment of a new state. In Kentucky that year a convention was petitioning Congress for recognition as a separate state. On the upper Ohio those first brazen intruders into the Indian country were at the same time demanding the right to form an independent state. The westward movement which continued through all the convulsions of the Revolution was made by people who had come as true conquerors. They had come to take and hold possession.

XIX

༅

The War without an End

As late in the peace negotiations as October 14, 1782, within five days of a full year after Yorktown, Charles, Comte de Vergennes, France's foreign minister, was writing Luzerne, his minister in Philadelphia who still enjoyed the grateful confidence of Congress, reiterating and re-emphasizing France's insistence that "the boundaries of the United States south of the Ohio" be "confined to the mountains, following the watershed." He threw in for good measure an appraisal of the American peace commissioners: "The American agents do not shine by the soundness of their views or the adaptation thereof to the political situation of Europe; they have all the presumption of ignorance. But there is reason to believe that experience will erelong enlighten and correct them."

It was the overconfident spokesmen for France and Spain, however, who were about to be enlightened and corrected. Months before, on April 12th, the English secret agent, Richard Oswald, a Scottish merchant, ex-army contractor and slave trader, had been sent to the continent to initiate informal conversations with Franklin. These conversations had been continued guardedly through the summer under the sanction of Lord Shelburne, whose long association with the opposition had ended with his return to the cabinet upon the fall of the North government which had conducted the war. No other Englishman of cabinet rank had had Shelburne's experience with the realities of the American wilderness and the American frontier. He had been Secretary for American Affairs during Pontiac's War, had taken the lead in drafting the Proclamation of 1763, and had thereafter been deeply involved in the extreme difficulties connected with land-company designs, the English army's disengagement from the wilderness, the first intrusions of American settlers into the transmountain region, and the Treaty of Fort Stanwix in 1768. Well aware of the full import of the issue, he understood the consequences contingent upon the definition of an American western boundary and felt little impulse to relinquish the enormous potential of the central valley to the rebels. The first indication of any possible shift in this attitude came in mid-September with the indiscreet revelation, in the course of equally secret and informal conversations being conducted concurrently with agents of the French foreign office, of France's devotion to Spanish interests at whatever expense to American interests. Shelburne with the cabinet's approval at once seized this opportunity to insert an entering wedge between the Americans and their allies, and at the same time to increase Franklin's carefully restrained interest in the proceedings by a concession regarded as an essential by the American commissioners. In the continuing conversations they were henceforth to be addressed not as representatives of colonies but of "the United States of America."

Even so striking a gain as this tacit recognition of independence proved insufficient bait immediately to lure Franklin from his French haven. To the increasing irritation of the less patient and so much younger Jay and Adams, he continued, almost placidly, to refer them to the congressional instructions to consult and be guided by French wishes. He clung to the position that the war was not yet over, that new need for French support could arise, that honor bound them to their great ally, and that this was not yet the moment to stray down a garden path with the English. His policy of prudence and procrastination was as successful as his long experience had led him to expect. The English cabinet became with each delay more eager to take advantage of the opportunity to sow discord among the allies. When at last on November 1st Franklin consented to deal directly and decisively with England without keeping France informed of the process, negotiations began immediately to progress at a pace that was all but indecent.

A great light had dawned over Whitehall. For centuries England's foreign policy had been shaped by the need to counter the perpetually hostile maneuvers of France and Spain. If France, in order to satisfy Spain, was now bent on limiting the future importance of the United States, this was of itself a sufficient demonstration that it was to England's interest to take a contrary view. The next step was obvious. Since independence must in any event be granted, there was the more need to salvage something from the wreckage. A strong and friendly offspring could conceivably become a future asset rather than a continuing threat. A first move in this direction must be the new republic's divorce from its French and Spanish ties by the offer of an independent and generous peace. England's ministers veered off on this unforeseen tangent with haste, zest, and few immediate qualms. On November 30th a provisional peace treaty was signed incorporating terms more favorable to the United States than the happily incredulous American commissioners could a few days before have dreamed a most distant possibility.

Of chief significance to the inhabitants of the frontier was the definition of the new nation's western boundary. The former English insistence on the legal sanctity of the Proclamation Line, on the obligation to protect the interests of England's faithful Indian allies, and on the geographical propriety of recognizing the crest line of the Appalachians as a natural western limit to the spread of a seaboard population was tossed aside almost without discussion. All former English territory west of the mountains and south of the Lakes was instead recognized to be as much a part of the United States as the more populated areas of the original thirteen colonies. The effect was dazzling to one who perceived the future consequences as clairvoyantly as did Franklin. Spanish territorial pretensions had been thrust back to the west bank of the Mississippi and in the south to the vicinity of Mobile. On the north the boundary between the United States and Canada had been made to conform to the median line of the Great Lakes, approximately as it does today. The homeland of every Indian nation which had been most actively hostile during the Revolution had been relegated to American sovereignty. Oswego, Niagara, Detroit, and Mackinac, for so many years the well springs from which had flowed innumerable Indian attacks, had been assigned to American control. An empire had been thrown open to American occupation and settlement.

By the forever astonishing legerdemain of eighteenth-century secret diplomacy, everything toward which the frontier people had been so desperately struggling had suddenly been offered them as an apparently free gift. But the jubilation with which news of the peace terms was received in the east had fainter echoes in the west. Prolonged misfortune had made every settler a suspicious and embittered realist. He sensed at once the difference between promises on paper and actual payment. Clark, writing Harrison April 30th, 1783, referred to the peace announcement as "the agreeable news." * This unexcited estimate well represented the general western view that the news of peace was wonderful if by any chance it was also true. It was a judgment soon proved sound but even at the moment not altogether prescient. It had already been amply demonstrated that, though the nation's war with England might have ended, their own with the Indians most decidedly had not.

Irvine's letter of April 1, 1783, from Carlisle to Major Isaac Craig, his commandant at Pittsburgh, acquainting him with "the glorious end to the war," was crossed en route westward over the mountains by two eastbound expresses. Lieutenant Colonel Stephen Bayard was reporting fresh attacks that spring which included "the Indians killing James Davis his son, and taking two prisoners about half a

---

* There was poignant testimony to the circumstances to which frontier inhabitants had been reduced by eight years of war in another of Clark's letters to Harrison that spring: "Nothing but necessity could Induce me to make the following Request of your Excellency, Which is to grant me a small sum of money on Acct, I can assure you Sr that I am Exceedingly destress,d for the want of necessary cloathing &c and dont know of any channell thro which I could procure any."

mile from Waltour's," "one man found killed and scalped and another taken prisoner at Wheat's Narrows," and "six persons being killed, six wounded and five made prisoners within seven miles of Catfish." In the other express Craig was reporting: "Notwithstanding General Carleton's assurance of the savages being restrained and the Indian partisans being called in, we have almost every day accounts of families being murdered or carried off. The frontier inhabitants of Washington and Ohio counties are moving into the interior settlements. The inhabitants of Westmoreland, it is said, will follow their example, and we have reason to believe that the post of Wheeling is or will shortly be evacuated. . . Prospects of peace on this side the mountains seem to vanish. The British either have very little influence over their savage allies or they are acting a most deceitful part." The capture of John Burkhart by Indians led by Simon Girty provided an incident precisely illustrating the anomalous situation. Upon his later release by order of De Peyster he reported that at the moment he was taken on Nine Mile Creek he could hear the guns of Fort Pitt firing a salute to celebrate the announcement of peace. In John Campbell's letter of April 5th to Clark, reporting to him the news of the preliminary peace terms as he had in 1778 reported to him the news of the French alliance, he was obliged also to report that "no less than 25 per Persons have been killed wounded & captivated in different parts of this Country in a few days past." During that first spring of peace the toll of dead on the Pennsylvania and Virginia frontier rose to more than 40. Clearly the Indians had not been impressed by agreements reached thousands of miles away by diplomats trading marks on a map at European bargaining tables.

Kentucky was having a similar experience with peace. Raids continued and a new threat was added. The Miami who had previously taken little part in the war had suddenly turned belligerent and from then on rivaled the Shawnee, Wyandot, and Delaware in the ferocity of their attacks. All Kentucky was stricken by one loss incurred in the raids of this spring. The heroic Floyd, who had been inseparably associated from the beginning with Kentucky's settlement, the leader of the first surveyors, a co-founder of Logan's Station, the colonel of Fayette County's militia, and one of Clark's most trusted lieutenants, was killed in a raid of April 12th.*

The frontier's premonition that the proclamation of peace promised little relief was borne out by other events of the summer even more menacing than the familiar raids. The Indians had been infuriated by England's cession of their homeland to their American enemy, a betrayal in their estimation in every way comparable to their betrayal by France in 1763 which had led to Pontiac's War. No Indian was more outraged than Brant. The callous abandonment by England of every essential Indian interest seemed to him a sad reward for his wartime services to the English cause. He wasted little time in useless recriminations, however, but threw himself into an attempt to fill the breach in Indian defenses left by England's second disengagement from the wilderness by the organization of such an Indian confederation as Pontiac had momentarily achieved. At a great council of 35 nations at Sandusky in September he strove to impress upon his disturbed listeners the overwhelmingly predominant fact that their sole hope of survival lay in their making a united resistance to further American aggression. Sir John Johnson, speaking with the authority of an English imperial official, advised them by any and every means to maintain the line of the Ohio, the limitation to the advance of settlement set by the Proclamation of 1763, as amended by the Treaty of Fort Stanwix, and which, he asserted, had been in no sense abrogated by the recent treaty of peace. In this endeavor he assured them of England's support.

Meanwhile the government in London had been compelled to give some second thought to their headlong cession of the west. Advisors more acquainted with the mysterious interior of America had reminded them of some of the wilderness realities which most ministers had overlooked in their anxiety to confound France and Spain the autumn before. Indian rage might very well lead to another such outbreak as Pontiac's which at the very least would disrupt the fur trade, at worst might threaten all Canada, and in

* His services to the frontier had been interrupted in 1776 and 1777 when he had shipped on a privateer, been captured, and held for a time a prisoner of war in England.

any event was bound to impose a new burden of expense on a war-depleted exchequer. Investors in the traditionally profitable fur trade had long enjoyed great political influence. The formation of the new Northwest Company had added to these commercial pressures. Rodney's defeat of De Grasse in the West Indies and the triumphant defense of Gibraltar had raised the spirits of every Englishman. To jettison every English concern with the future disposition of midcontinental America had begun to seem less rational than it had the year before. Discord between the United States and France and Spain had already been successfully provoked. The time had obviously come to look to England's more direct interests. American repudiation of one clause of the treaty, in the instance of every state's refusal to compensate loyalists for their confiscated properties, offered a convenient excuse for retaliation by English repudiation of another. When Washington sent Von Steuben to arrange for the orderly transfer of the Lake posts to the American army, he was rebuffed by Haldimand's suave explanation that he had as yet received no instructions to give them up. English garrisons remained at these principal Indian supply bases and were to continue to remain in them for another twelve years. The Indians, partially mollified by this show of English support, continued in a succession of major councils to perfect their plans for a united resistance.

To the settlers in the west the end of the Revolution thus brought little relief from any of the former dangers in their situation. They were still confronted by the same belligerently hostile Indian nations which were still being armed and supplied by the same English bases. Their fellow countrymen in the east, exhausted by the war and frustrated by a central government without political power to take any effective action, were as unable as during the war to extend them support. To these long-familiar perils had meanwhile been added new hazards. Spain, firmly ensconced at St. Louis, Natchez, New Orleans, Mobile, and Pensacola, had become an open enemy, able to set the southern Indians upon them and to close the Mississippi to their commerce. From all these dangers sprang another with which they were to find it yet more difficult to cope.

Taking form within their walls, it presented a more fearful threat than any aggression from without. This was the temptation after having come so far alone to go on alone. Their every most respected and influential leader was soon counseling them that the one sure way to solve their crushing problems, to end the Indian war, to find an outlet for their commerce, to provide for the safety and support of their families, was to cut their useless ties with the distant United States, to consider their situation with concern only for their own interests, and to accept one or the other of the eagerly extended helping hands offered by Spain, France, or England. This was a peril more insidious and more deadly than any they had survived and one from which their escape was to be more narrow.

In 1783 the frontier people had fulfilled the second of their great missions. The first had been their unaided success in forcing the mountain barrier to effect an American lodgment in the west at the last moment before the outbreak of the Revolution must otherwise have denied that opportunity, perhaps forever. Their second had been to hold that lodgment throughout the Revolution at a cost in suffering which amounted to a large share of the price paid for independence. A third and yet more challenging mission had been assigned them now. Upon their continued endurance, their continued fortitude, their continued capacity for making self-reliant decisions, depended the American opportunity to become one great nation in a continental area which might easily have been peopled instead by a covey of little ones of the sort soon to spring up in Latin America. Extraordinary as had been their past achievements, enormous as had been their services to their country, in the period now immediately ahead even greater contributions to the nation's future were to be demanded of them.

Bibliography

Among reasonably available published material casting light on the Revolutionary frontier the following have been found useful in the preparation of this work:

Abernethy, Thomas Perkins. *From Frontier to Plantation in Tennessee.* Chapel Hill, 1932.

Abernethy, Thomas Perkins. *Western Lands and the American Revolution.* New York, 1937.

Adair, James. *History of the American Indians.* London, 1775. Reprint (Samuel Cole Williams, ed.). Johnson City, 1930.

Alden, John R. *John Stuart and the Southern Colonial Frontier.* Ann Arbor, 1944.

Allen, Joel Asaph. *History of the American Bison.* Cambridge, 1876. Reprint. Washington, 1877.

Alvord, Clarence W. *The Illinois Country, 1673–1818.* Springfield, 1920.

Alvord, Clarence Walworth. *The Mississippi Valley in British Politics.* 2 vols. Cleveland, 1917.

Ambler, Charles H. *George Washington and the West.* Chapel Hill, 1936.

Annals of St. Louis. Frederick L. Billon, ed. 2 vols. St. Louis, 1886–88.

Annals of the West. James H. Perkins and J. M. Peck, eds. St. Louis, 1850.

Bailey, Kenneth P. *The Ohio Company of Virginia.* Glendale, 1939.

Bakeless, John. *Background to Glory.* Philadelphia, 1957.

Bakeless, John. *Daniel Boone.* New York, 1939.

Baldwin, Leland D. *The Keelboat Age on Western Waters.* Pittsburgh, 1941.

Bartram, William. *Travels.* Philadelphia, 1791. Reprint (Mark Van Doren, ed.). New York, 1940.

Beach, W. W. *The Indian Miscellany*. Albany, 1877.
Bemis, Samuel F. *The Diplomancy of the American Revolution*. New York, 1935.
Billington, Ray Allen. *Westward Expansion*. New York, 1949.
Bond, Beverly W. *The Foundations of Ohio*. Columbus, 1941.
Brebner, John Bartlet. *Explorers of North America*. New York, 1933.
Brown, John P. *Old Frontiers*. Kingsport, 1938.
Buck, Solon J. and Elizabeth H. *The Planting of Civilization in Western Pennsylvania*. Pittsburgh, 1939.
Butler, Mann. *A History of the Commonwealth of Kentucky*. Louisville, 1834.
Butterfield, Consul Willshire. *Crawford's Expedition Against Sandusky*. Cincinnati, 1873.
Butterfield, Consul Willshire. *History of the Girtys*. Cincinnati, 1890.
Butterfield, Consul Willshire. *Washington-Crawford Letters*. Cincinnati, 1877.
Butterfield, Consul Willshire. *Washington-Irvine Correspondence*. Madison, 1882.
Campbell, William W. *Annals of Tryon County*. New York, 1831. Reprint. New York, 1924.
Caughey, John W. *Bernardo de Galvez in Louisiana 1776–83*. Berkeley, 1934.
Chalmers, Harvey and Monture, Ethel Brant. *Joseph Brant, Mohawk*. East Lansing, 1955.
Cist, Charles. *Cincinnati Miscellany*. 2 vols. Cincinnati, 1846.
Clark, George Rogers. *Papers*. James Alton James, ed. 2 vols. Springfield, 1912 and 1926.
Clarke, T. Wood. *The Bloody Mohawk*. New York, 1940.
Collins, Richard H. *History of Kentucky*. 2 vols. Covington, 1877.
Cotterill, Robert S. *History of Pioneer Kentucky*. Cincinnati, 1917.
Cotterill, R. S. *The Southern Indians*. Norman, 1954.
Cruikshank, E. *Butler's Rangers*. Welland, 1893.
Dillon, John G. *The Kentucky Rifle*. Washington, 1924.
Doddridge, Joseph. *Notes on the Settlement and Indian Wars of Virginia and Pennsylvania*. Wellsburg, 1824. Reprint (Alfred Williams, ed.). Albany, 1876.
Downes, Randolph C. *Council Fires on the Upper Ohio*. Pittsburgh, 1940.
Drake, Samuel G. *The Book of the Indians*. Boston, 1841.
Dunbar, Seymour. *History of Travel in America*. 4 vols. Indianapolis, 1915.
English, William Hayden. *Conquest of the Country Northwest of the River Ohio, 1778–83 and Life of George Rogers Clark*. 2 vols. Indianapolis, 1896.
Filson, John. *The Discovery, Settlement and Present State of Kentucky*. Wilmington, 1784. Reprint (Willard Rouse Hillson, ed.). Louisville, 1929.
Franklin, Benjamin. *Writings*. Albert Henry Smith, ed. 10 vols. New York, 1907.
Gage, Thomas. *Correspondence*. Clarence E. Carter, ed. 2 vols. New Haven, 1931–33.
Gayarre, C. E. A. *History of Louisiana*. 4 vols. New Orleans, 1903.
Gilbert, Benjamin. *Captivity*. Philadelphia, 1784. Reprint (Frank H. Severance, ed.). Cleveland, 1904.

Halsey, Francis Whiting. *The Old New York Frontier.* New York, 1901.

Hanna, Charles A. *The Wilderness Trail.* 2 vols. New York, 1911.

Hart, Freeman H. *The Valley of Virginia in the American Revolution.* Chapel Hill, 1942.

Haywood, John. *Civil and Political History of Tennessee.* Nashville, 1823. Reprint. Nashville, 1891.

Heckewelder, John. *History, Manners and Customs of the Indian Nations.* Philadelphia, 1819. Reprint (William C. Reichel, ed.). Philadelphia, 1876.

Heckewelder, John. *Narrative of the Mission of the United Brethren.* Philadelphia, 1820. Reprint (William Elsey Connelley, ed.). Cleveland, 1907. (The latter edition also contains the Knight and Slover narratives of the burning of Colonel William Crawford.)

Hildreth, Samuel P. *Pioneer History: Being an Account of the First Examinations of the Ohio Valley and the Early Settlement of the Northwest Territory.* Cincinnati, 1848.

Hodge, Frederick Webb. *Handbook of the American Indians.* 2 vols. Washington, 1907–10.

Hornaday, William T. *Extermination of the American Bison.* Washington, 1889.

Houck, Louis. *History of Missouri.* 3 vols. Chicago, 1908.

Hubbard, J. Niles. *The Life and Times of Major Moses Van Campen.* John S. Minard, ed. Fillmore, 1893.

Hulbert, Archer Butler. *Historic Highways of America.* 16 vols. Cleveland, 1902–05.

Hunt, George T. *The Wars of the Iroquois.* Madison, 1940.

Hutchins, Thomas. *Topographical Description of Virginia, Pennsylvania, Maryland and North Carolina.* London, 1778. Reprint (Frederick Charles Hicks, ed.). Cleveland, 1904.

Imlay, Gilbert. *A Topographical Description of the Western Territory of North America.* London, 1792. Reprint. 2 vols. New York, 1793.

James, James Alton. *Life of George Rogers Clark.* Chicago, 1928.

Jefferson, Thomas. *Notes on Virginia.* Paris, 1785. Reprint (Paul L. Ford, ed.). Brooklyn, 1894.

Jeffries, Ewel. *A Short Biography of John Leeth.* Lancaster, 1831. Reprint. Cincinnati, 1883.

Jillson, Willard Rouse. *Pioneer Kentucky.* Frankfort, 1934.

Johnson, Sir William. *Papers.* James Sullivan and Alexander C. Flick, eds. 9 vols. Albany, 1921–39.

Kellogg, Louise Phelps. *Frontier Advance on the Upper Ohio.* Madison, 1916.

Kellogg, Louise Phelps. *Frontier Retreat on the Upper Ohio.* Madison, 1917.

Kellogg, Louise Phelps. *The British Regime in Wisconsin and the Northwest.* Madison, 1935.

Kenton, Edna. *Simon Kenton.* New York, 1930.

Kercheval, Samuel. *History of the Valley of Virginia.* Winchester, 1833. Reprint. Woodstock, 1850.

Kincaid, Robert L. *The Wilderness Road.* Indianapolis, 1947.

Lewis, George E. *The Indiana Company.* Glendale, 1941.

Long, John. *Voyages and Travels.* London, 1791. Reprint in Vol. II, *Early Western Travels,* Reuben Gold Thwaites, ed. Cleveland, 1904.

McKnight, Charles. *Our Western Border.* Philadelphia, 1875.

Marshall, Humphrey. *History of Kentucky.* 2 vols. Frankfort, 1824.

Mooney, James. *Myths of the Cherokee.* Washington, 1900.

Morgan, Lewis H. *League of the Iroquois.* 2 vols. Rochester, 1851. Reprint, 2 vols. in 1 (Herbert M. Lloyd, ed.). New York, 1904.

New York. *Documentary History.* E. B. O'Callaghan, ed. 4 vols. Albany, 1850–51.

Parkman, Francis. *The Conspiracy of Pontiac.* Boston, 1851. Many reprints.

Peckham, Howard H. *Pontiac and the Indian Uprising.* Princeton, 1947.

Pennsylvania. *Archives.* Samuel Hazard, ed. 12 vols. Philadelphia, 1852–56.

Pennsylvania. *Colonial Records.* Samuel Hazard, ed. 16 vols. Philadelphia, 1852.

Pennsylvania. *Frontier Forts.* Report of Commission to Locate Sites. 2 vols. Harrisburg, 1852.

Phillips, Paul C. *The West in the Diplomacy of the American Revolution.* Urbana, 1913.

Pittman, Philip. *European Settlements on the Mississippi.* London, 1770. Reprint (Frank Heywood Hodder, ed.). Cleveland, 1906.

Pound, Arthur and Day, R. E. *Johnson of the Mohawks.* New York, 1930.

Ramsey, J. G. M. *Annals of Tennessee.* Charleston, 1853. Reprint. Kingsport, 1926.

Ranck, G. W. *Boonesborough.* Louisville, 1901.

Riegal, Robert E. *America Moves West.* New York, 1930.

Robertson, James Alexander. *Louisiana Under Spain, France and the United States.* 2 vols. Cleveland, 1911.

Roosevelt, Theodore. *The Winning of the West.* 6 vols. New York, 1889–96.

Royce, Charles C. *Indian Land Cessions.* Washington, 1900.

Scheer, George F. and Rankin, Hugh F. *Rebels and Redcoats.* New York, 1957. Reprint. New York, 1959.

Seaver, James E. *Life of Mary Jemison.* New York, 1856.

Sipe, C. Hale. *The Indian Wars of Pennsylvania.* Harrisburg, 1931.

Smith, James. *An Account of the Remarkable Occurrences in the Life and Travels of Col. James Smith.* Lexington, 1799. Reprint (William M. Darlington, ed.). Cincinnati, 1870.

Smith, Richard. *A Tour of Four Great Rivers.* New York, 1906.

Steele, Zadok. *Captivity.* Montpelier, 1818. Reprint. Springfield, 1908.

Stevens, Wayne E. *The Northwest Fur Trade 1763–1800.* Urbana, 1926.

Stone, William L. *Life of Joseph Brant.* 2 vols. New York, 1838.

Sullivan Expedition, Journals of. Frederick Cook, ed. Auburn, 1887.

Thwaites, Reuben Gold. *Daniel Boone.* New York, 1903.

Thwaites, Reuben Gold (ed.). *Early Western Travels.* 32 vols. Cleveland, 1904–07.

Thwaites, Reuben Gold and Kellogg, Louise Phelps. *Documentary History of Dunmore's War.* Madison, 1905.

Thwaites, Reuben Gold and Kellogg, Louise Phelps. *Frontier Defense on the Upper Ohio*. Madison, 1912.

Thwaites, Reuben Gold and Kellogg, Louise Phelps. *The Revolution on the Upper Ohio*. Madison, 1908.

Turner, Frederick Jackson. *The Frontier in American History*. New York, 1920.

Turner, Frederick Jackson. *The Significance of Sections in American History*. New York, 1932.

Vail, R. W. G. *Voice of the Old Frontier*. New York, 1949.

Volwiler, Albert T. *George Croghan and the Westward Movement*. Cleveland, 1926.

Washington, George. *Diaries*. John C. Fitzpatrick, ed. 4 vols. New York, 1925.

Washington, George. *Writings*. W. C. Ford, ed. 14 vols. New York, 1893.

Whitaker, Arthur Preston. *The Spanish-American Frontier*. Boston and New York, 1927.

Williams, Samuel Cole. *Dawn of Tennessee Valley and Tennessee History*. Johnson City, 1937.

Williams, Samuel Cole. *Tennessee During the Revolutionary War*. Nashville, 1944.

Williams, Samuel Cole (ed.). *Early Travels in the Tennessee Country*. Johnson City, 1928.

Winsor, Justin. *Narrative and Critical History of America*. 8 vols. Boston and New York, 1889.

Winsor, Justin. *The Westward Movement*. Boston and New York, 1897.

Withers, Alexander Scott. *Chronicles of Border Warfare*. Clarksburg, 1831. Reprint (Reuben Gold Thwaites, ed.). Cincinnati, 1895.

Index

A Company of Heroes
The American Frontier
1775–1783

Dale Van Every

A Company of Heroes, the second book in Dale Van Every's sweeping chronicle of the American frontier, is a vivid and stirring account of life on the frontier during the Revolutionary War. Here is the story of the brave men and women who struggled against seemingly insurmountable odds eventually to win for themselves the right to call the frontier their home.

Praise for *A Company of Heroes:*

"A powerful story...He pulls no punches....Van Every's four-volume story promises to be a monumental achievement."
—New Haven *Register*

"[Van Every] brings to it the order, the search for meaning, and the readable style that mark the work of the expert historian."
—*Los Angeles Times*

"Told with great detail and facility by the author, with drama piled on drama...The writer knows of no other history of the tangled period which can equal it." —San Francisco *Sunday Chronicle*

"This is a fascinating volume. It is filled with colorful detail for the general reader and provocative conclusions and generalizations that should interest even the specialist."—*Annals of the American Academy of Political and Social Science*

"The author effectively dramatizes the turbulent eight years of Revolution, when the entire frontier was ravaged without respite by Indians incited by Tory leaders." —*Library Journal*

Cover painting "Daniel Boone Escorting Settlers Through the Cumberland Gap"

QUILL/105 Madison Avenue/New York, N.Y. 10016
An Imprint of William Morrow & Co.
Printed in U.S.A.

FPT   ISBN 0-688-07523-1   >>$9.95

30B1